Sean Christie was born in Zimbabwe in 1980. In 2015, he was awarded a special Taco Kuiper prize for his journalism on the Tanzanian stowaways whose world this book explores, and in 2014 he was a category winner at the CNN MultiChoice African Journalist of the Year Awards. He lives in Cape Town.

UNDER NELSON MANDELA BOULEVARD

Life Among the Stowaways

SEAN CHRISTIE

JONATHAN BALL PUBLISHERS
JOHANNESBURG & CAPE TOWN

Originally published in South Africa in 2016 by
JONATHAN BALL PUBLISHERS
A division of Media24 Limited
PO Box 33977
Jeppestown
2043

ISBN 978-1-86842-690-4
ebook ISBN 978-1-86842-691-1

Twitter: www.twitter.com/JonathanBallPub
Facebook: www.facebook.com/JonathanBallPublishers
Blog: http://jonathanball.bookslive.co.za/

Cover by publicide
Design and typesetting by Martine Barker
Printed and bound by CTP Printers, Cape Town
Set in Baskerville/Gill Sans 11/13.5

For all my Beachboy friends.
Especially for Adam Bashili.

PROLOGUE

This story about a community of African stowaways has several beginnings.

One lies in Tanzania in the late 1970s, in the port city of Dar es Salaam. Pushed by the collapse of the rural economy and pulled by the prospect of salaried work, rural Tanzanians are moving to the country's commercial capital in unprecedented numbers. Julius Nyerere's government has not planned for urbanisation on this scale and, by 1979, three quarters of Dar es Salaam's population lives in dusty, unplanned settlements on the southern and western fringes of the CBD. Working-age youths are absorbed into the ballooning informal economy. They sell cigarettes, peanuts, second-hand shoes.

Most will know little else.

Unwilling to accept such limitations, a group of young men discovers that they can sneak aboard the merchant ships that dock in Dar es Salaam's natural harbour. Some reach Europe this way, where they work in construction yards, or as stevedores in the ports. When they return, often many years later, they are treated like celebrities. The tales they tell inspire more young men to seek the ships; by the mid eighties, a significant stowaway sub-culture has taken root at the edges of Tanzania's principal port. Dockworkers and sailors dub these young men the Beachboys, because they spend all their time on the beaches below the city's promenade, watching the ships come and go.

The Beachboys quickly learn how to become useful to the visiting seafarers, running cigarettes, food and even prostitutes to and from the crew cabins. All they ask for in return is an opportunity to remain aboard, concealed, when the vessel departs. Port and ship security is lax, and it costs low-ranking crew members very little to offer their assistance. Ship captains do what they can to discourage these relationships, putting on shows of fury whenever the presence of a stowaway is discovered. But, if this happens when a ship is already out to sea, there is little to be done; ship captains frequently become enablers, too, by allowing the stowaways to slip off the ship unnoticed at the next port of call.

In the port cities of Europe, the presence of a growing number of East African men does not go unnoticed. Immigration officials warn ship captains that the disembarkation of African stowaways will no longer be tolerated. Increasingly, to avoid losing their jobs, ship captains make large detours to deposit Dar es Salaam's stowaways back onto East Africa's coastline. It is a short-sighted tactic, akin to pollination, because Beachboy communities are soon entrenched in Tanga and Mombasa, and as far north as Djibouti. As the Beachboy sub-culture expands, hearts begin to harden in the shipping industry. To avoid the cost and hassle of dealing with stowaways in a procedural manner, the captains and crews of some ships resort to extreme measures, forcing stowaways to jump overboard – often at gunpoint. The lucky ones are fitted with life jackets, the ship's name blacked out; the unlucky ones are attached to heavy objects and instantly disappear below the ocean's surface. Enough survive to tell the tale, advancing public awareness of crimes at sea. The survivors' stories also contribute to a deepening of the Beachboy mythology. In their communities, Beachboys are seen as hard cases and accorded a level of respect usually reserved for seasoned soldiers and gangsters.

For two decades, any southward spread of the Beachboy culture is blocked by civil war in Mozambique and racial apartheid in South Africa. By the mid nineties, however, these obstacles have fallen away, and not just for the Beachboys. Men and women from all parts of Tanzania set out for Africa's economic mecca. Most head for the El Dorado of Johannesburg, but the Beachboys continue on to the port cities: to Durban, East London, Port Elizabeth and Cape Town. They find the conditions in these places ideal for their purposes. Harbour security, untested for decades, is primitive. The CBDs verging on the ports are in varying phases of collapse, as wealthy residents and business owners continue to decamp to the suburbs, a process that had started in the eighties with the breakdown of apartheid-era influx laws. The Beachboys find they can melt into the shanty towns that have sprung up under city bridges, alongside railway lines and on vacant plots.

Incredibly, their presence goes virtually unnoticed for fifteen years.

◆

A more literal beginning for this book lies in Cape Town, in 2010. The South African-born photographer David Southwood was driving through Cape Town's Foreshore precinct one afternoon when he noticed a group of men gathered beneath the Nelson Mandela Boulevard bridge, then called Eastern Boulevard. They were cooking, washing their clothes, soaping their bodies, smoking, gambling – an intimate communal diorama in the unlikeliest of settings. Dave, whose photography limns both structures and social margins, pulled over. In his brief interactions, he was intrigued to hear the men speaking Swahili so many thousands of kilometres from Africa's Great Lakes region. He paid several more visits to the bridge and established that the men were Tanzanian nationals, come to Cape Town with the aim of stowing away on board the ships that dock in the city's harbour.

It was my good fortune to meet Dave not long afterwards, when he was on the lookout for a research partner. I knew a bit about the Foreshore precinct, having written about it years before. I knew, for example, that the area had been reclaimed from the ocean in the forties and was 194 hectares in size. And I was aware that the Foreshore's architecture, including two unfinished freeway bridges, had been a source of civic disappointment for decades – particularly the Eastern Boulevard, the development of which had led to the eviction of thousands of mainly non-white Capetonians in the sixties.

Its soaring overpasses had also disconnected the city from the sea, not only physically but psychologically, metaphorically.

I was also on the lookout for a Cape Town-based project, so meeting Dave felt like serendipity. I was instantly drawn to the historic irony embedded in his project: the suggestion that a structure frequently described as 'inhumane' and 'antisocial' had, for years, been leading a double life as a shelterer of undocumented African migrants. A singular hook, I felt, for a story about continuity and change in South Africa's oldest, most racially unreconstructed city.

There remained the considerable question of my ability to win the tolerance of the Beachboys. Dave had found that attitudes towards his interest varied greatly. When in smaller groups, or alone, most Beachboys seemed happy enough to talk with him. Around larger groups, he had experienced naked hostility, often from individuals who had been friendly to him the day before. Most of the Beachboys were junkies, which did not help; he said his access problems were further compounded by the fact that his most even-tempered contacts kept disappearing, presumably to sea.

Initially I struck the same problems, but as the weeks grew to months I found I was able to navigate the Beachboy community with ease. Friends puzzled over this, with one suggesting only half jokingly that my physical size was probably a factor, as if having the appearance of a lapsed lock forward may somehow help to override suspicion. But I knew there was more to their tolerance than this, and my research diaries became increasingly self-reflective as I strained to work it out. In effect, I began hunting for this story's third beginning: its source inside myself.

After much internal debate I settled on 2002, the year I moved to Cape Town with the intention of co-writing, with an old friend, a book about the city's Main Road, which starts under Nelson Mandela Boulevard and runs southwards out to Simon's Town. It was a precocious project. We were both 21 and so ignorant of local history that the first words I typed into the University of Cape Town's library search were 'Cape' and 'Town'.

We did a lot of work, though. We spent hours in the city's libraries, reading all the social histories, the Cape novels, the poetry of place. And, for several hours each day, we walked the streets. It soon became apparent that very little in Cape literature connected with our pavement experiences. K. Sello Duiker's *Thirteen Cents* had just been published, and came closest. It tells the story of a preadolescent boy named Azure and his search for a way out of the city's underworld. Psychopathic gangsters loom large, as do pigeons, rats and taxis. Instead of mountains, we are shown bridge underpasses and toilet blocks. The stench of fire-smoke masks the smell of the ocean.

It was a landmark portrayal of a city that had slipped the frame of touristic representation and run wild into a new century. But it was also narrow, as any story narrated by a 13-year-old is bound to be. There is no recognition, for example, of the great social change being wrought in the city by the arrival of foreign-born Africans. Also absent is any sense of the city's new security pact with big business, which quickly saw to the dispersal of the squatter camps under certain overpasses while clamping down hard on its growing informal sector.

I remember feeling inspired to take up Duiker's lead, but doubted I was qualified to do so. My Afrikaans was poor, my Xhosa, French and Swahili almost non-existent. I was a student of literature, not of history, anthropology or political science, and I had grown up privileged and loved, not bullied and stymied on every level imaginable. Through his excoriating depictions of white Capetonians (as pederasts, hard-hearts, hedonists or impotent do-gooders), Duiker himself seemed to be suggesting that I – a person like me – should leave this kind of work to others. And he would not have been wrong, I don't think.

At any rate, the student loan I took on as a way of financing the Main Road project ran out, and my friend and collaborator left for Scotland and the start of a PhD. I remained in Cape Town without direction, working in a series of bars, exacerbating a drink and drug problem that was older and greyer than it had any right to be. I was arrested and put behind bars a few times, and moved from digs to digs, leaving behind broken relationships and unpaid bills. I was slipping. The pavements I had so enjoyed walking beckoned in an entirely new way; I avoided them as if my life depended on it, using the freeways to move in and out of the city, shunning public transport.

When I decided to take a stab at journalism in 2008, I had very little left in the way of self-belief. I felt my life had spoiled at the near end, possibly beyond saving. I soon discovered, however, that wrong turns and trodden-on turds count for a great deal in certain lines of work. People respond well to humility, especially in a region still shaking off the trauma of minority rule, and I was meek in the presence of just about everyone – especially those who have achieved the miracle of self-sufficiency in the face of great odds. Embarrassed by my own inability to do the same off the foundations of a loving home and an excellent education, I dedicated more of my time to recording the stories of others than made economic sense. To make up the shortfall, I continued to work in bars and, to save on travel costs, I learnt how to work the region's trucking network. My departure point was frequently the Slabbert Burger Transport depot in Wellington. My way stations were tolling points to the east of Johannesburg, repair yards outside dusty towns. I started seeing the world through the eyes of long hauliers, turn boys and petrol station attendants.

My extreme enthusiasm for this work led to new opportunities and, by the start of 2011, I was – in a sense – professionally established. I had secured a job with a renowned local newspaper writing about foreign policy matters and, since the post was externally funded by an American philanthropic organisation, I was able to bounce between the major capitals of the world, spending no more than a week a month in

Cape Town. I stayed in luxurious hotels, wore Italian suits and handed out beautiful business cards left, right and centre. I proposed to my girlfriend of eight years and she accepted. We moved out of our small apartment into a house with a garden, front and back.

Marriage agreed with both of us, but the work I had signed on for began to drag me down.

At the outset, I had imagined myself a soul after Whitman, comfortable everywhere and comrade to all. I was soon cured of this fantasy. After years of interacting with African survivalists, mostly warm and trusting people, I was all at sea in the chanceries of the world, where advantage is constantly being calculated at the expense of basic decency. I stopped feeling like myself – or, rather, I experienced the creeping return of the panic I had carried around in my stomach for most of my twenties. I started drinking heavily again and developed a bad habit of walking through unfamiliar neighbourhoods at dangerous hours.

Too often, I woke up in strange places, not able to recall how I got there. The prow of a boat moored at the side of the Potomac River. The bucket seat of a grader parked inside a construction yard in Juba. And, once, beside a subterranean swimming pool in Antananarivo.

◆

I was several months into this whorl of work and wine when Dave Southwood introduced me to the stowaway Adam Bashili in 2011. We sized each other up for a few weeks, and found little to dislike. We even discovered some unlikely overlaps in our experience of the world: an out-of-the-way truck stop or two, the insides of certain police holding cells. We shared personality traits, too, like an acute recklessness around money, narcotics and figures of authority, joined to a naïve belief in our own ability to avert self-destruction in almost any event.

Adam once admitted to bursting into tears at strange times for no discernible reason. I knew exactly what he was talking about.

I like to think that our friendship was inevitable, and that it was built from an early stage on the delight taken in each other's stories. It was also symbiotic: Adam connected me to the wider Beachboy world, and I helped to keep him connected to his daughter many thousands of miles away. In time, he introduced me to the slums of Dar es Salaam, and I helped to put his half-brother Mohamed through school and, later, college. None of this was conditional.

◆

In place of a choice between tropes and genres – the ethnography of a community of stowaways or the biography of one stowaway in particular – *Under Nelson Mandela Boulevard* is part history, part ethnography, and part biography, with a measure of memoir mixed in. It is also as much a book about 21st-century Dar es Salaam and Tanzania as it is about contemporary Cape Town and South Africa.

Its four sections, delineated as seasons of the year, incorporate several years of research. I chose to write this book as a series of vignettes, because so many of the scenes are lifted almost word for word from my research diaries, and because this approach seemed best suited to the narration of these episodic and peripatetic Beachboy lives. For obvious reasons I have slightly fudged the co-ordinates of certain Beachboy locales, but in truth Cape Town's Foreshore has changed so dramatically since 2011 that most of the encampments I describe no longer exist.

To protect individual identities I have mostly used the monikers that the Beachboys give each other, which are nothing like the names given to them by their mothers and fathers. Adam wanted his real name used, arguing that Cape Town's authorities could hardly make his life more difficult than they already do.

I spent several weeks reading the manuscript to him and to dozens of other Beachboys, and the reception was positive; Adam declared the book his greatest achievement.

If nothing else, I hope I have demonstrated how artfully – intuitively – he guided me through his world. Without Adam, these stories do not exist.

SHC
19 May 2016

WINTER

And Cape Town is not what it used to be. Foreigners have left their imprint on our culture.

– K. Sello Duiker

City gardener Karabo Moshoeshoe's orders were to clean, and then cut, the grass embankments around the intersection of Oswald Pirow Street and Hertzog Boulevard, though the routine trim wasn't supposed to happen for another week.

'I don't want to see a single Simba packet when I'm down there,' were his overseer's words.

It had something to do with the new sign the traffic department had put up alongside the highway on-ramp and covered with a black sack. The city's new mayor, Patricia de Lille, would be coming down to the intersection to make a speech, apparently. A tent for the VIPs was already going up next to the wild olive trees alongside the on-ramp. Nothing like this had happened in the eight years for which Moshoeshoe had been tending the area.

It was not a nice area, in his opinion. The room in the concrete substructure of the highway bridge, in which he kept his clothes and his tools, was an especially ugly place. There were always people sleeping around it on flattened cardboard boxes, under sheets of plastic. They cooked in the shelter of the bridge, blackening the concrete with smoke, then drew everywhere using the charcoal from their fires.

'They draw ships,' Moshoeshoe once told his wife, but he could not say why – nor was he particularly interested. These people, these bridge men, made work for him. Plus, they were foreigners, drug-smokers.

Michael Bakili, a Congolese-born member of the Central City Improvement District's (CCID) security detail, had orders of his own: get rid of the bridge men before the VIPs arrive.

It would not be easy. With the sun shining for the first time in a week, the bridge men had come out from under the Foreshore flyovers and slumped down on the grass embankments, where they smoked a procession of cocktails – marijuana joints laced with heroin. These, with the sunshine, would make the bridge men very difficult to deal with; Bakili knew this from experience. One group in particular was likely to test him – the youngsters who had made their sleeping places right there in the plants on the intersection's traffic island, squashing the Agapanthuses to reedmat thinness.

But, if anyone could get them going, Bakili knew it was him. He could speak to them in Swahili, their own language, which he had learnt from his father, whose people were from Arusha in Tanzania. Over the years, he had established an understanding with the bridge men: he would leave them be, as far as it was in his power to do so; they, in turn, would clean their living areas each morning, sweeping away the coals from their night-fires, rolling up their flattened cardboard boxes and returning the boulders they used as chairs back to the bridge abutment walls from which they had prised them.

When Bakili arrived at the traffic island, one of the men – just out of adolescence, really, and wearing a red overall with reflective strips at the knees – was lying back in the warm sand between the Restios. In one hand he held up a news poster for that day's *Die Son*, using it as a parasol. The other arm, missing from the long sleeve lying across his chest, was working up and down inside the overall pants. '*Ngunga*!' shouted Bakili – wanker – and made as if to stamp on the boy, who giggled when he realised his lewd joke prevented him from freeing his hand to defend himself. Some of the others joined in the laughter, then they all picked up their personal items – their torn jackets, beanies, water bottles and sun-bleached backpacks – and wandered off in the direction of the Grand Parade.

Across the road, Moshoeshoe had not enjoyed the same success. He had been cutting the grass with his weed eater, but was now staring gravely off in the direction of the civic centre.

'Everything okay?' Bakili shouted across to him. The old man shook his head, and looked down between his city-issue gumboots.

'Your friends shit everywhere,' Moshoeshoe said. 'Mess, man, mess.'

In the ankle-high grass he'd struck a crap with his weed eater, spraying the stuff all over his work trousers.

'Sorry baba,' Bakili said, meaning it.

By the time the mayor arrived in a bright-red suit everything was in order, or looked to be. The people seated before her in the tent were a mixture of MPs in their black suits, faith leaders in their white dog collars and African National Congress members in gold, black and green T-shirts. The mayor greeted them in English, Afrikaans and Xhosa, and said that it was a great day for the City of Cape Town.

'Today,' she said, 'we take a step towards making our city even more inclusive.'

From his position behind the tent, Bakili noticed a group of bridge men approaching down Oswald Pirow, unmistakable in their multicoloured overalls and woollen hats. He glanced nervously at his superior. The media were all over the event, their camera lenses trained on the mayor and the shrouded sign behind her. This was not the time for a scene.

'The apartheid government,' the mayor was saying, 'knew full well what it meant to claim ownership of our public spaces. Through a careful strategy of selective naming and selective cultural recognition, it sought to stamp its interpretation of the world on future generations.'

The group of bridge men reached the intersection and waved at Bakili, who opened both his palms to signal they should come no nearer. They did not. Instead they followed one of their many paths around the bridge off-ramp and disappeared into the gloom beneath the soaring overpasses. There, Bakili knew, they would light their lunch fires, remove from their backpacks the chicken pieces they had just shoplifted from the Shoprite on Adderley Street.

'That apartheid planning,' the mayor continued, 'sought to keep us divided, even long after the apartheid government was gone. As such, we have an imbalance in our named public spaces. We recognise some histories, but not our shared history. We are changing that today.'

With this, the mayor pulled on a cord and the black cover slipped from the sign: 'Nelson Mandela Boulevard', the stacked words forming a neat isosceles trapezium. The ANC members began singing out the iconic name as the mayor moved over to the red ribbon across the on-ramp to the former Eastern Boulevard, the bow of which clung awkwardly to the ceremonial scissors after she had snipped it. Behind her, a chorus of Cape Minstrels struck up a spirited rendition of 'Daar Kom Die Alibama', the classic goema paean to the 1863 arrival in Cape waters of the confederate warship the CSS *Alabama*. When the twanging banjos started on the chorus the mayor joined in:

Nooi, nooi, die rietkooi, nooi, die rietkooi is gemaak,
Die rietkooi is vir my gemaak, om daarop te slaap.

With the minstrels still playing De Lille bade farewell to her audience, clambered into the mayoral Prius, and swept up the Nelson Mandela Boulevard on-ramp in a cavalcade of blue lights. The crowd began to disperse just as the first curlicues of smoke began to waft from the underpasses.

'Get those fuckers out of here,' grunted Bakili's superior, but like the other VIPs he was on his way back to an office, and Bakili was not about to come between a group of hungry bridge men and their *ugali*.

By sunset the new sign, like almost every other flat surface in the area, had gained a strapline.

NELSON
MANDELA
BOULEVARD
Memory Card. me like ship no like pussy

◆

An afternoon, in March 2011, spent leafing through photographs that my friend David Southwood has taken of the Foreshore, an area of freeway bridges and railway yards at the foot of the city.

I kept returning to one in particular. It showed the underparts of the Eastern Boulevard flyover, which divides the tall buildings off Martin Hammerschlag from the cold stores and grain chutes of the port. At first, I saw only the towering concrete pillars and, in the background, the Duncan Dock's gantry cranes, like the beaks of gigantic wading birds. But looking again I noticed the man in the foreground, soaping his head and shoulders over a white paint bucket; to his right, what I had thought were printing imperfections resolved into sticks suspended by bits of string from the branches of a tree.

'Handmade clothes hangers,' said Dave.

I started again with the image, the way fighter pilots are supposed to scan the horizon: sweeping left to right, from top to bottom. Each pass struck some surprising new detail: a man sitting alone on the highway bank, his head adorned with a white *taqiyah*. A tree stuffed with backpacks and, near to it, two concentric rings of men, the inner circle seated and the outer on their feet. Doing what? I felt caught out by these hidden scenes and confessed as much to Dave, telling him he could surely find someone more suitable to help him with his project. He assured me that they had all said no.

'The last writer I took down there was mugged at knifepoint,' he said.

Looking again, I noticed the shadow of the bridge on the far embankment, and also the shadows thrown by the trees. From their length and angle, I felt I knew the time of day at which the photograph had been taken, and in which season.

'Yes, midsummer,' Dave confirmed. 'Early January.'

This, at least, is a start: some sense of the seasons here.

◆

The men living under the Foreshore bridges are stowaways. To be precise, they live where they do because it is near to the port, and they are constantly trying to stow away on the ships that dock there. They are, to a man, from Tanzania – youngsters in their twenties and thirties from the slums of Dar es Salaam and Tanga. They want nothing from Cape Town other than the means to leave the continent for good.

All of this according to Dave, who derived evident satisfaction from supplying these details only after I had agreed to accompany him on one of his visits.

To get as near to the bridges as possible, he suggested we park outside the Toyota garage in an area of the Foreshore called Culemborg, after the town in Holland in which Jan van Riebeeck was born. I knew the garage well. For many years, before I found somewhere less expensive, it was where I would take my maroon Conquest to be serviced. Getting there was never easy. You first had to overshoot the garage in the permanently busy outbound lanes of Oswald Pirow Drive, and then duck into a secretive gap in the traffic island to await an opportunity (usually several minutes in coming) to motor across Oswald Pirow's three incoming lanes to the service road that lies alongside the Eastern Boulevard on-ramp. The entrance to the garage was immediately on the left, overhead signs guiding you in towards a smiling service adviser and a complimentary cappuccino. I was always happy to hear the squeak of my car's tyres on the service centre's brightly painted floor. No doubt the effect was deliberate – a psycho-acoustic ploy to make you forget about the environment just beyond the garage walls, which was easily one of the most squalid in the city.

Little has changed in the ten years since I last visited, except that today I had to leave the Conquest in a public bay opposite the garage entrance, my tyres crunching on broken glass as I parked. I had forgotten how intimidating the Eastern Boulevard looks from here, rising thirty metres up above the garage's backyard. The bases of the nearest pillars were blackened by cooking fires, and slogans had been scraped into the soot.

I was curious to read this bridge literature, but reluctant to go any nearer. Cape Town is a city of many borderlines and this bridge, right at the point where the service road passes beneath on its way to the rail yards, is one of the more defined ones. To know this, you only have to observe the reactions of motorists who travel this way by mistake. The three-point turns are positively cinematic, the speeds at which they backtrack reminiscent of drag racing. It is hard to say why the fear comes on so quickly here. After all, this is not gangland, where hard faces stare into car windows from scrappy corners. 'Semi-derelict' is how city planners describe the land here; the road does crumble away fantastically, overlooked by warehouse windows that are shattered, boarded up, or painted white.

There are no signs at all, not anywhere. The functioning part of the city bristles with them, telling you where to go, where not to smoke, and where the stopcocks are located beneath the pavements. Their sudden absence suggests abandonment, and a kind of permissiveness for which few people have any use.

Dave arrived. Instead of leading me this way, as I expected he would, we headed down Oswald Pirow in the direction of the port. Where the Eastern Boulevard passes over the city's last set of traffic lights, we crossed to a hectare of landfill where patches of lurid-green grass vied with oily puddles. As we clodded along, Dave pointed out a surface deposit of beer-bottle sherd and bone chip.

'Cow molars,' he said. 'Large groups of stowaways used to gather here every Sunday to boil cow heads, bought for R1 a pop from a Pakistani butchery near the Salt River Circle.'

When we reached the far end, he turned to his right and began climbing the bridge's steep abutment wall, digging the toes of his boots into the stone facing and pointing out slogans written here and there in permanent marker or white paint.

The power of sea forever and ever
Today Africa Tomorrow Yurope
Sea never dry
Escape from cape

We paused by one inscrutable message – Aver Theang Isgoabe Orite – but then noticed three men sitting above us on the Armco barrier of the highway bridge, their faces deep in their hoodies. We collided with their knees at the top of the wall and jostled against one another uncomfortably, bounded on the left by a sheer drop to the road feeding out from under the flyover and on the right by the cars rushing down the bridge off-ramp to join it. Sandwiched between these two converging roads was a hundred-metre slice of downward-sloping land, open to the port's cold storage terminal like a viewing embankment in a sports stadium. More traffic poured off the bridge than out from under it, giving me the impression of an eye being narrowed by a heavy lid. Three trees marched down the slope; beneath the first of these, several men lay submerged in a mound of dirty blankets. At the sound of our voices, one of the sleepers wriggled out and pissed against the nearest tree, all the while squinting in our direction.

He shouted across. 'Haiyo Dave.'

'Adam!'

'Yeah, is me bruv.'

'Where did you disappear to?'

'I've been in Russia, Dave, in St Petersburg.'

An icy breeze was blowing off the Atlantic and the man's holey black T-shirt afforded no protection against it. He clutched his hands together at his groin for warmth, presenting a rough tattoo of a container ship when he turned his right forearm outwards.

'We call this place The Freezer, because it's so fucking cold,' he said. Two gold-plated incisors glinted in his smile. 'Some others call it Scrapper, because ships come to load scrap metal just here.'

Skirting back around the knees of the three sitters, Dave pointed at the alien-speak on the abutment wall: *Aver Theang Isgoabe Orite.*

'Tha's not Swahili, Dave, tha's Bob Marley,' said Adam, in the tailings of what I'd have said was a Brummie accent if the likelihood of his ever having lived in Birmingham, England, were not so infinitesimally small.

'Baby don't worry, about a thing. Because every li'l thin', isgoabe orite,' he croaked. The three sitters cracked wide grins. 'These are my seamen brothers. This big brother here is Barak Hussen. He's been in Cape Town since 2008. This shorter brother is called Sudi Brando. He's from Magomeni in Dar es Salaam. Nobody fuck with Sudi, I'm telling you. And this younger brother is Daniel Peter, he's only 19 but he already stowed many boats.'

Beachboy, Dave explained, is the name taken by Tanzanian stowaways everywhere.

'Tha's true,' said Adam. 'You will find Beachboys from here to Mombasa, all following the Sea Power way. It's like our Qur'an, only nobody ever wrote it down.'

While Dave and the stowaway caught up, I absent-mindedly rolled an anvil-shaped rock under my foot. Beneath it, in a sweating plastic sleeve, were the emergency travel documents of one Kham'si Swaleh Kigomba. The ink had bled and the Beachboys who had gathered around to see said that Kigomba had possibly caught a ship, or had more likely been arrested and deported. Nobody could say for sure what had become of him.

'Take it, as a memory,' Adam advised, and I did want to get the find somewhere nicer, drier. In the end, though, I put it back on the flattened yellow grass, next to a blanched snail shell, and placed the ship-shaped rock back on top.

◆

That was no ordinary place, the narrowing eyelid. The Beachboys say they go there because it is a nice, private spot from which to check out the ships coming and going from the Port of Cape Town's Duncan Dock. If they are seen at all by passing motorists, they figure as little more than flecks in the corner of the eye.

I realised, suddenly, that for years I had carried around more information about the corner of the eye than I have ever known what to do with. I know, for example, that it is called the corneal limbus, *limbus* being Latin for 'edge' or 'border'. The ablative of *limbus* is *limbo*, which, in the Middle Ages, described the region that supposedly exists on the borders of Hell, reserved for pre-Christian saints (*Limbus patrum*) and unbaptised infants (*Limbus infantum*). Today, the definition is more figurative. If you're in limbo, you're in an uncertain space, neither here nor there.

There is also a more poetic derivation. The limbus of the moon, first described by the 16th-century Italian poet Ludovico Ariosto, is all that we fail to notice or care about on earth. According to the legend, such things end up stored in moon craters. 'The Courtiers Promises, and Sick Man's Pray'rs', suggested the English poet Alexander Pope.

The Smiles of Harlots, and the Tears of Heirs.
Cages for Gnats, and Chains to Yoak a Flea.
Dry'd butterflies, and tomes of casuistry [...]

He would have done much better out of Cape Town's Foreshore, I think, among the cow molars and the pidgin graffiti, scribbled by men caught somewhere between their dreams of Europe and the homes they had left in the slums of Dar es Salaam, six thousand kilometres away.

Limbus Tanzanium.

◆

Dave is away on one of his frequent cross-country drives, so I went looking for the Beachboys alone today, but found The Freezer deserted, possibly because a Central City Improvement District (CCID) 'information and safety' trailer had been towed to beneath the bridge, where it looked like an ice cream kiosk that got lost on its way to the beach. The guard, his reflective flak jacket glinting in the open hatch, cut a forlorn figure.

'I'm looking for the Beachboys,' I said, introducing myself.

'Michael Bakili,' the guard said, in a thickish Congolese accent. 'You are looking for the Bongomen?'

'The Beachboys,' I clarified.

'They are the same,' he said, explaining that people from Dar es Salaam have a reputation for being schemers, and that this has attracted the nickname 'bongo', after *ubongo* – Swahili for 'brain'. Dar es Salaam, he said, is often referred to as Bongoland, even within Tanzania. He opened the trailer door and stepped out, all six foot five of him. He said his superiors had posted the trailer under the flyover in an attempt to keep the Bongomen away.

'The City does not want them here. They think all Bongo steal and sell drugs.'

'Do they steal and sell drugs?'

'Yes, but not here.'

Bakili claimed that he and the Tanzanians had an understanding: he left them alone, sometimes even tipped them off if he knew the police were about to raid the bridges; in return, they kept their living areas clean, even rolling back the boulders they prise from the bridge abutments each night to use as seats around their fires.

'The Bongo are similar to my people from Kinshasa. We are both, how do you say … *la débrouille* – always coming up with a plan to make money.'

As to where they had all disappeared to today, Bakili explained that the Bongomen only slept and cooked around the bridges.

'Any other time you will find them at the Grand Parade,' he said.

◆

For most Beachboys the day starts at about 6 a.m., often under the cover of fog reaching over from Table Bay. Those who sleep under the Foreshore bridges roll out of their middens beside the concrete pillars and wander over to the irrigation spray heads on the Hertzog Boulevard traffic island, which have been jimmied so that they leak constantly – just enough to keep the depressions in the ground full of drinkable water. Those who have chosen to make their camps directly across from the port, alongside Table Bay Boulevard, clamber out of their home-made tents, or *mchondolos*, and wander into the railway reserve to empty their bowels beside the tracks before joining the bridge-dwelling Beachboys on the walk into town.

Up Oswald Pirow they go, over the top of Old Marine Drive and on, tracing the perimeter of the Castle of Good Hope in the direction of the city centre. Breaking left up Harrington Street, they arrive at the warehouses in which Cape Town's informal traders store their wares overnight. The trolleys in which the goods are stowed are taller than a man and half as long as a car, and their four tiny wheels make them extremely hard to manoeuvre on the city's cracked and congested streets. For a R10 fee, the Beachboys will wrestle the trolleys down to the daily market on the Grand Parade. For another R10, they will erect the traders' stalls, cover them with green shade net and arrange the wares on tables and hangers. In the evenings, for the same fees, they will do it all in reverse.

This was explained to me by Adam's friend Barak, who has extremely long eyelashes and, today, a cut to the bone across the knuckle of his right index finger.

'Bullshit thing this, pushing trolleys. Just look what it done to me,' he said, wiggling the wound so that it opened and closed like a fish's mouth. 'But what else must I do? If I don't push trolleys I have to pick pockets, or sell drugs.'

We wandered down Buitenkant Street together, passing a string of hooting sedans held up by a caravan of slow-moving trolleys. Barak wanted a smoke so we bought a few singles from a Somali tuck shop outside Mavericks, the city's most notorious strip club. A fashion model came mincing out of a nearby salon in pedicurist's slippers, cotton wool between her delicate toes, and further along a stout woman yelled 'Marthinus, Marthinus, Marthinus!' at the bomb-catching grates over the holding-cell windows of the Magistrate's Court. Just before the Universal Church of the Kingdom of God we turned left down Longmarket Street and stepped onto the Grand Parade at its southern corner, passing Chapmac Traders and AB's Fast Foods.

If Cape Town has a crucible of cultures, then the Grand Parade is it. Here, the Italianate City Hall overlooks a market in which francophone immigrants display knock-off handbags alongside Rastafarians in sackcloth clothes, who put out tubers harvested from the slopes of Table Mountain for the interest of commuters between the railway station and the inner city. After serving as the city's social heart for centuries, the Parade, like much of the CBD, had started to deteriorate by the late eighties. In the early nineties it was possibly the most dangerous block in the city, described by a contributor to local history as 'somewhere you would have expected to be in downtown Beirut'. In an attempt to regain control of the area, the South African Police Service erected a scaffold tower at one end of the square so that information about crimes in progress could be relayed to ground-level policemen via radio. Today, the Parade is no longer the gauntlet of violent crime it once was, but it remains the perfect place to hide in plain sight if you happen to be foreign-born and undocumented.

'See that stone? That is where you will always find Beachboys,' said Barak, pointing at the large statue of Edward VII, which rises out of the encampment of market stalls like a smoker's finger. On the plinth's granite steps, some twenty Beachboys were lounging in the weak winter sun, some betting on a card game with R1 coins, others sleeping, their faces puckered inside tightly drawn hoodies. We took a seat among them, directly across from the balcony from which Nelson Mandela had addressed a crowd of approximately two hundred thousand people just hours after being released from prison on 11 February 1990. On that day, the elevation of the statue steps had provided the best views of the iconic leader. The Beachboys, Barak explained, were drawn to Edward VII's feet by the same logic.

'From here it is easy to see where the police are moving, in case we need to warn some of our brothers, you know.'

Most of the Beachboys on the steps were wearing overalls, the pants and sleeves turgid with underclothes. There were blue overalls and green ones, white and red and orange ones, but all so filthy it was the grime you noticed first. The ubiquity of this uniform intrigued me. I assumed the Beachboys favoured the overall for the same reason it was created: to stop dirt from entering the lower half of one's clothing through the gap in the middle. Their living environments are, after all, extremely grubby.

Barak set me straight.

'These clothes come from inside the ships, from the stores. About five years ago the captains started using dogs to search their ships before they left the harbour. This made it very difficult for us. It is easy to stow a ship, but most of us are found before the ship can leave the dock. But even if he finds us, the captain still has a problem, because the South African government will not believe him when he says, This stowaway came on board this ship in Cape Town. The government says, No, this person must have come on at another port. The government tells the captain, This stowaway is actually your problem, you must find out what country he comes from and send him back there. Some captains don't like to take this responsibility because they know the South African government is lying. Instead, they take us to the storeroom and give us an overall and some work boots, sometimes even a helmet and protection glasses, so that we look like a dockworker. The crew makes us wait for the change in the security shift and then they walk with us off the ship. On the ground they turn one way, and we must turn another way. If we get caught on the ground, they will say they have never seen us before.'

The stink of foul cotton intensified as, one by one, the Beachboys gathered around us.

Barak started to describe his journey to Cape Town but the chatter became angry. He clucked his tongue. 'Some of these brothers have a small mind, they don't want me to tell you anything about the Beachboy life,' he said.

I was about to leave when I felt it, faint but unmistakable: the stirring of fingers in the pocket of my coat. Barak looked away and wiggled his forefinger nervously.

'Everything all right?' I asked the Beachboy seated above me, whose hand I had trapped in my pocket with an elbow.

'Everything all right,' he said, retrieving his fingers slowly.

In the sullen moments that followed I noticed, for the first time, the crude skull-and-crossbones drawings on the granite steps, dozens of them, somewhat lost in the dark stains left by greasy pants.

◆

Dull light pours into the city in advance of cold fronts, displacing, at a certain pitch, all human activity from the Grand Parade. It sweeps up everything from the perimeter bollards to the massive rectangular form of the civic centre and, while the traders tie down their wares, commuters hurry into the mouths of the tunnels leading down into the Golden Acre.

Even the Edward VII steps were deserted today, though I found Adam at the toilet block at the Parade's northern end, under the Golden Arrow bus shelters.

'Careful, tha's not water,' he said, pointing out the stream of fluid coursing across the grey paving. 'The city keeps the toilet locked, you see, so we have to piss against the wall.'

He was wearing an orange overall and, with his caramel skin, gold-plated incisors and home-made tattoos, looked like a prison-gang general. The policeman frisking him completed the image quite nicely.

'He's searching me for drugs,' Adam explained matter-of-factly as the policeman finished patting him down.

'I take it you're not carrying?'

Adam opened his mouth, rolled a white plastic cube around with his tongue, and winked. The policeman wandered off.

'Coke?'

'Heroin.'

'Don't swallow.'

'It's no problem. I'll just throw it up later.'

Not for Adam the arduous pushing of trolleys. Between ships, he hustles quarter grams of heroin behind the Parade's chip and *salomie* stalls – *kattes*, he calls them. He'll shift buttons or tik, too, but heroin is what he knows best.

'Heroin is the Beachboy drug,' he said. 'We call it *unga*, which means flour, because that is what heroin looks like.' He pronounced 'heroin' softly, with an almost Gaelic delicacy: nÉirinn. His pronunciation of *unga*, by contrast, was deep and round, a sound not unlike the lowing of a lion.

'In Dar es Salaam you can get *unga* anywhere. It comes by boat, mainly from Karachi in Pakistan. The boats dock at the island of Zanzibar, and from here the *unga* is split into smaller boats and brought to the city.'

Adam felt like a smoke, so we headed for The Freezer via the chaotic taxi deck above the train station, where he spent more time walking backwards than forwards, cursing people at the top of his voice and making enquiries about their narcotic wares. 'You got Swazi? No, don't talk to me about Swazi, don't ever talk to me about fucking Swazi!' Everyone seemed to be on something, or looking to get on. I'd been up on the deck a hundred times and the people around me had always seemed like ordinary folk, on their way to or from jobs at Edgars, Foschini or Shoprite. In Adam's company it was an entirely different relational dimension, alive with criminal opportunity.

'Sean, watch out for your *balaza*, I heard one of the brothers tried to pick it the other day.'

'What's a *balaza*?'

'It's Swahili for living room, the place where people keep their TV and DVD player. If you break into a house it's the easiest room to hit. Beachboys use this word for the outside pocket of your jacket, because it's the easiest to pick.'

Adam demonstrated how, by using his one hand to hold up my jacket pocket, he could imperceptibly remove my cellphone.

'Impressive.'

'That brother who tried to rob you got a beating, by the way.'

'Why?'

'Because it is too easy to pick the *balaza*. The others were ashamed that you caught 'im so they cuffed 'im a few times.'

We descended to the Foreshore, aiming for the port, and came once more below the Nelson Mandela Boulevard flyover, where Adam lifted a metal lid in the pavement and revealed a washing-machine tumble of rags.

'Tha's my bed folded up in there. Tha's my wardrobe.'

Up on the ledge at The Freezer, we ran into young Daniel Peter, who pointed to a vessel moored in the Duncan Dock, a Jamaican flag painted on the smokestack. He said something to Adam in Swahili.

'The boy says it's a good ship because it is low in the water. That means it's loaded and ready to go. We're going to try to stow that ship tonight, me and this boy.'

Notebook against a knee, pen poised, I asked Adam for a short summary of his career as a stowaway. He finished mulling his weed and quickly rolled a cocktail – marijuana laced with heroin. He lit up and puffed a few times before beginning theatrically in the third person.

'Adam is a poor outcast boy from Tanzania. His daddy, who he never knew, is from Greece. His mummy is a black girl from a place in the south called Mbwera. One day some witches cast a spell on her and she went totally *chizi*, so this boy had to run away, and he ran all the way to Cape Town. Tha's the end of my story.'

I took the hint and closed the notebook.

'Daniel, show Sean what is in your bag.'

The youngster did as he was told, reaching into a small blue rucksack and pulling out a large blue faux-leather 2010 diary, the corners of which had swollen and burst. This he opened first at the pastel-coloured continental maps that large diaries have at front and back, where he pointed out Dakar, Jakarta, Singapore, Dubai – some of the cities to which, he said, he had already travelled. On almost every other page he had drawn cargo and container ships in pencil and pen. He began jabbing at them with his callused fighters' fingers, pointing out the engine room, the lifeboats, the tonnage hatches and even the bulbed area above the rudder – all established Beachboy hiding places. Lastly, he pointed out the portal to the anchor chain locker, and cut his hand across his throat to indicate danger.

'Fire.'

'Fire?'

'Anchor out, fire in,' he clarified and, to demonstrate what a gigantic anchor chain would do to a human body as it went sparking out through its portal, he scooped up a handful of dirt from between his feet and threw it out over Table Bay Boulevard.

◆

Walking along the port's perimeter fence, I noticed a tarpaulin snagged between the stanchions that separate the incoming lanes of Table Bay Boulevard from the outgoing ones. Crossing between traffic to this concrete seam, I realised that it was, in fact, a home-made tent, not much bigger than an airstrip windsock. The mouth of the tube had been tied to the base of a gigantic floodlight, #HMCT102, which no doubt afforded some protection from the icy Atlantic air. The other end had been attached by strips of denim to the trunk of a short palm, the fronds of which had been split and stripped by the snapping of the cords in the winter north-wester. Shattered glass, pools of oil and buckled sections of crash barrier all up and down the freeway spelled out the risks of sleeping in such a structure, which in its way was every bit as extreme as the doss platforms that rock climbers affix to cliff faces.

Continuing out of town I came to the Lower Church Street overpass, passing articles of clothing that had been left out to dry in the wind. From the elevation of the bridge the neatly arranged laundry items constituted a perfect exploded view of Beachboy attire in winter: tasselled beanie, hoodie, overshirt, second overshirt, undershirt, second undershirt, a pair of baggy jeans and the ubiquitous overall. Strains of reggae were audible in the sonic lulls between passing vehicles, and I followed these beneath the bridge to find Rashidi Omari and his friend Ngaribo Masters wedged like overgrown pigeons up where the abutment wall meets the bridge's belly. They were in good spirits, having just smoked a joint, the smell of which temporarily overpowered the acrid highway gases. I opened my notebook on some mystifying Beachboy graffiti I had seen on the retaining wall.

TMK
CTR/018729/03
Junior No More

'TMK is for Temeke in Dar es Salaam, where we are both from,' Rashidi began. 'This number – CTR/018729/03 – is an asylum permit number. Some of us write out permit numbers on the walls in case we go to sea, or prison, and lose our papers.'

'Who is Junior?'

'Junior no more,' Ngaribo whispered.

'He means Junior is dead,' Rashidi clarified. 'He was crushed last year by a truck, crossing the highway. He was Ngaribo's main man.'

Ngaribo looked away and I noticed the three tattoo tears that spilled from the corner of his right eye.

'Some lost, some win, some die. It's no fucking joke,' said Rashidi.

◆

Graffiti of the Beachboy areas

Grand Parade

Wa Beach
Waa hop 2 Sea
God Yucken Bless Mi
Don't West Your Time
BALTI MORE
Sad boy say time will tell

Nelson Mandela Boulevard bridge

The power of sea forever and ever
Fuck you dog stowaway
Life goes on
Easy to die tuff to get Beter to die young.
Some win Some lost Some die
Seaman life no story only action
Who to trust now?

In god we trust
In thug we trust
Days goes on
No way to escape my life without ship
More time to get catch me if can fine

The Freezer

Aver theang isgoabe orite
Don't trust a woman because a woman is a snake and a snake is a dangerous animal
Things never be the same
IM TWO AMECA
Time will tell life is going on
God Bless my people we pray for you to get good time
Jesus fails
Thuff to get easy to die One time you gonna die
Push life to sea
Sherney TMK hate all wizard
Stiff necked fools

Woodstock railway reserve

Die or save Seamanlife is not story. Action
Nothing is tough Accept tough is yourself
Try to make friend not enemy you never no
Memory Card
Corder Sailor Never big Up
Opportunity Never Come Twise
One day 2c
Kacho Lee I'm 2 the ROP
Bremen
To Stavanga
Ohio States Miami New York City

◆

Being so heavily overlaid with transport infrastructure, Cape Town's Foreshore is light on formal identity. The very definition of 'foreshore' – the part of any seashore between the high- and low-water marks – suggests an area constantly sliding between different states, a place unfit for human settlement, too liminal to name. The few designations that the area had been given were, without exception, dull or directional: Boulevard East, Table Bay Boulevard, Beach Road, Ocean Road. Tide Road. Dock Road. Portside.

In recent months, however, some of these had been changed to reflect a more digestible heritage for the city. In addition to Eastern Boulevard having become Nelson Mandela Boulevard, Oswald Pirow Drive, named for an apartheid-era admirer of Adolf Hitler, had been renamed Christiaan Barnard Street, after the local surgeon who performed the first human-to-human heart transplant surgery in 1967.

But as worthy as these substitutions are, they, too, float on the Foreshore's history like oil on harbour water. Today, with Adam's help, I marked the area's informal place names on a 1:10 000 orthophoto map I recently fetched from the National Geo-spatial Information office in Mowbray.

'We call this place Maskani,' said Adam, putting his finger on an area of the railway reserve in lower Woodstock. 'In Dar es Salaam, a *maskani* is a street corner where boys do their hustling and gambling. In Cape Town, we do this stuff here in the railways. All the street people know this place as Maskani. It is a Beachboy area, but the coloured gangsters and junkies come here too. Also the prostitutes and the white people who beg at the traffic lights, they know it.'

In a similar act of transference, the Grand Parade is known to hundreds as Kijiweni, Dar-Swahili for 'place of work'. The landscaped area outside the Ford Imperial dealership off Christiaan Barnard Street, where an ever-leaking sprinkler system has created a fetid, unnatural wetland, is known as Msimbazi, after a particularly polluted river in Dar es Salaam.

Other names include:

Vietnam – the manicured area on the port side of Table Bay Boulevard, called this on account of the large palm trees that flourish there.

The Kitchen – a Beachboy living area on the rail yard side of Table Bay Boulevard, above which smoke from large communal cooking fires always rises.

Beachboy Office – the parking bays outside WOMAG (World of Marble & Granite), on the corner of Marine Drive and N1 Paarden Eiland. This is the place where Woodstock Beachboys meet the drivers of vehicles, be they paramedics responding to a Beachboy emergency or heroin suppliers.

Old Maskani – the vacant lot alongside Fuel44, off Tide Street in lower Woodstock. This was once a shanty town inhabited mainly by coloured Capetonians and Tanzanians. The community was evicted from the land in 2009, in advance of the 2010 FIFA World Cup. Many of those evicted were relocated to the Symphony Way Temporary Relocation Area in Delft, where they became known as the Woodstock Pavement Dwellers.

Arches – the railway tunnels that lead into the Port of Cape Town beneath Table Bay Boulevard. The name is a trans-verbalisation of hatches, specifically the dark and cavernous hatches found in cargo ships, in which Beachboys seek to stow away.

Wa Tony – the Port of Cape Town's container dock, named after a Beachboy called Tony, who has the Cape Town record for stowing away successfully on container ships.

Seaman Bar – the pool hall off Draklow Street, lower Woodstock.

Only in respect of the gigantic vertebral shapes that constitute the Foreshore's breakwater is the Beachboy bent for naming outdone. 'We call that place Stones,' said Adam, 'as in, we're going to the Stones tonight to try stow a ship.' Locally, the shapes are known as dolosse, derived from *dolos*: a South African term for the animal knucklebones used by indigenous medicine men in their divinisation rituals.

◆

'What does Memory Card mean?' I asked Adam today, noticing that he had the words tattooed in crack-cocaine font on his skinny right biceps. We were again seated on the cold highway ledge, which had become our unofficial meeting place.

'That is what people call me.'

'Why?'

'Because I'm a peacemaker. I remind the boys what is good and what is bad Beachboy behaviour. I remind them that everyone else is against us, so why fight each other?'

He took off his shirt and revealed a torso covered in tattoos.

'This is my life story here. I had this done when I was 17,' he said, indicating the container ship tattoo on his right forearm. 'That was after I stowed away for the first time in a ship like this, in Durban harbour.'

Shortly before this, Adam had been picked off the streets of Durban and incarcerated in Westville prison for having no documents – his first stretch of time. It was an experience that drove him to commission the outline of the African continent on his abdomen, enclosing the words **Getto youth wil neva hav no peace Jah know.**

'Who is Aniya?' I asked, pointing at a tattoo on his shoulder.

'Princess Aniya is me daughter,' he said, pronouncing the word 'door-ah' and putting the provenance of his accent – Birmingham – beyond doubt. He went on to relate, speedily, the story of his passage to England: how he had entered through the Port of Hull in 1999 concealed in a Maltese bulk carrier called *Global Victory*, which he had boarded in the Port of Richards Bay on KwaZulu-Natal's north coast. In his first months in the United Kingdom, he had lived in Sheffield with a benevolent Cameroonian before bussing to Birmingham, where the Jamaican gangsters around Handsworth had permitted him to hustle small amounts of marijuana. Aniya's mother, a second-generation Jamaican immigrant called Rochelle ____, had tried to save him from the streets by convincing her own mother to take him in. But, with no other means of making money, Adam had continued to hustle by day and was eventually arrested for dealing. He had met Aniya for the first time in the visitors' room of Birmingham's Winson Green prison. Two months later – seven years after his arrival – he was put on a flight back to Dar es Salaam.

I scratched it all down.

'Tell them,' said Adam, peering into my notebook, 'that I'm fucken West Brom for life. Up the Baggies, yeah!'

◆

On two occasions, now, Adam has asked me to account for my interest in the Beachboys. The first time he did this, I fell back on a pitch I had recently submitted to a number of foundations, companies and philanthropic individuals in the hope of securing project funding.

'Cape Town's Foreshore has a historical reputation for being inhumane and anti-human,' I said, reading aloud from my phone. 'This is partly because the earth here was dredged up from under the ocean during the port expansion works of the 1940s and, to this day, the soil, where it surfaces, retains a pelagic texture and appearance. The monumental bridges and boulevards that were subsequently developed in this reclaimed part of the city only added to this extraterrestrial mystique by making it difficult and frankly dangerous to travel the area on foot.'

At a point I quoted from a popular photo-history book called *Cape Town in the Twentieth Century*, in which the authors describe how the development of the Foreshore bridges and boulevards 'snipped the city away from the sea' producing 'a soulless city centre, virtually lifeless after office hours save for some restaurants and clubs catering for visiting sailors'.

I did not need to look up to know that I had lost Adam. I couldn't blame him. As an accounting for my interest, the piece was worse than insincere, and I hadn't even arrived at my references to Heidegger's work on bridges. I ploughed on anyway, approximating David Attenborough's accent in self-mockery.

'Exposed as it is to the stormy Atlantic, the Foreshore has become a zone of inexorable disintegration, a place where abandoned anchor chains flake away into oil-drenched sands and retired trawlers sag on their stocks – everything succumbing slowly to the rasp of the south-easter and the lash of the winter rains. And yet, as harsh and neglected as this environment is, a community of young men have found shelter here these past 15 years. They live under the forbidding bridges and in the freeway culverts in small tents constructed from plastic and wood. They are from a faraway place – Dar es Salaam on the Swahili Coast – but their stories illuminate a side of the city that is absent from the tourist brochures: an underworld on the rise, complete with its own laws and codes and comprising mostly foreign-born Africans …'

'Sounds nice, man,' said Adam.

'It needs work. I'll think about it some more.'

When we next talked, I overcorrected and reduced my interest to professional pragmatism. I said that I did not expect my current job to last the year, and it was for this reason that I had jumped at the opportunity to start on a project closer to home, which would leave me with something to do when my employers let me go.

'You mess up?'

'You could say that. I'm not doing very well at my work,' I said, and began confessing, for the first time, the deep feelings of insufficiency with which I had been living since assuming the impressively titled post of Foreign Policy Correspondent for a major local newspaper. It was a position that was handsomely funded by an international foundation, enabling me to spend weeks at a time in New York, Washington, Antananarivo, Juba – any place I wished to visit, really, as long as I could convince my handlers that the jaunt would serve a deeper understanding of how the South African government conducts its relations with other governments, and towards which ends.

'Nobody in that world says what they really mean,' I complained. 'If you write what you think they really mean, their people call and tell you, That's it, you messed up, don't ever call us again.'

'Tha's politics. Sounds like it isn't for you,' said Adam.

I shook my head.

'No, it's deeper than that. I seldom prepare adequately before I speak to these diplomats and negotiators. As a result, when I play back the recordings of these conversations, it's mainly just my own voice that I hear, talking in a wide circle about the things I'm supposed to be getting at. In fact, I have a problem with planning in general. I leave everything to the last second. Usually everything works out, but when things go wrong they go spectacularly wrong.'

I winced as my professional mishaps played back to me, ending, as always, with the first of them, the Ur-fuck-up.

'I was arrested for border jumping once. I spent a few days in a Zambian jail cell. I think I still have a criminal record there.'

Adam sat up slowly.

'How'd it 'appen?'

Over the years, the story has become my great mock-heroic dinner piece, gauged to scandalise and entertain friends and family. But seated next to Adam, the two of us gazing out at the shipping in Table Bay, I put it back together more or less as it happened.

'In 2008, I decided to try journalism. I had no training but I was desperate to make a change in my life. I had been working in bars and restaurants for seven years and that left me with a drinking and drug problem.'

'*Unga*?'

'No.'

'Tik?'

'No.'

'Buttons?'

'No.'

'Okay.'

'I was moving from house to house, not settling. I got myself arrested a few times. One morning, after a very bad weekend, I drove out of Johannesburg and ended up in a place called Wadeville, stuck in a traffic jam. I went through the radio stations, listening out for news, and eventually heard on Highveld FM that a truck had overturned somewhere up ahead and chemicals had splashed over the tarmac. The highway had been closed and the other drivers were going mental, hooting at each other and shouting into their phones.

'Ahead, there was this truck with a tall load under an orange and white tarpaulin. I watched the driver climb out of his cab with a bucket and walk to a nearby petrol station to fetch water. When he returned he started washing his cab, humming along to the radio, which was playing nineties hits by Whitney Houston and Bryan Adams. He really made an impression on me because he was so calm, like he was washing his car in his own driveway. When the other people saw what he was doing they started to relax as well. They climbed out of their cars and bummed cigarettes from one another. Others walked off to the garage to use the toilet and buy sweets for their kids.

'At that moment, I wanted to be that trucker. I wanted this so badly that I called the number on the truck's tarp, and told the receptionist that I was a journalist with an interest in life on the road. The receptionist put me through to the operations manager, a man called Bennett Pillay, who listened to my request and said, "Right … right, I can do that for you. When do you want to go?"'

The following day I was placed in a left-hand-drive International Eagle Pro Sleeper 9800i, bound for Zambia's Copperbelt with a load of massive paper rolls. The driver was a guy called Willie Phiri, a Zambian in his early fifties who had on a neat blue windbreaker, shorts and long khaki socks. We waited out the evening traffic in the depot and then went rocking through a cold highveld night, northward bound. Almost immediately I was fighting to keep my eyes open and, since Willie seemed to prefer silence while he concentrated on the city roads and traffic, I gave in. For the remaining hours of darkness I slept deeply, warmed by the 15-litre engine below us.

When I woke up, it was the last moments before dawn. Mist filled the hollows in the landscape and a thin red bar spread across the horizon on the right. A truck passed inches from my face, which was still pressed against the window. I realised we had left the highway, toll dodging. Baobabs started to appear, and giant millipedes streamed before us on the tarmac. We stopped to piss among some low koppies and Willie got a rag, bucket and bottle of Sunlight out and washed the bugs off his windscreen ahead of our arrival at his usual truck stop near the Zimbabwean border. I felt better than I had in months. After a very long period of feeling trapped, I was moving and in the care of this very competent, very experienced guy.

'We stayed just outside Beit Bridge for three days while Willie waited for his clearance papers to come through. I spent a lot of time playing pool and drinking Black Label with the other truck drivers, who were all Zimbabweans. Talking to them was easy because I was born in Zimbabwe, and spent a lot of my childhood there.'

'I never knew,' Adam interjected.

'I've been living in South Africa for a long time. My parents moved here in the mid eighties. My mother's family remained but their farms were taken for the government's land reform programme in the early 2000s, and now they're here, too.'

'I heard about that.'

It had been eight years between visits, and the truckers told stories that were painful to hear: the spectacular collapse of the economy; the hunger in the rural areas and the use of food aid as political patronage; the torture and murder of opposition leaders. The impoverishment of the countryside had turned the truckers into small gods – Big Men who were paid in forex and could bring goods in that nobody in Zimbabwe was selling, like rice, and soap. Family, friends, policemen, teachers and even tribal leaders came before them to grovel for favours. Going home had become complicated, and many of the truckers had taken to meeting their wives in places where they would not be recognised.

Personally, I felt nothing but joy when we crossed the border at last. I could identify the roadside cattle by breed, and could judge from the trees which soil type we were travelling on. Outside Bulawayo, I remembered about the baobab into which soldiers on furlough had hammered empty FM shell casings during the war, standing on their transports to do this so that it would be difficult for passers-by to prise them out. Willie wanted to see this for himself and, by a process of elimination, we found the place. He inched the cab right up to the vast trunk and sure enough, standing on our seats, we could see the casings. Twenty-five years after they had been hammered in, the African giant was busy spitting them out like pips.

We reached Victoria Falls on the border with Zambia at dawn on a Saturday morning, and already the queue of trucks stretched from the border post through the town to its outskirts, a distance of about two kilometres. Willie said that since it would take all day to reach the post, and another to clear no-man's land, I should stay in Victoria Falls and join him in Livingstone on the Monday morning. After four nights in the cramped cab I readily agreed, and took a bunk in a lodge called Shoestrings, located where the town gives way to bushveld. I had a wash and an English breakfast priced in US dollars, and set about getting drunk.

The barman marked each beer in his ledger with a pencil, a small 'I'. Occasionally, he'd draw a stripe through a few, which meant I'd had another five. As the day wore on, the lodge filled up with big-game hunters and tour guides who had left their clients on the Zambian side. The political and economic crisis in Zimbabwe had turned Victoria Falls into a virtual ghost town, but the few who had remained gathered each day at Shoestrings, giving the place the manic energy of a speakeasy.

Full of booze and encouraged by the colourful stories the guides were telling, I made pretentious use of my recent trucking experiences, flaunting them the way a dandy might flaunt his father's old jeans. In the morning, I felt ashamed and very hungover. I returned to the bar and confronted the forest of crossed-through 'I's in the ledger next to my name. The barman whistled, not at the cost of my tab but at the sight of my passport.

'It is a pity,' he said, 'that you did not arrive a week earlier, before the Zambian government doubled the cost of the visa you will require.'

Without having to make any calculations, I knew that I did not have enough money left to move forwards – or backwards, for that matter. ATMs were no longer dispensing cash in Zimbabwe and, even if they had been, I had nothing in my accounts. I thought of asking my long-suffering parents to send me some money through Western Union, but it was Sunday and the local outlet was closed. I had no way of contacting Willie in Livingstone, and knew that he would carry on without me if I had not materialised by 9 a.m. This would effectively kill the story I intended telling, and I would be able to add journalism to my own personal forest of crossed-through opportunities.

The thought made me feel desperate, and I spent the day trying to outwalk my anxieties on the silent railway line to Dar es Salaam. By the time I reached the big baobab where Livingstone is said to have carved his name it was almost dark, not that it had deterred a young German lad, in all the emptiness of that corner of a wrecked country, from climbing all the way to the top. I had checked out of Shoestrings that morning but returned to the bar after sunset, saying I was there to drink and have dinner. In actual fact, I spent the night reading a Redmond O'Hanlon book locked in a toilet cubicle in the communal shower block. When the security guard finally locked the gates, I sneaked down to the bottom of the garden and tried to snag some sleep in a hammock.

An hour before dawn, to get away from the mosquitoes I walked down to the river and milled around in the darkness with the curio sellers who were on their way to the busy tourist market in Livingstone. When the border post opened we crossed the bridge as a group, watching the Zambezi spill over the kilometre length of the falls in the soft morning light. A troop of baboons patrolled the queue of trucks parked in no-man's land on the other side, climbing up the lashings like pirates, the littler ones getting beneath tarps and riffling around. I envied them their ability to move wherever they wished.

'When I arrived at the Zambian post, an official looked at my small pile of rands and told me I needed US dollars to pay for my visa. "It is not a problem," he said. "Just carry on to the Royal Livingstone Hotel and change your money there. Then come back, and we will give you your visa." He handed me back my passport.

'I stopped thinking after that. I simply walked around the boom, hailed a taxi and, fifteen minutes later, was back in the passenger seat in Willie's cab.'

'Amazing,' said Adam. 'You took your chance.'

We reached the depot in Lusaka after midnight. In the morning, I showered in an open cubicle with several other truckers, all of us semi-hiding our genitals. When I came out I bumped into a thickset white woman, who looked me up and down and said, 'Yes, okay, I know who you are.' She handed me a coffee and took me to meet her green-eyed mother, who led us to her brother, the boss of the company. He insisted we take breakfast with him on the veranda of his home, which overlooked a crystal-clear pool paved with glitter stone. A Zambian youth in a frayed chef's outfit took my order. I told them I thought Willie was marvellous, and the big-bottomed daughter said, 'Yes, they're great guys, but man, they steal. Tyres, diesel, you name it. Zambians are the worst thieves in the world.' Her mother agreed wholeheartedly. 'And this one,' she said, indicating the cook with her head, 'is the worst of the lot. I've put locks on the fridges!'

They explained that they were Zimbabweans who had, like my relatives, lost their properties to the government's land reform programme a decade before. At first they had emigrated to Cape Town, and later to London, but they had been unable to find happiness in these places.

'We're from the bush, you know,' the mother said. 'The coast, for all its prettiness, leaves us cold.'

The cook came over to clear our dishes and announced that Willie was about to leave for the Copperbelt. I had managed, by this point, to borrow enough for a flight home, so we were parting ways.

'Do you want me to tell him to drop your bags at the office?' the daughter asked. 'Mind you, you'll probably want to check them before he leaves.'

Adam shook his head in disgust. 'Yow, I can't hardly believe that.'

Her attitude upset me, but I had also experienced a kind of personal clarification. This woman, her mother and her uncle had assumed that I viewed the world as they did, but they were wrong. I regarded these truckers the way most others did, as Big Men – men to be respected, and envied. The R20 000 or so that Willie earned a month was more than I made in three. He and the other veteran cross-border drivers required no books or news broadcasts to make sense of the world outdoors, because they were out in it day and night.

Adam, who had listened with great patience while I rehashed the identity crises of my late twenties, now urged me on to the story's end.

'So they caught you at the airport?'

'Yes. The immigration officer who checked my passport could not find any visa stamp and, when I insisted that I had paid for one in Livingstone, she sent me to speak to the deputy chief – a big, intelligent man who had launched an ambitious crackdown on corruption in the service while his boss was on vacation. I repeated my lie to him and he apologised on behalf of the Zambian government before picking up his phone to call Livingstone. "This might take a while," said the deputy chief, "the line to Livingstone is very bad." It was a brown Bakelite with a rotary dial, and I thought perhaps there was a chance he would make a mistake while dialling with his big fingers. A flight attendant from my flight was waiting in the doorway, pleading with this guy to let me go so that the plane could leave. "Hang on, sister," he said, "hang on. We are working on corruption here. It takes time."

'Eventually someone picked up, and the deputy chief started laying into him, bumping his fist on the table while he talked. But after a minute his face cleared and instead of shouting he started to listen, keeping his eyes on me all this time. Zambians are the world masters of expressing astonishment, and the deputy chief had a particularly expressive voice, deep like an oboe. "Ohhh, all right," he said. "Ah-ah. Okay, okay." After another couple of minutes he gave a short laugh and said, "Fine, thank you very much, officer. *Tsalani bwino*." He put the phone back slowly and fell way back into his chair. "Christie," he said, "the officers in Livingstone remember you verrrry well."'

Adam flicked his fingers in delight. 'He got you. That man was too clever.'

'He told the flight attendant she could go, but that I would be staying. Then he told me I could either pay a US$350 admission of guilt fine, or go to court. I had no money left, so he sent me to the airport police station and knocked off for the day. The duty officers took my fingerprints and locked me in a dark cell with three Zambians. The prisoners were lying crossways when I entered, and when they saw from the light outside how tall I was they kindly shifted lengthways, so that I could lie next to them and extend my legs. I was happy enough, lying in the dark. I remembered the truck driver from the highway in Wadeville, how he had just accepted the situation and found something constructive to do. I used the time to write my article about Willie, in my head. After three days, I was released. When I arrived home, I wrote a story about Willie and the cross-border truckers, and a newspaper published it. I've been writing stories ever since.'

Adam laughed out loud. 'Tha's beautiful, man.'

'I often wonder where I would be if that trip hadn't worked out. Not happily married, I don't think. Almost certainly a junkie. I don't know …'

Adam pulled deeply on his joint and exhaled a large cone of white smoke.

'You know what I'm thinking? I'm thinking it don't matter if you're not doing your job proper. I'm not a seaman, but I travel all over the world in ships, and it costs me nothing. Seem to me you found your way, too, so fair play. Maybe we gonna travel together some day. You never know, it can happen. Inshallah.'

And so, we have a gentleman's agreement. The next time Adam is deported he will call me, and if I have not yet been fired I will fly to Dar es Salaam, where he says we will spend time with his mother and some other people from his past, before returning to South Africa, overland.

◆

Many of the Beachboys claim they like living in Cape Town.

'I love Cape Town,' Adam often says.

It is a phrase echoed everywhere you turn in this city. 'I Love Cape Town' is, at present, a private tour company's URL, a Facebook page with over three hundred thousand likes, a purveyor of kiddies' clothes located in the Victoria & Alfred Waterfront, and also Cape Town Tourism's Twitter handle. Earlier in the year, the city launched a campaign to scrub graffiti from city walls, and now many of these spaces are crowded with city-sanctioned purple, black and red heart stickers 'designed' by an artist called Michael Elion. These and other flowerings of the café class attract criticism, much of it deserved, though coming from an undocumented Tanzanian the sentiment is not so easily skipped over.

To understand the affection Adam feels for the city, it is necessary to go back to the early nineties and the arrival of the first Tanzanian migrants in South Africa.

'Most of them came from Quelimane in Mozambique, not far from Nampula,' Adam explained today, lying back in the grass beside the Nelson Mandela Boulevard on-ramp.

'They were traders there, bringing stuff in over the Tanzanian border near Mtwara. It was the time of the Mozambique civil war, and so the conditions were bad. The Renamo soldiers would beat them, steal their things and even rape them. If you tried to struggle they would kill you straight. There was no law.'

By the early nineties, a coincidence of profound events had opened a way for the Tanzanian traders to cross into South Africa: Nelson Mandela was released from Victor Verster Prison in 1990, signalling the demise of apartheid South Africa, and in 1992 the long civil war in Mozambique ended. The Tanzanian traders travelled south with their psychological baggage, though, and in Adam's analysis it was inevitable that the communities they established in South African cities ended up mistrustful and vicious, characterised by high levels of 'bongo-to-bongo' violence.

'You know, we used to rob the new boys,' he said. 'I'm talking about the Tanzanian boys who come to South Africa for the first time. We would bring them to a place like this and ask them questions. Where you from? What are you doing here? Where's your money? Then we would search the guys. In 1999 this Tanzanian boy came to Durban, 19 or so. Nobody knew him so we took his clothes, his phone, his shoes. Later that night this young boy went to the port after midnight and stowed a big ship. Three other Beachboys also stowed away in the engine room of the same ship. The crew found them after a few days but they only found the youngster at the next port, when they opened the hatches. The ship was full of *mayolo* – maize – and this boy was too young to know that they spray the maize with chemicals to kill the insects. You can't breathe that air so this guy had been dead a long time. They put his body on the deck and the captain called the other guys and said, "Do you know him?" The guys said they did not know him but then the one Beachboy started to cry. You see, that night back in Durban when they stole that boy's things this guy felt bad and took the clothes back to him. The dead person was wearing those clothes so he knew it was the same boy.'

The practice of robbing new arrivals is still alive and well in Durban, by all accounts, but Adam said something changed in Cape Town in 2008.

'The xenophobia that happened in Johannesburg pushed a lot of Tanzanian boys down here,' he said. 'The newcomers had a different mind. They had seen for themselves how South Africans were killing foreigners, and so they knew we had to stick together to survive.'

By the time Adam reached Cape Town in early 2011, this new Beachboy generation was in the ascendant.

'At this time most of the nineties Beachboys had died or gone to prison, so we changed our Beachboy ways. We stopped robbing the new boys, and now if two Beachboys want to fight we try first to make peace. No Beachboy can tell another Beachboy what to do any more. You can just be yourself. This is why I love Cape Town.'

Hoping for a kind of narrative perfection, I asked Adam whether he was the Beachboy with the conscience, who had returned the clothes to the young man. He shook his head.

'No, that was another guy.'

◆

'If you want my story we must talk soon,' Adam told me today, 'before I go somewhere. Taking a ship isn't like taking a taxi. If I get the chance, I will go, and after that you never know, I might not come back.'

His only condition was that we talked somewhere nearer to his corner outside the Grand Parade Spar than our usual spot at The Freezer, so that he could keep an eye on his stringers.

'Beachboys will fight each other over any little thing,' he explained, 'even the foils we sell for R1, which some use to smoke their *unga*. I've saw this 'appen last week. One boy sold another boy a dirty piece of foil, and the guy came back and said, "*Kuma mama ake* [mother fucker], you sold me dirty foil," and when he got close the other guy bit his lip, the bottom one, until it was hanging off his face like a piece of bacon.'

I suggested we meet outside the headquarters of Woolworths on Longmarket Street. Although separated from the Parade by just a single row of buildings, this is a parallel world of brick avenues and Chinese infinity balls, the air perforated by the click of stiletto heels. Adam appeared trailing a CCID guard, who did not hesitate to ask me, 'Is this your friend?'

'Yes.'

'You see, I told you. Now *fokof*,' said Adam, deploying that beautiful palindrome of Cape Afrikaans. It was drizzling and I had thought we could talk under the grocer's eaves, but the guard insisted we move out under the naked plane trees.

'I'm going to start in 1999,' said Adam, pulling two news posters off nearby streetlights to cover the wet metal of a nearby public bench. 'That was the year I stowed my first ship, in Durban. Before that I was in Dar es Salaam. That's another story, which you will learn when you meet me there. If I tell you now you will not understand, not really.'

I nodded, happy to go along with the pretence that we may actually meet in Tanzania one day.

'I don't remember the name of the first ship I stowed. I've stowed nine ships since and I remember all their names but not the first one. I was in a hurry at the time. I was 17. I had been living with the Durban Beachboys for six months, trying to get a ship every night. Nobody was trying harder than me. One night, February I think, a cargo ship docked at Pier 2. I was with a friend called Nnanani, and another guy called Bambo. Nnanani had already stowed a ship about a month before. He was caught and deported to Dar es Salaam, and he had just arrived back in Durban that day, and already he wanted to stow another ship. We came closer to the port and noticed that the crew was Chinese. Bambo decided to turn back when he saw this because Beachboys were too afraid of Chinese crews at this time. A lot of our guys had already been thrown in the sea by Chinese seamen in the nineties. It is better now, but in 1999 people were proper scared, especially of the mainland Chinese crews. Hong Kong Chinese are better, but you can't tell who is who from a distance, so Bambo left,' said Adam.

When Adam and Nnanani saw that the gangway of the bulk carrier at Pier 2 was unguarded, they sprinted up the steps and made it onto the deck, which, at 1 a.m., was clear. Skirting the cabins, they came to a place where fuel drums had been stacked one on top of the other.

'We each climbed in a drum and made our bodies small,' said Adam, folding his arms against his chest. 'After an hour a guy came and shook the drums but he never looked inside. Afterwards I felt the ship going. I don't know what he was thinking but Nnanani climbed out of his drum and came and shook my drum. I thought I had been caught until I heard him whispering to me. When I came out I saw the sea all around the ship, and the land far away. I thought, *What the fuck, Durban is leaving. I'm at sea for the first time.* It's a feeling I can't really explain.'

The two friends needed to find somewhere better to hide, and decided to climb the tower of the ship's cargo crane hand over hand on the vertical ladder until they reached a platform which, if they kept their bodies flattened, shielded them from view.

'It is very high, if you drop you're dead, but I grew up climbing coconut trees in Tanzania so it wasn't a problem,' said Adam.

The ship tracked South Africa's east coast in the darkness and by mid morning drew towards another port.

'Nnanani knew what was going on. He said, "Yow, we're docking at Richards Bay," a South African port in the forest, near the border with Mozambique. He said we needed to stay hidden until the ship left, but after five days we were still there. I said, "Nnanani, we don't know when this ship is going to leave and we can't go on like this. I'm going to try and escape."'

Having observed the deck-top activity for days, the stowaways knew exactly when the crew took lunch and, at this time, scuttled down and made for the gangway. Rounding the cabin block once more, they ran into a Congolese security guard.

'The security officer radioed for chief officer, who came and said, "Where you stow?" I said, "Durban." He said, "You sure?" and then he punched me. He asked again. Nnanani said, "Durban," so he punched him too, and almost broke Nnanani's thumb. After that he locked us in a cabin and brought us food and water.'

The Beachboys slept for hours, and when they woke it was to the barking of sniffer dogs, searching the ship for other stowaways. When this process had been concluded, the cabin door was opened and a man the boys had never seen before ordered them down the gangway and into a minibus with the name of a stowaway detection service written on the side. The sniffer dogs went in the back, and Adam was guided into the passenger seat, with Nnanani behind him on a bench.

'I had big amount of ganja in my sock, seventy grams or so. I was thinking, *They're going to take us to the police station straight*, so I decided to leave it under the seat of the car. But they just stopped the car outside the port area and said, "Come off." Richards Bay harbour is surrounded by a big forest and they just left us there in the bushes. We hugged each other then, me and my brother, because we were free to carry on with our lives.'

Adam and Nnanani were too naïve to know it then, but their sudden release was not out of the ordinary. One of the unlisted services that stowaway detection outfits provide to shipmasters is the removal of stowaways from under the noses of port authorities. The procedural processing of stowaways costs a great deal of time and money – up to R100 000 a case, according to insurers – and shipping companies happily pay for alternative outcomes.

Adam and Nnanani were dropped on the side of Harbour Arterial, just before the on-ramp to the John Ross Highway, and were advised that a left turn and a fifteen-kilometre walk in the direction of Durban would get them to Empangeni, the nearest town. This was a lie. If the boys had walked just two kilometres in the other direction, they would have reached the town of Richards Bay. Here, they would have encountered some of Richards Bay's Beachboys, who would have conducted them to the secret encampment in the dense forest near Lake Mzingazi.

Instead, they arrived in Empangeni after dark and slept in some bushes. In the morning, they listened out for voices they could understand.

'We heard one guy speaking Swahili, name of Sylvester,' said Adam. 'This guy was from Mtwara on Tanzania's south coast. In 2003 Sylvester made a successful drug run to Brazil, and became one of the area's biggest drug dealers, but in 1999 he was still a barber, working out of a shipping container. He looked at me and said, "*Unahitaji kula*, you must eat." I said, "We need to get to Richards Bay, so that we can try stow another ship," and he said, "No, *wewe ni kwenda kufa*." So I said, "Okay, we will go with you and eat food."'

Nnanani soon caught a taxi back to Durban, but it was a month before Sylvester gave Adam his blessing to carry on to Richards Bay.

'I think he wanted me to stay and help him with his business, but the only thing I could think of was ships.'

When Adam left for Richards Bay, he was not alone. A week before, a young Tanzanian called Hussen Chiza had come to Empangeni, seeking his cousin. When the young man heard that his cousin had moved to Maputo, he asked Adam if he could join his next stowaway attempt.

'I told this boy it was going to be difficult. I knew I could walk into Richards Bay and nobody would touch me because I arrived in a ship, not in a taxi or a bus. I was already Sea Power but Hussen was nobody, just a boy, and I knew they were going to rob him. When I told Hussen this, he said he had R3 000. I said, "Okay, give it to me and let's see what is going to happen."'

Adam's strategy was simple. When he and Hussen came among the Richards Bay Beachboys, he announced that they had R3 000 between them, and that they planned to spend all of it on beer and food for the others. All they wanted in return was a chance to try their luck at the port.

'Richards Bay is not like the other ports,' Adam explained. 'In Cape Town and Durban, nobody cares if you walk along the fence, but Richards Bay port is surrounded by forest, and to get there from where the Beachboys stay you have to walk all night. Because of these conditions they have a rule that only two or three guys can go to the port at one time, and they're only allowed to stay there for four days. If they haven't stowed a ship in four days they must come back, to give the next group a chance.'

A group had departed hours before Adam and Hussen's arrival, led by the Beachboy called Dullah Macho Mzungu – Dullah because his first name was Abdullah, and Macho Mzungu because his eyes (*macho*) were blue, 'like the eyes of a white person (*mzungu*)'.

'The others said we would have to ask Dullah. I could see they were afraid of him. Dullah and his friends had killed another Bongoman and buried the body on the beach not long before, so he was in power at the time. We waited four days for Dullah to return, and when he did we were proper nervous, I can't lie, but I spoke to him and he was an all right guy. I remember he gave me one of the apples he had taken with him to the port. I took him straight to the Beachboy bar and bought him a drink. I said, "You give me hope, Dullah Macho Mzungu. You didn't make it, but me, I'm going to make it." And we drank. After dinner we walked: me, Hussen and two other guys called Chilli and Gift, who I chose because they knew the way. We bought everything for them: glucose, water, food. I remember there was a tin of fish in there, some biscuits, bread, even beer. We also had some ganja and a torch, because it's dark in the jungle. When we left I didn't have a penny left.'

The party walked for most of the night and, at 4 a.m., came to the shore of a small bay beside the multipurpose terminal. There were no ships docked at the terminal, so the men crawled into the enormous dolosse scattered nearby and smoked joint after joint.

'I put my head up in the morning and saw two ships out at sea. I went back down and smoked another spliff, and when I came up I saw the biggest ship I ever seen in my life, coming towards the terminal. I went down and said, "Guys, we need to make quick d'ua [prayer]." Nobody knew how to make a d'ua, so I said three allahamdus [alhamdullilah – God is great], and then we jumped the harbour fence.'

The ship the four stowaways approached with stealthy speed was a behemoth – the 260-metre-long bulk carrier *Global Victory*, just three years at sea. It had a bright-red hull, which loomed over the men like a planet. When the Tanzanians reached the bottom of the steps, the guard at the top of the gangway walked away from his post, as if on cue. They were aboard in moments.

'We saw this door in the ship, with handles and locks that looked like scissors. I said, "Yow, Chilli, open this," and he did. The room was full of paint tins, like a *ghala*, or hardware store. Hussen and me hid ourselves on the bottom level, and the other two hid on top. We stayed there all day but at night Chilli and Gift came down and said, "We have to leave, it isn't safe." I said, "What the fuck, are you crazy? We are safe here. Outside, anyone can come from any direction." I told Hussen, "Go if you want," but he said, "Memory, I came with you, I trust you, I'm going to stay." The other two made it to the engine room but a guy saw them and told them to get off the ship. That is what I found out when I bumped into Chilli in Johannesburg in 2010. After thirty minutes, a guy came to our room and opened the door. He shone his torch a bit and then he closed the door. After another twenty minutes, the ship started shaking. In two hours, the ship was moving. I came out. There was a small hole in the door, just big enough for one eye to see outside. I saw people were busy folding the ropes. I came back and said, "Yow, we're going, the ship is fucking going." We hugged each other.'

Adam knew from conversations with other stowaways that it was not enough to make it out to sea, and that to stand any chance of reaching Europe they would have to remain concealed until the vessel was well clear of the port of Cape Town – if, indeed, it would be travelling that way. He knew that the journey from Richards Bay around Cape Point took roughly five days, so the pair counted five nights and, on the sixth day, left their hiding place and hailed the first crew member they spotted.

'When this guy saw me he shouted, "Stowaway!" and held his chest here, like he was 'avin a heart attack. He told us, "Wait here, wait here!" and ran to fetch the captain, an old Korean guy called Jay Jeong.

Captain Jeong looked at us and said, "Don't worry, boys. We are very far from Africa already."'

The benevolent captain put Adam and Hussen in a cabin, and ensured that they were well fed and kept in beer and cigarettes.

'He was like my father,' said Adam, 'that is what I thought at the time.'

The two friends were not confined to their cabin, but they happily spent most of each day there, swapping stories. Adam learnt that Hussen was from a village near Kigoma, on the shores of Lake Tanganyika.

'He started telling me about his family – his mother and his sisters. He'd had a hard life, same like me. He never knew his daddy.'

Adam, who likes nothing better than an escape story, was enchanted by Hussen's flight from Kigoma at the age of 12.

'Hussen's aunt, who he was living with, was renting a room to this old shopkeeper, and he used to give Hussen money and tell him to buy stuff for the shop. One day Hussen took that money and rented a bike, which he pedalled to the next village. He left it there in some bushes and paid for a space in a car to Dar es Salaam. He never bin back since that day.'

On board the *Global Victory*, Adam maintained he was from Somalia and Hussen, who was darker skinned, said he was from Burundi. They had been told by other Beachboys that this was the way things were done, though between them they had no clue why. Their ignorance probably worked in their favour, because the experienced captain believed them and radioed ahead to Rotterdam, the next port of call, to inform the Dutch authorities that he had two bona fide asylum seekers on board his ship.

'I knew nothing at all about seeking asylum,' said Adam, 'and I didn't speak a word of English. When we arrived in Rotterdam, the Holland authorities sent a guy to communicate with us in Swahili, and because it was the only thing I could speak they found out that I wasn't a Somalian guy. That fucked me up, and they sent us back to the ship. When the Dutch police handed us over to Captain Jeong they said, "Here we go, sir, we're returning your crew." Mr Jeong looked like was going to cry. He said, "You told me you from Somalia, but you from Tanzania. You lied to me!" He wasn't happy with us for a bit, but then he came to our cabin and gave us each a cigarette and he said, "You know where the ship is going next?" I said, "No, I don't know. You tell me, Captain." He said, "England." He said if we got off at England they would send us back to Africa. I'm not sure if he was warning us to stay on the ship or encouraging us to leave, but anyway, he gave us that information.'

A day later, the *Global Victory* was at anchor off the 12th-century city of Kingston upon Hull. Adam and Hussen, who caught sight of the shoreline every time they used the outside toilet, were underwhelmed.

'I told Hussen, "Yow, if this is all we can tell the people at home about Holland and England, it is better we die right here on the ship."'

After two weeks at anchor, the ship started shaking again and moved into a berth in the Albert Dock.

'After half an hour nobody had come to fetch us, so I told Hussen, "Come, let's pretend to pee and see if we can escape." We saw there was nobody at the top of the gangway, so we just walked down. There was a guy at an electronic gate at the bottom but the gate opened automatically and he just let us walk through. Outside the port we saw signs on the highway saying Liverpool, Manchester, just like the football teams, and that gave us big nervousness. We felt like everyone who passed us in a car was looking, so we ducked into a park and just chilled there. We had no plan, but Allah was looking after us because in all of the white city of Hull here comes this black guy. Hussen could speak some English and he found out that this guy was a Cameroon guy called Simone, and he was in the park to meet his ganja dealer before going to work a night shift somewhere in Sheffield. He took us to his place and said we could stay the night, then he left and locked the door.'

I had been writing furiously the whole time Adam had been speaking, shielding my notebook from the spitting sky with my coat. I hadn't looked at Adam in all this time, and when I did I saw that he was shaking with cold.

'Sorry, Adam, you're freezing.'

'I am freezing my fucking balls off.'

'Let's stop there. It's a good place to stop, anyway. You can tell me about England tomorrow, if you have time.'

'No problem. I have time. I got *fokol* to do, to be honest with you.'

Passing an electronics store on the way back to the Parade, Adam casually mentioned that he had robbed the place back in 2011. 'Me and some boys knocked the bottom glass out with a wheelie bin and I crawled in and filled the bin with stuff and left. I got about R10 000 for the gear. We had a big party under the bridge.'

At the Darling Street KFC, Adam crossed to his corner, eyes

narrow against the weather, which had steadily worsened. I climbed into the Conquest and turned upslope, heading home.

◆

Adam has been arrested.

We were sitting with Barak and Sudi against the fence of the Ford Imperial dealership off Hertzog Boulevard when a police cruiser stopped in the panhandle of Old Marine Drive. Two male officers stepped out, one paunchy, the other diminutive. Adam broke off telling me about England and watched as the officers walked over to a nearby Cape Willow and peered into its dense canopy.

'*Wapashesha*,' Adam grumbled. 'That's what we call the railway police. They always *shesha shesha*, you know, trying to catch us with drugs. They make life very difficult for Beachboys.'

Shesha is Zulu for 'rush', one of many local words absorbed into Beachboy lingo.

'That fat one is called Wellington, but we call him Kichwa because he has such a big head. The other one is called Prince. We've known them for a long time now.'

After a small conference, the little cop meshed his fingers and boosted the big one up to the crook of the tree. A lot of branch shaking ensued and then, to my great surprise, two backpacks fell to the ground. This brought several Beachboys running from the direction of the Nelson Mandela Boulevard off-ramp, Daniel Peter among them. Slung around his shoulder was a large straight-shackle padlock attached to a heavy-duty chain – the type used for locking up traders' trolleys. The officers quickly wrestled him to the ground, where the smaller of the two – Sergeant Prince – remained sitting on his back. In the hope that we might intervene somehow, Daniel Peter shouted over that one of the bags was his and that it contained his prize sketchbook. The notebook came fluttering to earth when the bag was upended.

Adam stormed over, yelling that the boy had done nothing wrong. 'You just want money again, *kuma mama ake*.'

'Trouble now,' Barak whispered as the little cop rose, allowing Daniel Peter to wriggle free. Sudi urged restraint – 'Memory, *twende*' – and clucked his tongue.

Prince moved forwards a few steps. 'You want to get fucked up?'

'I'm not from this country so you better kill me because if you don't

I will kill you,' Adam yelled, standing his ground. The threat of mortal violence took the officer by surprise. He looked over at his associate in pure amazement before launching a kick that Adam had anticipated. Adam swayed sideways and the policeman's kick merely grazed his side before reaching the limits of its force beneath his armpit, at which point Adam reflexively clamped down and began pulling Prince around on one leg, a scene so farcical that even the big cop laughed, until Prince let out a scream of pain.

'He just had an operation, you *poes*,' said Sergeant Kichwa. Adam relaxed his grip and Prince slumped to the ground, clutching the knee that had taken his weight.

'It's his second operation on the same leg.'

'I'm sorry, I didn't know.' Adam sounded genuinely contrite.

'You can tell the court you are sorry. I'm putting you under arrest. What you did is a Section 67 offence, assaulting an officer. The judge is going to give you one year for this.'

Adam walked forward with his wrists together.

'Come, let's go. Your police station is my hotel. Fuck you both.'

Later, after Adam had been bundled into the back of the van and taken off to Cape Town Central, up the road from the Grand Parade, Barak said it was unusual that the *wapashesha* had actually made the arrest.

'Normally we just pay them some money, whatever we have, and they leave us. Or they take our cellphones. I think maybe they saw that you were watching them and thought it must be better to make the arrest this time.'

I asked if there was anything I could do.

'Memory will call you from Pollsmoor,' said Barak.

Sudi nodded but said nothing.

'I think I'm going to go now.'

'In a bit,' said Barak.

I walked off.

◆

Adam called from Pollsmoor Prison to say that he had been charged with interference.

Over a background din of singing inmates, he asked whether I could buy R60 worth of MTN airtime and SMS the code to the number he was calling from. The phone, he said – an *enjin* in prison parlance – belonged to another inmate, who would take half the airtime as his own and then allow Adam, effectively, to rent the device out to other inmates for as long as the airtime lasted, swinging it between cells with lengths of string. The inmates would pay him in marijuana stops or bowls of rice.

Since Pollsmoor is the largest prison in the Western Cape and the institution most associated with the enigmatic and notoriously violent Numbers gang, I asked after his safety.

'I'm in the Muslim cell, which is quieter, and the food is better. There are many Tanzanians inside the cell with me, and even two or three Sea Power, so nobody gonna mess around. It's just boring, you know. Nothing to do.'

I asked whether telling me more of his story over the phone would help to pass the hours.

'Of course. Where did we leave it?'

'You and Hussen had just left the Port of Hull, where you met a Cameroonian called Simone who gave you a place to stay.'

'Okay. Strange to hear that name … Hussen.'

'That's what you've been calling him.'

'I actually know him better as Dawoodi, Dawoodi Chisa. You see, Simone introduced us to some Arab Sudanese guys who were very serious Muslims, praying five times every day. We needed their help so we pretended we were very serious Muslims too. Hussen became so good at praying that I started to call him Dawoodi, because everybody knows the Dawoodi Bohra people from India are the most strict Muslims you can find anywhere. Soon everyone was calling him Dawoodi, but he wasn't really serious about Islam. The Sudanese guys gave us money, and we would use it to secretly go drinking. But a funny thing 'appened you know. After a while Dawoodi started living with these guys, and they took him to Birmingham where there are many more Sudanese refugees. I think he's still living with them until today, in Birmingham or maybe Middlesbrough, still praying five times.'

Adam had stayed on at Simone's place until Dawoodi sent cash for the bus journey to Birmingham. The moment the bus had pulled into Birmingham Coach Station, he'd known he was in the right place.

'On the streets it was just blacks and Indians, nothing white. In Hull City everyone used to look at me but in Birmingham I was invisible. Memory Card had arrived in black town.'

Adam had lived with Dawoodi's Sudanese connections for several months, but increasingly spent his time with British-Jamaican dealers and bookies on Soho Road in the suburb of Handsworth. To fit in, he had adopted a Jamaican identity.

'I learnt how to speak Jamaica patois before I knew English. If anyone asked me where I was from, I told them *miya Mobay*, which means Montego Bay. I never been there but I could describe it like a natural.'

By December 1999, he was also learning Nigerian pidgin from a Lagosian called Felicia, who had employed him to fry chicken and chips in her takeaway restaurant in Walsall.

'I worked in that chippy until I understood the streets of Birmingham. Felicia wanted me to stay working but it was not for me, to be honest, frying chips all day, so one morning I took all the money in the till and walked out and bought some ganja with it. The Jamaican dealers knew I arrived on a ship with nothing so they didn't get jealous, they let me hustle. They used to call me Afro Boy, short for African boy. They adopted me, I think I can say that.'

Selling marijuana had enabled Adam to rent a squalid room from a Jamaican dealer. He spent most of his free time in Ladbrokes, 'betting horses, football, roulette, even dogs'.

Adam's other major pastime had been riding buses – his way of exploring the new environment. In Hull, he had been afraid to go outside. In Birmingham, he'd made up for months of confinement.

'I remember the routes like it was yesterday,' he said. 'The 79 was my main bus, the Birmingham to Wolverhampton. The 74 was Birmingham to Dudley and the 55 was Birmingham to Walsall. I met Rochelle on the 79.'

Rochelle and her cousin Lisa had clambered aboard the 79 one afternoon in early 2000. Adam was sitting in his usual position, in the middle of the back row, when they came up the steps.

'They were also bus riders,' he said. 'They would just get on and go anywhere, just to see what was going to happen. I remember Rochelle came and pushed past my knees and sat next to the left window. She said hullo but that was all. Her friend sat in the seat in front and turned to talk. She said, "Do you like me?" I said, "No, but I like your friend." Rochelle just smiled and kept looking out the window. I didn't have a phone at that time so I went all over the bus looking for a pen so I could take her number. Nobody 'ad one, so I lost her.'

Adam had bumped into Lisa several more times on the buses, but never Rochelle. One morning, with nothing better to do, he had bought and downed a half-jack of Russian Bear vodka before boarding the 79. He usually stepped off at Wolverhampton, but had decided on a whim to get out at West Bromwich; the moment he gathered his senses, he'd spotted Rochelle and her cousin in a phone booth.

'I had a phone by this time so I went straight to Rochelle and said, "Put your number please." She put it in. I said, "Okay, see you later, I'll call you."'

Adam had wanted to call her that afternoon, but he didn't have enough cash for airtime. A week had gone by and every time he'd thought of calling Rochelle, which was every other minute, he'd found some reason to put it off. In the meantime, he'd picked a young man's pocket on the 79 and come away with another phone.

'At that time people called that type of phone a 3, because it was a phone, a camera and it played music. I saw there was airtime, so I called Rochelle. She said, "Who this?" I said, "Adam." She said, "I'm not your baby no more, you never called me until now, whatever happened to you?" I said I was sorry, and then I explained the truth of myself. I told her I was a stowaway boy from Africa, with no documents at all. I described how me and Dawoodi came to the *Global Victory* through the forest in South Africa. She felt sad for me. She said, "You make me cry, bwoy."'

They had made a plan to meet the next morning at the McDonald's on Holyhead Road. It was, said Adam, a compromise venue, 'halfway from the ghetto areas of Handsworth and the nice part of West Brom, where Rochelle lived with her mother and stepdaddy.'

The meeting had gone well. Adam had talked again of his childhood, telling Rochelle about his absent father and troubled relationship with his mother. Rochelle had said that her father had also been absent most of her life.

'We became friends after that, meeting up nearly every day to talk.'

After a year, Rochelle had agreed to go on a date with Adam in the Winson Green area. They slept together for the first time that day, in Adam's squat.

'On the second day she saw me again, and the day after that she came with her mum and her stepfather and said, "I done speak to me mum and you're going to stay with us. Pack your stuff, we going." I said, "Fair play," and we jumped in her mum's car, a Ford Focus two-door, and went back to West Brom and put my things in her room.

That was my new life. Before I had to take a bus to get to my corner but now I could walk there in five minutes.'

Adam's living conditions may have improved, but the new situation had come with its challenges. He still had to hustle by day. When Rochelle's stepfather had learnt of this, he had started supplying Adam with high-quality skunk – 'real Dutch stuff' – in greater quantities than Adam was used to moving.

'Before, I would sell maybe a quarter ounce a day, just enough to live, but now I was selling an ounce or two, even supplying some of the other hustlers and having enough left to sell two or three hens myself.'

'What's a hen?'

'It's what South Africans call a stop. A small section of maybe one or two grams.'

Adam would make anything between £50 and £100 a day. If he was having a good week at the bookies, his roll of cash could grow to £2 000 or more. With Rochelle's help, he had sent money back to his mother and elder half-brother. He had visited a tattoo parlour and had a nautical wheel inscribed on the back of his right hand. He had visited a jeweller and had gold caps fashioned and applied to his incisors. But he found that he was not nearly as happy as he had been in his first years in Birmingham.

'Rochelle's stepdaddy was always cussin' me, always trying to control me. Even his own daughter – because he had two daughters with Rochelle's mum – said, "Watch out, he will try to bully you." He even told me I should leave Rochelle and go stay by him. I didn't like that and neither did Rochelle, so we moved to a small house in Dudley and I left him and went back to work for myself.'

The split had left Adam in a quandary, because he could not go back to selling inferior weed on Soho Road without suffering serious reputation damage. To get by, he had started breaking into homes in his new neighbourhood, gaining access by sliding a skinny arm through the mail slot and turning the Yale locks.

'I got a big camera from this one house, where the guy had a small weed plant in his office. Another time I opened the door and saw a stack of £20 notes on the sofa, like they had been left there for me.'

Adam had also started selling crack cocaine and abusing alcohol, especially after he'd learnt that Rochelle was pregnant.

'I was happy for her, but I also felt bad in my own self. When I was a boy I swore I would never give a child a life like mine. Me and

Rochelle used to talk about what we gonna do to raise that baby but in my mind I already knew I was going to go down sometime, and that she would be left alone. Maybe not tomorrow but sometime, because I 'ad no status.'

And there'd been something else. Although he was no longer in contact with Rochelle's stepfather, he'd felt the man's rage all around him, like a curse searching for the right moment. To him, this curse was as real as the air he was breathing. What else could explain the fact that 16-year-old Brummies were suddenly harassing him on Soho Road, when for years he had experienced no troubles? He had been jumped on the 79, and had narrowly escaped arrest after a fight had broken out on the pavement.

In 2007, he had smoked heroin for the first time. It had made him sick but he'd smoked again the next day and felt wonderful, at peace with the world. Rochelle was seven months pregnant, healthy and happy.

'When I smoked everything was clear,' said Adam, 'and the truth was I felt bad because I hadn't spoken to my mother for seven years. We were fighting when I left for South Africa but I was a boy then, and in England I became a man. I could see her struggles in a new way and I forgave her everything. I had to make peace with 'er, I knew that. I was going to call 'er that week but before I could do it I got nicked for dealing in the city centre.'

Adam had been charged with possession of a Class A substance and held for the weekend. After he had been released on bail, his fellow dealers on Soho Road had advised him to avoid his court date in a month's time.

'They said, "The police don't know who you are, Afro bwoy. You're not in the system, so never go back there again." But to be honest I was tired of life on the streets. If I could have had a decent job then fine, but all I could do was keep hustling. That is not life, not really. So I went back to court, and they told me to go and sign in with the immigration officer. I told this guy straight: "My name is Daniel Solomon Belete from Ethiopia, and I'm seeking asylum." He gave me the asylum forms to fill out and then he said, "Tomorrow you're going to court. They will give you bail and after that we will give you accommodation." I told him, "Fair play," but before I left his office I put my fingerprints in his computer. Five minutes later he came to my cell and said, "Adam, why you fucking around, man?" He found my details in the computer. Holland, Germany and the UK share a system, you see, and in Rotterdam I gave my name and my story, and this officer saw everything.'

Adam had posted bail the next day, but had been instructed to sign in at the immigration office in nearby Solihull every Thursday until his next court date in another month. He had made the trip only once, and it had cost him.

'When I went back to court, the judge set another court date for two months' time. He was about to let me go when he read a paper in my file telling him that I had not been visiting Solihull. He said, "Mr Adam, you did not go and sign with the immigration officer, so I'm going to remand you in fooken custard-y." So, I had to go down to Winson Green Prison.'

At his trial the judge had rejected Adam's claim that the drugs had been for his personal use, and had handed him a three-year sentence.

'I went straight to Shrewsbury Prison, which was full of white boys from Stoke City. I loved those guys. They called me Captain 'cos of the tattoo on my hand. To be honest with you, all the time I was in England I got on with white guys more than black guys. If you say you're from Africa the black British treat you differently, they diss you. The white guys don't care.'

While Adam was awaiting trial, Rochelle had visited him twice a week, and she had kept these visits up when he had been moved to HM Prison Shrewsbury. One morning, he'd broken down and told her how sorry he was that she would give birth to their child while he was locked up. Her response had taken him by surprise.

'She said, "Don't worry, my daddy was locked up when my mum had me. My mum and me was fine. Your baby will be fine and so will I."'

When Rochelle was eight and a half months pregnant, Adam had been moved to HM Prison Stafford. In the early hours of 9 December 2007, he had been roused by one of the wardens.

'He said, "Adam, are you expecting a baby?" I said, "Yeah." He said, "Congratulations, you're a father."'

Adam had celebrated by drinking prison hooch with his Pakistani cellmate. He had met Aniya for the first time a week later, in the visitor's centre. Eighteen months into his sentence he had been informed that his release was imminent, but that he would be taken directly to Heathrow Airport and put on a plane back to Africa. The news had come as a great shock to Rochelle, but Adam had not been surprised.

'For six years I never thought about Tanzania but in prison I started dreaming about Dar es Salaam every night. I would see my uncles and aunts praying in a circle for me to come home. I have a difficult family, to be honest. If you get somewhere in life they want to pull you back. It was them who gave me those dreams, I swear, and I knew that no matter what I was going to try with the British government, my family would pull me home.'

This was not the first time that Adam had characterised his family as a kind of negative force, bent on keeping him from happiness. I wondered whether he hadn't just processed his homesickness in this manner, as a way of staving off his guilt about leaving Rochelle and Aniya. I pressed for clarity.

'Did you dream that your family members were worried about you, and praying that you would return safely?'

'No, not worried about me – worried that I might be doing something good with my life. They do not want me to go forward. It would drive them mad and they would not sleep until I came back down. You can't understand my family until you come to Tanzania with me and meet them.'

I left it there, remembering that he was, once again, in a cell, three years and half a world away from his daughter.

The last time he had seen Aniya was in Harmondsworth Immigration Removal Centre, near Heathrow. Adam had called a former girlfriend called Nanette and begged her to bring Rochelle and Aniya across the country for one last visit. Rochelle had packed Adam's possessions into a single backpack.

'I gave her a hug when she arrived and said, "I'm going, nothing I can do." I picked Aniya up and hugged her, then let her play on the floor for two minutes while I talked to her mother. Rochelle was crying. I told her, "Don't worry about me, just look after the baby, do everything you can."'

Adam had called Rochelle hours after he landed in Dar es Salaam.

'She said, "Are you already there?" I said, "I'm here, I don't know what to do."'

In fact, Adam had known exactly what he was going to do. He had caught a bus to Mbagala Road in the township of Temeke, where he had spent his teenage years. Here, he had scouted the street scene and found a vacant plot bordered by derelict buildings – an ideal spot for developing his own *maskani*. To ensure that his *maskani* was instantly and permanently busy, he had cooked breakfast, lunch and dinner, and shared his meals with anyone who stopped by. Before long, he'd commanded a network of confederates, mostly men in their late teens – the age Adam had been when he had left Tanzania. They had found his stories of ships and British cities intoxicating, and had been awed by his golden teeth and his nautical tattoos. The area's residents had been appalled, but, since Adam had issued strict instructions that no crime be committed in the immediate neighbourhood, there had been little that anybody could do about the increasingly busy *maskani*.

That had changed one evening after a football derby. The local team had lost, and a player from the winning side had come to Adam's *maskani* to gloat. He had worked the younger men into a frenzy of indignation by the time Adam had intervened.

'I told the guys, "Forget about it, that's football, sometimes you win and sometimes you lose." It's like the white people say, sometimes tea, sometimes coffee. This guy stood up out of nowhere and said, "*Msenge*, what does *msenge* know about football?" *Msenge* means "gay" in Swahili, that's what he called me. I just stood and put him three times in the chest with my screwdriver, bup bup bup. He screamed, "Aah, you're killing me, please, please." One of my friends said, "Yow, you need to go, Memory," so I left but I didn't like to run away because of this boy, so I came back and the police were waiting for me. They hit me with a big stick – bang, on my head – and took me to Chang'ombe police station. I thought, *If this guy dies I'm going down*, so I was preparing myself to go to Keko Prison by robbing the new people coming into the police cells. Anyone in Dar es Salaam will tell you that you can't go to Keko with nothing and expect to survive. You need something to trade. On the third day in Chang'ombe, the older brother of the guy I stabbed came to talk to me. He was an old Beachboy, and we talked nicely for an hour. Afterwards he said, "I see you have no problem, you're a peaceful guy, maybe my brother has the problem." He told the police his family was dropping the case.'

In a gush of relief, Adam had divided all of his money between the inmates, and had even stepped out of his clothes and handed them to the men he had robbed.

'When I left by the back entrance I was wearing only my boxers, and the policemen who were playing cards there stood up and ran, shouting, "*Chizi ana kimbiya*, a madman has escaped." I walked straight to the house of the guy I stabbed, and he also started shouting, "Memory, I'm sorry, I'm sorry, don't kill me." I told him, "Please, settle down,

I'm here to apologise. I lost my temper and I stabbed you. You're lucky you lived, but I'm also lucky because if you died my life would be over as well, so let us give thanks to Allah." He prayed with me and even gave me some clothes to wear, but the residents around my *maskani* now believed I was a monster. I knew that they would keep calling the police until I was in prison, so I decided to come back to South Africa.'

Adam had set forth without money or emergency travel documents, planning to hitch or hide away in trucks.

'Beachboys call this *chukua safari ki*, to stow away on land,' he said.

He had made it through Malawi and reached Inchope in central Mozambique before he had been arrested for having no papers. It was 13 March 2010. He had spent the next three months in Beira Prison, where he had attained a measure of local fame by claiming that he was a Jamaican citizen who had been robbed while on his way from Johannesburg to Nairobi, where, he claimed, he was due to meet his girlfriend.

'Some newspaper people came and interviewed me, and after the story was published the police sent a real Rasta woman from Jamaica to suss me out. That was in early June and she told me she was going back to Jamaica in July. I said, "I wish me was you mum, going home. Miya suffer here you know, sista, no food to nyam." The police asked her, "Is he really Jamaican?" and she said, "He sound Jamaican. I think he Jamaican." The next day they let me out and gave me emergency travel documents and a ticket to Maputo, pocket money as well. I arrived around 9 p.m. in the centre of Maputo.'

The first person Adam had spoken with was an old man, who wore big yellow-framed glasses like a clown.

'"Where you from?" he asked. I showed him my emergency travel documents and he said, "You from Jamaica? You're welcome. No *jaja* no muse." Tha's what Bob Marley told the people – no weed, no music. He took me to an old house to sleep. I woke up in the morning and I saw there was a shit next to my head. In Swahili we call a place like this a *gofu* house: no windows, no water, no electricity, pure ghetto. In Maputo so many people live in *gofu* houses.'

The elderly tramp had insisted on buying food for Adam the following day, and the day after that. He had bought *kachasu* and invited others around to drink and meet the curious, tattooed traveller. A woman a few years younger than Adam had taken his hand and wouldn't let it go. Through the elderly man she had said she wanted him to stay – that she knew of a room in a nearby house where they could live. Adam had lied and told her he would think about it. The following day he'd risen and was on the road to the South African border before dawn.

'I feel bad I never said goodbye. They were good people and they loved me. I should 'ave at least let them know where I was, because maybe the next guy who comes to them will be treated differently. Maybe they rob 'im instead of love him.'

Adam had genuinely been in a hurry, though. It had been his plan all along to make it to South Africa for the FIFA World Cup and, what with all the delays, he had been in real danger of missing out. He had jumped the border at Komatipoort the same day, and arrived in Johannesburg two days later. When the World Cup had officially opened on 11 June he'd been cruising the crowds outside Soccer City, the calabash-shaped stadium near Soweto. He had picked a few pockets and thought smugly that nobody had travelled a harder road to be there. The following day he had worked the crowds outside the Ellis Park Stadium, where Nigeria played Argentina. At night he had stayed with some Tanzanians he knew in Braamfontein, swapping the phones he had pulled for *unga*. He'd impressed a lot of people with his stories, and become over-enthused – bolshy, even – like a student on a much-anticipated summer break. After the 2–2 Slovenia–USA draw, he'd joined an ecstatic circle of American supporters in chanting U-S-A, U-S-A on the streets of Doornfontein.

'I was watching this young man in a white T-shirt with Brooklyn written across his chest in red,' said Adam. 'He had a nice camera, which I took eventually. I walked away from the group. That was my mistake – I was supposed to run. He saw me going and followed, so I put the camera down the back of my pants and said, "What are you talking about?" He called the other guys and they all started shouting at me. I started running and suddenly everyone in that whole valley was after me, including security guards and police. I dropped the camera in a bin and twenty yards on they caught me.'

The camera was never found but the South African government had established special courts and extraordinary legal procedures with a view to keeping people like Adam off the city streets for the duration of the World Cup. The judge had dismissed the theft charges, but sentenced Adam to three months in Johannesburg Central Prison for failing to prove that he was in South Africa legally. When the last of the World Cup crowds had drained back to their home countries, Adam had been transported to Lindela Repatriation Centre outside Pretoria, where he'd been incarcerated for another two months. Once again, he'd claimed he was an asylum-seeking Somali, but rather than investigate his case the authorities had released him on 26 November.

Adam had arrived in Cape Town on 15 February 2011, almost a year after he had set out from Dar es Salaam.

'It felt familiar, like I already been here before. The air smelled like the sea in Hull. The buildings looked British but the palms growing near the Castle reminded me of Sheikilango Road in Dar es Salaam. There were police everywhere but also many, many hustlers. I saw a guy pick a pocket right in front of my eyes.'

And then he had spotted a short, muscular man in jeans and a T-shirt, with a backpack over his shoulders and a white *taqiyah* on his square head.

'I knew he was a Beachboy. I said, "*Oya vipi Munungu*," and he said, "*Poa, poa, mambo vipi*." That was Sudi. He's been my *achoose* since that day. That's what Beachboys call the guy you stow away with. It comes from prison language. In prison, your *achoose* is the person you trust with your life.'

◆

Facebook confirms much of what Adam has told me.

Rochelle ____ from West Bromwich, Birmingham, regularly posts pictures of herself in revealing dresses, often arching her back when she directs a glossy pout at the camera. At a point in her timeline, the selfies cease and she begins channelling her feelings through a cartooning app called Bitstrips.

Cartoon Rochelle seems to be lonely a lot of the time. One pictogram has her cartoon likeness carrying the world on its shoulders. In another, she sits alone in a room, thinking, *Could do wid sum company. Oh well!* In a happier scene, she holds a bouquet of flowers to her chest and says, 'I love you Princess Aniya'. The only photo album on the page is tagged with this name – Princess Aniya – and it charts the life of a five-year-old girl, from hospital wraps to the face-paint party she attended last week.

There is no Facebook page for Adam Bashili, but a page for Adam Chazili carries a thumbnail image that is unmistakably him. And although his location is given as Donaldsonville, Louisiana, his friends comment in Swahili and have taken pseudonyms like Mzee Seaman, Jimmy London, Dr Seapower and Sex Man Chateka. Group photographs taken on Cape Town's Grand Parade dominate the timeline. At one point Adam writes 'I miss England man', to which Rochelle replies 'ya Yoo taking too long'.

In a more recent comment, he rants about his mother and father, swearing he wishes he could line them up and shoot them for 'giving me this life'. His timeline cuts short in 2010 with a simple 'Fuck life', below which Facebook informs Adam that 'Sea Side Katuni likes this'.

◆

This morning Adam's name was the last on the roll for Court 17 in the Cape Town Magistrate's Court, which is two streets upslope from the Grand Parade. As far as courtrooms go, it is pleasant enough: a colonial relic complete with Palladian windows and Tuscan pillars, the latter painted a cheerful green. In the atrium outside, the branches of a Ficus reach up above the level of the courthouse gutters, promoting fantasies of escape even in the innocent.

I scanned the gallery on entry and recognised Sudi and Barak, who motioned me over. It is increasingly clear that the three friends constitute an underworld troika, and a well-rounded one at that, with Adam as the principal decision-maker and breadwinner and Sudi and Barak supplying many of the qualities in which he is deficient, such as physical menace and restraint. Barak, particularly, is a born diplomat. Never boisterous or over-hearty, he always strikes me – at over six foot tall and with his thick beard and Cushitic features – as a man among boys. Sudi is considerably shorter, his skull and features as compressed as Barak's are aquiline. He is the group heavy, a former boxer with pectorals like balloons and a reputation for resolving disputes with his fists. As the only one of the three to have attended madrassa, he is also the group's spiritual adviser, the moralist.

'Sit here,' Barak mouthed, shifting down the bench to make space. Sudi reached into his pants and pulled out a bag of weed. Adding a 'y' to the end of every fifth word, he explained that he knew a policeman who would take it down to Adam in the holding cell for a small fee.

'Court is one of the only ways to take weed-y into prison,' he whispered. 'The police don't mind-y, because it keeps the prisoners quiet.'

The judge, a coloured woman in her forties, worked through the roll in a stern but understanding manner, shaking her head in dismay whenever the prosecutor failed to produce a docket.

'There can be no excuse,' she vented at one point. 'The police station is across the road. Please see to it that the dockets start arriving on time from now on, okay?'

It is a warning she issues daily, yet the dockets fail to appear, leaving her with little choice but to order the release of an endless succession of suspects, most of whom are almost certainly guilty of the crimes with which they were charged. She is correspondingly short-tempered, and intolerant of bombast and cheek. For this reason, I feared the worst when the clerk of the court cried, 'Chazili, Adam Chazili.' Sudi and Barak raised their heads from their arms as Adam came clinking up from the cells, wearing a white Bob Marley T-shirt. He turned his grin on us before facing the judge, who asked him to confirm his residential address.

In a shockingly loud voice he said, 'No problem your worship,' and gave a street name and number in Delft, a township of greater Cape Town situated among the dunes behind the airport.

'A lot of us use that address,' said Barak. 'The guy who stays there used to be a Beachboy. He don't mind telling the police anything.'

'Do you have any family?' the judge asked, and the entire gallery stood up.

'Tha's my family right there, your worship,' said Adam, his face a mask of seriousness.

It was a master class in dock diplomacy: his body language open but communicating no challenge, his answers short and bold without sounding schooled. I had to leave before judgment was passed, but Sudi called soon afterwards to say that the judge had ordered Adam's release.

'Free bail-y.'

◆

At 3 a.m. last Sunday, the Beachboy called Manyama Kiziwe was stabbed to death on the corner of Castle and Darling, alongside the Grand Parade. A local tabloid reported that Kiziwe had come to South Africa five years before in search of economic opportunity. In all that time, ran the article, he had struggled to find a job, and had endured the most degrading living conditions imaginable. Now he had been murdered, apparently for no reason.

When Adam read the report, he was amazed.

'It shows you can write any shit in the newspaper. Kiziwe was a dealer, and a robber. He was one of the nineties generation, so he actually bin here in Cape Town longer than he ever lived in Dar es Salaam. If your eyes were closed when he speak, you would think he was a coloured.'

Even in adolescence, in Dar es Salaam, the deceased had been a troublemaker. It was the reason he was *kiziwe* – deaf. He had been caught thieving by members of his own community, who had beaten him until his ears had stopped working.

On the night of his murder, he had been out drinking with his coloured girlfriend in the Rainbow Tavern off Albert Road in lower Woodstock. This is territory controlled by the Hard Livings gang, but since the Beachboys constitute the most loyal customer base for crystal methamphetamine, both as street dealers and as users, a mutual respect is observed. Kiziwe had sold a good quantity of heroin during the day and had money to burn. His girlfriend knew that he kept his money stowed in his sock, though, and let this slip to some gangsters, who followed Kiziwe as he made for the Foreshore underpasses in the early hours of the morning. They caught up with him at the Grand Parade, pulled their weapons and demanded that he hand over the money. Kiziwe was knifed when he fought back.

At dawn, the city's underworld was tense as large bands of Beachboys scoured Woodstock and Salt River, knocking on the doors of known gangsters and threatening death if it were discovered that the murderers had been sheltered there. By mid morning it was clear that the killers were long gone. A different form of mobilisation was now initiated: Kiziwe's closest comrades went around the Beachboy areas asking for donations towards the cost of repatriating the body. They extracted peace payments from Hard Livings notables and from the Tanzanian drug syndicates, too. Everyone gave something, and the amounts went into a notebook next to the names of those who had donated.

By lunchtime, R25 000 had been raised and paid over to Deo Gloria Funeral Services ('Doing all things as if unto God'). Manyama Kiziwe's body was returned to his mother in Dar es Salaam two days later.

◆

To get to The Kitchen, you must head down Tide Road and turn onto Beach. Park at the dumpster in the panhandle at the oil recycling company, and look for the gap between the palisade struts. Turn your body sideways and slide through. Cross the multiple tracks heading directly into the city, and then pick out the path that leads, at this time of the year, through a field of knee-high purple loosestrife. Ahead, you will see the mouths of two railway tunnels, leading under the highway. Take the right tunnel. The overhead power cables have been cut, leaving stubs of cable dangling from the tunnel walls. Small stalactites are forming there along the concrete seams. The blue stone beneath the tracks will be dusty and everywhere around you will see old shoes, bottles and other discarded items – a breccia of refuse and decaying cotton. Do not be fooled by appearances, though – the tracks are in use. Stay near to the walls, which have been overpainted with slogans and tags going back many years. As the orb of light grows at the tunnel's end you will smell wood smoke, acrid marijuana, perhaps. On a normal day you will emerge into the blinding coastal light to find a handful of young men seated on crates and old cable wheels around a fire that never goes out.

On an abnormal day, you might find upwards of a hundred young men lining the highway embankment, their faces bowed and their eyes closed. A tall, dark man in a white robe chants a du'a above the sound of gulls and hammer blows in the nearby port.

'Allahumma inna Manyama Kiziwe fi dhimmatika, wa habli jiwaarika, faqi-hi min fitnaltil qabri, qa adhaban-naari, wa anta ahlul Wafaa'i wal-Haqqi. Fagh-fir lahu warhamhu. Innaka antal Ghafurur-Raheem.'

O Allah! Surely Manyama Kiziwe is under Your protection, and in the rope of Your security, so save him from the trial of the grave and from the punishment of the Fire. You fulfil promises and grant rights, so forgive him and have mercy on him. Surely You are Most Forgiving, Most Merciful.

◆

Adam called to say that he had seen a ship he liked the look of in the Ben Schoeman Dock, and that he would probably be gone before the end of the day.

We met at The Freezer, where he smoked the usual series of joints and unpacked his travel bag at my request.

Of the two two-litre Coke bottles of cloudy water that emerged first he said, 'The glucose makes it like that. You must have glucose to survive. Some people prefer Jive [a locally produced soft drink] but old-school Beachboys use glucose.' Two packets of Tennis biscuits followed some Jungle Oats yoghurt bars, and that was it for food and drink.

'It lasts me maybe ten days.'

He also had a torch, a short length of tubular metal and five or six empty plastic packets.

'The best place to hide is inside the cargo hold,' he explained. 'The only problem is they lock the hatch and don't open it again. It's dark down there so you need a light.'

The length of metal had a more vital function. 'When your food and water run out, you need to use a small iron like this to hit the hatch, so that the sailors can hear and let you out. Otherwise you will die.'

The packets would serve a less vital, but still very important, function.

'The first thing the crew will do is report you to the captain, and the first thing the captain will ask is, "Where did you shit in my ship?" That is why I have these,' said Adam, holding up a plastic bag in each hand and flashing his golden grin, much the way he would, I imagine, when presenting a week's worth of shit to some surprised shipmaster.

◆

Woken by a text message at 5:46 a.m.

Yow i m going last night i jup on ship name bluu sky. pls keep on touch with me family. fhone me daughter mum pls. pls tell her what is hapen. Memory Card. sea power.

Five minutes later the phone went again.

Sean can feel the ship is moven braa sound so nice. alone this time and have no food. i have only wotar but still me go make.

A quick search on MarineTraffic returns the following information for the *Blue Sky*:

Vessel Type: Tanker
Flag: Liberia
Next port of call: Doula, Cameroon
Estimated time of arrival: 10 August

SPRING

It is hard for us today to imagine the expectations that Cape Town harbour once aroused in the breasts of all who passed through it, whether arriving at the quasi-mythical foot of Africa, or departing from it certain only of one thing: the difficulty, perhaps the impossibility, of ever returning. The vacancy between two landfalls, the void that the ocean used to represent to those crossing it, its tedium and formlessness which engendered a longing for the shore, for any shore – all that has been lost. The difference between the Cape and the 'real world' once amounted to 7 000 nautical miles; at sea it was experienced as an apparently interminable period of suspension, a yawning hiatus in the lives of all who were on board.

– *Henk van Woerden*, A Mouthful of Glass

I'm officially out of a job.

Some weeks back, I was informed by my editor that the position of Foreign Policy Correspondent would be terminated at the end of the month and that I would not be re-employed in another role. The news came as no surprise (no assurances had ever been given that the gig would become permanent), but since I had spent only a fraction of the travel budget I asked to be allowed to make one last trip. Permission was granted and, since Adam has not made contact, I booked myself to Zambia to coincide with the run-up to the national elections there.

It ended up a fitting coda: a true *chukua safari ki*. The escapade had its beginnings in an intriguing call from a Zambian number – an elderly woman with a thick Afrikaans accent, who claimed it was within her power to facilitate an introduction to the Zambian president. When I hesitated she told me an extraordinary story, which I feel I ought to record since it is unlikely that anyone else will.

Andrea Breytenbach and her husband Wynand had trekked into Zambia from Zimbabwe in the early 2000s, pushed by the loss of their farm and the collapse of the Zimbabwean economy. After living in a tent for a lengthy period, they had bought a dilapidated property on the outskirts of Chipata, which they had duly developed into a lodge called Mama Rula's. The business was well positioned on the East African backpackers' route from Nairobi to Cape Town, and had become instantly popular with both overland tour guides and moneyed locals.

Among the first regulars had been a large-bodied man in his sixties, who always ate alone and with great relish. If he used his wonderfully deep voice it was to thank Andrea for another delicious meal, or to share with her the recipes of his childhood: fried tilapia with sides of *nsima* and *kachumbari*; black-eyed peas and Bambara groundnuts.

Andrea had taken notes and added the dishes to the menu. Their enigmatic guest had been delighted. In fact, he had insisted that the Breytenbachs take their evening meals at his table. In the course of these nightly engagements, the Breytenbachs had discovered that their new friend was Rupiah Banda, former Minister of State Mines and Governor-General of Lusaka Province. In 2000, after 40 years in politics, Banda had taken the decision to retire to his cattle farm near Chipata, only to find his home beset by supplicants day and night. The opening of Mama Rula's had been well timed to provide Banda with a few hours of sanctuary each evening. It pleased him that the elderly Afrikaners knew nothing of his past, yet delighted in his company.

In 2006, to the surprise of many, Banda had become the country's deputy president, apparently in repayment for his help in delivering President Levy Mwanawasa's party the vote in the eastern province. 'We were very happy for him,' said Andrea, 'but also sad because we realised we would probably lose a dear friend. He said, "No, you have an important job now, and your job is to keep me humble, because humility is often the first thing to go when one rises suddenly like this."' Henceforth, Mama Rula's functioned as a de facto state house, with Banda and his entourage taking over the entire lodge whenever his duties brought him to the eastern border. This situation persisted when Mwanawasa had suffered a stroke in 2008, at which point Banda had automatically become the country's president, a role he assumed formally after the 2008 national elections.

Banda was now seeking a second term, and the Breytenbachs had decided to do their bit for their friend's international image by reaching out to as many non-Zambian journalists as they could find numbers for. I was the only one to have called back, apparently.

Days later, I was seated in a hardwood and blackened leather chair overlooking the atrium in Zambia's State House. Cleaners and orderlies moved carefully to and fro in the corridors, while tilapia in a large rectangular tank gazed out at swaying papyrus. Occasionally, the presidential spokesperson appeared and shot me a withering look. He had been against the idea of an in-person interview at this late stage of the re-election campaign, feeling it could serve no purpose. His entirely reasonable objections were overruled, however – apparently by Banda himself. This left the spokesperson with the job of securing me a precious place on the president's final campaign trip. By noon that day I was in Zambian Air Force One, being served miniature Mars bars and a copy of the *Lusaka Times*. The president – referred to as HE (His Excellency) by his aides – had come shuffling down the centre aisle in a blue Mandela shirt, his face at once grandfatherly and spry. The ever-scowling spokesperson took the seat next to me.

'I need you to listen carefully,' he said. 'We will be making several stops and, when it is time to leave, the president's men care only for their principal. Whichever car they tell you to get into, get into it fast, because once the doors shut on HE they will leave anyone who has been daydreaming behind. And I'm afraid they do not take Visa or MasterCard where we are going.'

I heard titters from the secretary of state, who was seated behind me. The president's Indian doctor was two rows down, playing Tetris on his phone.

It did not take long to reach the northern town of Kasami where, after a short rally, I was ushered into the smallest of three helicopters leaving for Mbala on the Tanzanian border. From Mbala the cavalcade of choppers hopped along the eastern border to Chinsali, Lundazi and, finally, Chipata. In each of these dusty towns a dozen or more SUVs would storm towards the nearest secondary school, where the president would be greeted with song by the local choir while his aides distributed *chitenges* bearing Banda's pleasant face with its dented bottom lip. At the start of every short speech, HE would form the thumb and index finger of his right hand into a bird-like shape and sing out *chwe*, *chwe*, *chwe*, to which the crowd would respond in kind, apparently to signify common instinct and purpose, as of flocking birds. This was explained to me by Banda's American campaign consultant, who had come up with the idea.

Banda's campaign was certainly well funded. On this last tour of the countryside, those who turned out for his rallies received skirts, shirts and head wraps, but in other places it had been bicycles. Banda, furthermore, had the full apparatus of state at his disposal: its planes and helicopters, even a dedicated team of videographers and presenters from the Zambia National Broadcasting Corporation. Of the other candidates in the contest, only the firebrand politician Michael Sata had been able to rent a helicopter for campaign purposes, and only for a short time. The playing field was so uneven that Sata's party, the Patriotic Front, had decided to contest the election with a single line: *Donchi kubeba*, meaning 'don't tell' (anyone who you are going to vote for, and on election day make your mark for Sata). The strategy had made a mockery of the polling process, and most political analysts seemed to feel this was an error, a bit like flying at night without navigational instruments.

I wasn't so sure. Banda himself seemed authentically pleasant and humble, but his support staff exuded an unsavoury overconfidence. In the smallest of the helicopters, into which I was sandwiched with the communications team, northern Zambia was denigrated as cassava country, its inhabitants as cassava munchers. They waved white handkerchiefs regally in the windows as we descended towards waiting crowds and, giggling, said things like, 'Peaceful Zambians. My people. Zambia is one.'

Leaving Chinsali I was invited to travel in the presidential helicopter, which was easily twice the size of the others, with plush leather seats and luxurious carpeting. I sat with my back to the pilots, facing the president, our legs interlocked for want of room. This was the time accorded for our interview, but the large, elderly man fell asleep immediately and without any preamble of self-consciousness. All conversation in the aircraft ceased immediately. The sun set as we coasted over the eastern hills, where fires burned out of control in every direction, lines of orange on a black canvas.

We spent that night at Mama Rula's, where I joined the president and the Breytenbachs for dinner. HE seemed genuinely happy in their company, and insisted that a photo be taken of himself with their granddaughter, Saartje, who entered the restaurant wearing a Rupiah Banda head wrap. I realised, as dinner concluded, that there would be no formal interview, that our small talk over fried *kampango* fillets (brought in for the occasion from Lake Malawi) was as close as I'd come. I was comfortable with this.

Lying in a horrible bed that night, blonde hairs criss-crossing the pillow and someone else's toothbrush in the shower, I felt giddy. In fact, I felt I had glimpsed, for the first time, how power might become a subject of study – how the thing might be inhabited, explored from within. I believed I could start right away – I could push the two bedsteads in the room together and, by 3 a.m., have something written that would, within 24 hours, be read by influential people all over the world. But I was equally certain I wanted nothing to do with it, not if miniature Mars bars were involved, and sophistic news crews, and white handkerchiefs. I was with the president's spokesperson: where's the upside?

The news broke shortly after I landed in Johannesburg: Michael

Sata's Patriotic Front victorious, by a margin of 45 per cent to Banda's 35. *Donchi kubeba* had triumphed over *chwe, chwe, chwe*. Banda, to his credit, conceded, and returned to his cattle farm outside Chipata.

Not my pick. Not in ten guesses.

◆

I returned to find a number of Please Call Me messages on my phone.

Adam, I thought.

'Yeah big man,' said the voice that answered my call.

Barak.

'How you doing?'

'Good,' I said.

'How's your mummy and daddy?'

'They're good.'

'How's your wife?'

'Good.'

Beachboy decorum. It gets me every time that I can't reciprocate when Barak is on the other end of the line. Barak has no family. He's unlike the other Beachboys in this respect. Most have somebody at home in Tanzania: a mother, sisters.

In fact, Barak is not from Tanzania. He was born on one of the Bajuni islands, off the coast of Somalia. His fisherman father, he'd been told, had died at sea. His memories of his mother are equally vague; she, too, had died when he was very young, leaving him in the care of relatives who had relocated to Mombasa in Kenya, and later to a desperate Dar es Salaam slum called Mburahati. His adoptive family had not applied for legal status. They had simply disappeared into the fast-growing city, kept their heads low.

Barak's earliest memories are of being chronically hungry, and 'not knowing what life is for'. He had known how to move, though, and at the age of 13 had run away to Mbeya in southern Tanzania. A week later he had jumped the border into Malawi, where he'd spent some time in Dzaleka Refugee Camp in the brown hills near Dowa. Life in that camp had been desperate, so Barak had pushed southwards into Mozambique, across Tete Province to the Nyamapanda border post with Zimbabwe.

Here, he had applied for asylum, claiming he was from the south of Sudan, fleeing the war. The Sudanese national who had interviewed

Barak on behalf of the Zimbabwean government had quickly established that Barak could not understand Arabic – or Dinka, for that matter. Barak had explained that he had grown up in a town called Nimule, on the border of Sudan and Uganda, where Swahili is the spoken language. It was a story he had picked up in Dzaleka, and it had worked. Barak had been handed his asylum papers and transported down the country's eastern roads to Tongogara Refugee Camp, near the town of Chipinge. Here, for two years, he had attended the camp's primary school, learning to speak English among classmates who had been considerably younger than he was.

He had spent the next two years in Harare, hustling marijuana on a street called Rotten Row. He remembers this as a good time, though the Zimbabwean economy had been in free fall, and it was becoming difficult to find food in the shops and markets. By mid 2008, the Zimbabwean dollar was registering the highest monthly inflation rate not attributable to a war: 79 600 000 000 per cent. In all of history, only the Hungarian pengö had shed value at a faster rate, thanks to the wrack of the Great Depression and the ruin of World War II. Barak had heard on the refugee grapevine that people were starving in Tongogara, and that the governments of Canada and Australia planned to take all the children. He had bussed back to the camp and been placed in the third of three groups due for extraction. The first group had been flown to Canada, but before the second and third groups could go the Zimbabwean government, embarrassed by international media coverage of the conditions in the camp, had bussed the Tongogara refugees to Botswana. The government of Botswana had kicked them back into Zimbabwe a few days later, at which point Barak had decided to continue on to South Africa. The blue-uniformed policemen at the Beit Bridge border checkpoint had studied his refugee pass and waved him up to the Immigration Control office on the hill overlooking the Limpopo River. Here, he had been issued an asylum permit, and told to report to the Refugee Processing Centre in the nearby town of Musina. He had observed the long queues of people there, sleeping night after night in the red dust, and decided to continue his southern trek.

Six months later, at the age of 19, he had entered the Beachboy community in Cape Town.

Unlike the Tanzanian youths he lived among under the freeway bridges, Barak felt little desire to escape to sea. Compared with what he had known, Cape Town seemed a nice place. It was relatively safe, and making enough money to buy food was not difficult. He tried a few times, but quickly gave it up.

By the time Adam had arrived, Barak, although just 21 (and with no ships to his name), was already a mainstay of the local Beachboy community. His time in the refugee camps of Malawi and Zimbabwe had taught him the value of alliances, and he had been quick to recognise Adam's strengths as a social animal. It was through Barak that Adam had been introduced to a heroin supplier called Mas Bato. Mas, Barak and Adam had soon gone into business, practically running the trade in heroin on the Grand Parade. Barak and Adam had hustled at night, sometimes all night. The only formal business open after 11 p.m. had been a small shop called Hot Chicken and Chips, and Barak would buy coffee there. On quiet nights he would talk to the cashier, who had been unfailingly nice to him. She had listened to his story, and told some of her own stories. They had become friends, then lovers.

And now they planned to marry – the reason for Barak's many messages.

'Morieda and me invite you to come to our wedding,' he said, and gave me a time – 10 a.m. the next day – and a place.

A Tanzanian drug dealer's room off Page Street in lower Woodstock.

◆

I met Sudi on Main Road an hour before the ceremony was scheduled to begin, and followed him into a squalid apartment block, the ground floor of which comprised dim, doorless rooms subdivided many times by holey blankets, grubby sheets and large pieces of plywood. We climbed two flights of stairs to the makeshift venue and helped to move the dealer's furniture out into the stairwell, leaving a two-person couch covered in a grubby salmon-coloured material.

The original plan, Sudi explained, had been for him to officiate, but Morieda had insisted that the ceremony be led by an imam from her home suburb of Kraaifontein and for Sudi to function merely as witness to the nikah. The only other guest was Kabila, Barak's one-time *achoose*; both Kabila and Sudi had gone to significant efforts to clean up for the occasion, having bathed from a bucket of icy water early that morning and borrowed decent, collared shirts and jeans from fellow Beachboys.

'We don't mind. We support our brother any way we can,' said Sudi.

In due course, we heard voices on the stairs and stood in anticipation of the couple's arrival. Barak entered first, dressed in a flowing white *kanzu*, his closely shaven head topped with a white *kofia*, the traditional brimless hat of the Swahili coast.

He was followed by the imam, a greybeard in a button-down khaki robe, and a woman in a turquoise hijab, who took Barak's hand. The ceremony began with Barak proposing marriage to her in front of his friends. From his jeans pocket, Sudi took out a ring and handed it to Barak, who raised his partner's left hand and worked the ring up her little finger above the knuckle, over the mehndi designs that snaked across her brown, wrinkled skin into the cuff of her dress. Her fingernails had been chewed back into the soft shelves of her fingers, and what was left had been painted orange.

'Barak was supposed to give his wife a proper gift but she knows he got *fokol* to give her and she don't mind,' whispered Sudi.

Without further ado, the imam recited from the Qur'an and blessed the couple. A minute afterwards, the little wedding party was out on the balcony, congratulating Barak with shoulder hugs and shaking his new wife's hands solemnly. The imam left; we watched him limp up the pavement to the Main Road. A box of cigarettes went around and everyone took one and lit up.

'This is Morieda,' said Barak.

'Nice to meet you,' his wife said softly, smoke pouring from her nose and hazing over her green eyes, which were all the more striking for the thick stripes of black eyeliner she had applied to her lower lids.

The newlyweds returned indoors to sit together on the pink couch.

Sudi grinned at me. 'Sean-y, I can see you can't believe it,' he said.

I mouthed the question that had occurred to me the moment Morieda had appeared in the doorway: *How old is she?*

'We don't know. Kabila thinks around fifty but I think fifty-five at least. She got no teeth of her own, you know, just fake teeth. Sometimes, when she talks fast-y, it looks like they will fly out of her mouth. I try to tell her, mummy, please, slow down.'

I was eager to stick around for the makeshift *walimah* Sudi and Kabila had planned for their friend, but I was late for a meeting. I pressed a few hundred-rand notes into Barak's hand and ran down the stairs, passing the open rooms again.

Candles flickered here and there in the gloom. It seemed as if the rooms just went on and on, one false wall after another, sliding away under Main Road, under upper Woodstock, running deep into the darkness of the mountain.

◆

The issue of asylum permits is enigmatic: some Beachboys have them, whereas others do not. In an attempt to get to the bottom of this, at Barak's request – Morieda has advised him to seek asylum – Dave and I ventured down to the Legal Resources Centre off Greenmarket Square, where migrant traders have, for years, attracted tourists with a multiplicity of African cultural artefacts ranging from Congolese face masks to polished tanzanite.

The LRC foyer, smelling faintly of paraffin, was crowded with foreign nationals, too, though in contrast with the market hubbub, nobody spoke. At the reception desk, the secretary stared at us for quite a time without saying a word.

'We've had a bad week,' she said eventually. 'The state is closing down the asylum centres in the cities and moving them to the borders. There's a protest happening right now outside the Cape Town Refugee Centre on the Foreshore.' We had passed it on the way over, a group of discouraged-looking people gathered outside a locked building.

'This means genuine asylum seekers from Somalia, Burundi and the DR Congo, after risking their lives to get here, are now expected to reverse thousands of kilometres northwards, without resources, just to fill in forms. It's positively Kafkaesque,' the secretary spat.

The fancy term figured in several laminated clippings pinned to the wall next to her desk.

'We are here to see Mr Kerfoot,' we said.

'He's swamped, as always,' said the secretary, though Kerfoot – an LRC lawyer – stepped out just then, wearing the beatific smile of a doctor seeking the day's last patients. In appearance he reminded me of Marlon Brando's character in *A Dry White Season*, or possibly his office did, with its topographies of documents, its wooden fixtures and its metal wastepaper basket. He took his chair and rubbed his eyes and face dramatically as he said, 'I suppose you know the story of modern immigration to this country.'

When we hesitated he embarked on a summary, reminding us that, under apartheid, the Aliens Control Act had made it nearly impossible for foreign-born Africans to enter South Africa in any capacity other than as migrant labourers contracted to the mines.

Perhaps the most powerful embodiment of the apartheid government's attitude to black foreigners, he said, was the three-hundred-odd kilometres of fencing it had erected along parts of South Africa's border with Zimbabwe and Mozambique in the mid eighties. The fence – three coils of electrified razor wire stacked in a pyramid – had been nicknamed the snake of fire by border-dwelling Mozambicans.

'If you touched it, chances were you would be electrocuted to death.'

When the voltage was cut in 1990, holes began to appear. With the country's leadership preoccupied with the transfer of political power from white to black hands, the holes widened until eventually entire sections of fence were being carted off by metal thieves. Drawn by the relative wealth of South Africa's cities and pushed by war, repression and poverty, northerly Africans poured into the country in great numbers, some through the border posts on tourist visas, which they overstayed, with many more bypassing the entry points altogether.

Attempts to address the situation had, by the early 2000s, led to the entrenchment of an ugly detention and deportation system, said Kerfoot. In no time at all it had become corrupt to the core. Foreign nationals detained for not being in possession of the correct documentation found that they could bribe their way back onto the streets with ease. Those who were deported had little difficulty re-entering the country within days. The consequence was universal frustration. African migrants found themselves caught up in a bureaucratic limbo – 'a Kafkaesque state' – whereas working-class South Africans increasingly felt that the government was failing to prevent foreigners from taking jobs and pressurising welfare systems. The outbreak of xenophobic violence in 2008 left nobody in any doubt as to the stakes.

'Which brings us to the question of your stowaways' asylum permits,' said Kerfoot. 'Most of the undocumented migrants who have entered the country since the nineties have not qualified for asylum under the Refugee Act, but many of them applied anyway and received asylum seekers' permits, otherwise known as Section 22 permits, which allowed them to remain in the country legally pending the outcome of their application process. I'd warrant that the Tanzanians you mentioned are Section 22 holders, and the reason some have them and others do not is easily explained by the fact that the Home Affairs department no longer dishes them out like it used to. It makes little difference either way,' he continued, 'because Tanzania is a peaceful country, and any Tanzanian who applies for asylum is almost certain to have his application rejected. To be frank, it is hard for me to imagine a group of foreigners being more at odds with the current dispensation, given what little you've told me about their habits and intentions.

'And just out of personal interest,' he said, changing tack, 'how do you envisage presenting your research, ultimately? If, as you say, this community values little more than secrecy and anonymity, surely anything you intend to publish about them will be deleterious to their cause?'

Kerfoot gave his face another long rub and thanked us for stopping by. In the waiting room, the worried asylum seekers glanced up momentarily before returning their gaze to the ends of their shoes. It had been our intention to join the protest outside the Foreshore asylum centre, but we passed it without discussion now, our mouths possibly over-filled with difficult syllables.

Kafkaesque: having a nightmarishly complex, bizarre, or illogical quality.

Deleterious: from the Ancient Greek *dēlētḗr*, 'a destroyer'.

◆

I suspect our LRC visit could mark the end of our collaboration.

Dave's visits to the Foreshore have become infrequent of late, as other work projects keep him out of Cape Town for half of every month. He has also said, on more than one occasion, that he was aware of certain limitations at the start – that there would always be a point beyond which his camera would not be able to follow.

More than this, something appears to have shifted in his relationships with the Beachboys. Possibly I am understanding, for the first time, what a burden a camera can be in contexts of fragile trust. A few weeks ago, for example, we were with a group of Beachboys when a waxy-faced man with a broad nose and short dreads hauled off his jacket and hoodie, and any number of subsidiary layers, and turned away from us to show off a dolphin tattoo on a shoulder blade. It was, he said, his protection against drowning. He introduced himself as Juma, a name as common in Dar es Salaam as David is elsewhere; when Dave asked whether he would mind posing for a photograph, Juma nodded, pulled his layers back on, removed his grubby Peruvian beanie, and posed.

After taking his portrait, Dave asked Juma if he could photograph the protective charm – which, of course, is what he'd meant initially. Without hesitation, Juma asked for money; just as reflexively, Dave refused. Dave and Juma have bumped into each other two or three times since. Each time Dave asks Juma if he wouldn't mind taking his shirt off, and just as reliably Juma grins and asks for money. For R50, possibly even R20, Juma would happily expose his shoulder to the lens, but Rhodes will return to govern the Cape before either man – the seaman from Dar es Salaam or the photographer from Pietermaritzburg – backs off from a principle.

◆

Some months back, Sudi had fallen from the port's fence and cracked a couple of his ribs.

Adam had called for an ambulance and, with Barak's help, had walked Sudi to the place beneath the elevated freeways where the state paramedics know to meet the sick and wounded of the lower city. The ambulance had traversed the line of skyscrapers that overlook the harbour and entered the Victoria & Alfred Waterfront precinct, an ever-tightening crush of business schools, five-star hotels and shopping malls.

The Somerset Hospital squats stubbornly in the centre of this district, a monument, in many ways, to the city's finer inclinations. A doctor named Samuel Bailey had used his own money to establish the place – the region's first civil hospital – after the city's governor at the time, Lord Charles Somerset, had refused him funding.

From its opening day – 1 August 1818 – the old Somerset Hospital and Lunatic Asylum had been open to both civilian burghers and slaves. This basic humanitarian principle had been carried over to the new Somerset Hospital, built in the 1860s, and has survived intact until today. In fact, free hospital treatment for all is a policy of the South African government. Patients are supposed to provide proof of South African citizenship, but in practice state doctors treat all comers. As a consequence, the Somerset Hospital, along with every other state-run medical facility, is overstretched at most hours to the point of barely contained chaos.

When I had arrived, Sudi and Adam had been in the processing queue for three hours. Another three passed before any doctor could get around to assessing Sudi, and in that time two gunshot victims had come in, escorted by the policeman who had shot them. A drug-addled teen with a strikingly deep tan had walked around and around the casualty ward, her feet bare and her forehead ever so slightly creased in confusion. One the far side of the ward, a middle-aged woman with arms like biltong sticks had addressed nurses with a yellow fan in front of her face, saying, 'No black doctors please, I'm warning you.'

Sudi had eventually been seen by a female intern from Athens, Texas, a smiling sylph in bright-pink scrubs. She had helped Sudi to remove his shirt and praised his tattoos while examining him. They are some of the better Beachboy markings I've seen. A container ship sails over his bulging pectorals, faded to a ghostly pentimento. A pirate grins off a muscular shoulder, complete with tricorn hat.

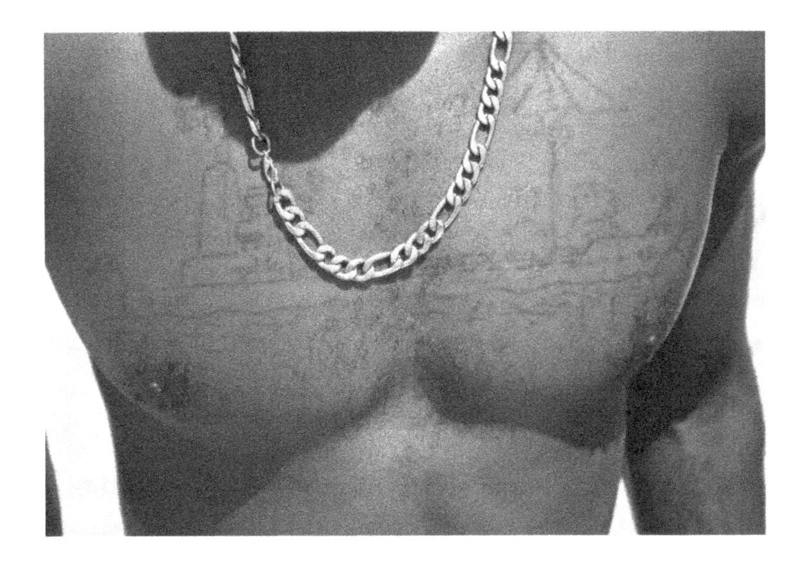

X-rays had revealed hairline cracks in two of Sudi's ribs. By the time the doctor had written a prescription for Tramadol and signed Sudi's discharge chit, the sun had been setting beyond the kelp beds off nearby Mouille Point.

Today, Sudi called to say that his chest was swollen in the same area.

'My blood,' he said, 'bad blood,' and went on to explain about a dreadlocked Beachboy called Juma who had used one of the communal *kisus* at The Kitchen to pick at the thick papules on his forehead. It is widely suspected that Juma has Aids – 'H' in Beachboy parlance – and Sudi had inadvertently used the same *kisu* to lance a boil on his back.

He is now convinced that the swelling around his ribcage is not a coincidence – that he is, in fact, infected.

To avoid spending another day in hospital waiting rooms, I took Sudi to see Dr Deon Cabano, who has a small private practice off the Marine Drive service road in the industrial precinct of Paarden Eiland, overlooking the port's breakwater. In recent years the South African-Italian doctor, whose sleek waterfall of sandy blonde hair would not be out of place in a cosmetic plastic surgeon's rooms, has seen and treated (at no charge) several Beachboys among his regular paying stream of dockworkers, seafarers and machinists. This has earned him the Beachboy moniker Dr Sea.

Sudi's chest, when Cabano lifted his shirt, looked far more gruesome than I had expected. Where the inside of his left bicep would have touched his ribs a small volcano of swollen skin jutted out, ending in a bloody point. The lump looked worse for whatever cream Sudi had applied to it, which was now flaking off in little black and white clumps.

'It's one of two things,' said Cabano, writing a script for antibiotics. 'It's either a dermal or a bone infection – let's pray it's the former. If the problem is in the bone, then I'm afraid, Mr Brando, that you will have to return to Somerset Hospital, where the orthopaedists will probably run a mile because bone infections are a nightmare to treat.'

Armed with penicillin we returned to the car, where Barak sat smoking a joint. I asked where to.

'Can you drop us at the Beachboy sick house?' Sudi asked.

I had heard the place described before – a rustic shack in a place called Blikkiesdorp, where sick and injured Beachboys can stay until they are strong enough to return to the bridges. Quite who the structure belongs to, or what the terms of residence might be, I had no idea. I did know that Blikkiesdorp was an unlikely site for a sanctuary. Formally called Symphony Way Temporary Relocation Area (TRA), Blikkiesdorp (Tin Can Town) has been notorious since its inception. The TRAs – there are several of them scattered around the poorest parts of the Cape Flats – were developed to house surplus people: victims of natural disasters, private property squatters, foreigners displaced by xenophobic violence and, in the case of Blikkiesdorp, men and women who were living rough on the streets of Cape Town ahead of the 2010 FIFA World Cup. The fact that Blikkiesdorp was used in this way, as the back end of a city's touristic makeover, had turned the place into a cause célèbre; any follower of the local news is likely to know one or all of the following facts:

That Blikkiesdorp is twenty kilometres outside the city, in the dunes behind the Cape Town International Airport;

That the settlement comprises one thousand six hundred or so single-room structures – steel cubes (*blikkies*) wrapped in zinc sheets, divided into alphabetical blocks running from west to east and A to Q;

That nothing grows from the dune sands on which the camp is built;

That temperatures inside the structures soar into the fifties in summer;

That movement in and out of the camp was initially controlled by a barbed-wire fence and a police presence; and

That drug abuse and violent crime are daily realities.

With Table Mountain receding in the rear-view mirror, I asked how the Beachboy sick house had come about.

'In 2006,' said Sudi, 'there was a big *maskani* at Culemborg, under the bridges, maybe one hundred, two hundred people. We were Bongomen and coloureds living together, but mainly Bongomen. I was staying in a small *mchondolo* with three other guys. One day, some white people came and took our names. They said they were going to give us a bigger house in another place. They didn't ask us where we were from, or if we had permits. In 2009, they came back to the bridge and called out the names. If you were still living there in the Beachboy areas, they took you to your new house in Blikkiesdorp. This is why there are so many Bongomen in Blikkiesdorp. Some are married to South African women now, others have become big drug dealers.'

We peeled off the N2 onto the R300, took the Blue Downs exit and doubled back through Delft, an epicentre of violent crime on the Cape Flats with an annual murder rate three times the national average.

'Turn left here,' said Sudi, as we approached the Golden Crust bakery.

We made our way on rock-strewn streets through rows of newly constructed tenements, crossed the M171 and entered Blikkiesdorp through a wetland suffocating under trash. We followed the perimeter road around the eastern end of the camp and stopped at a place where several concrete bars had been knocked out of the boundary palisade, creating a body-sized exit into the surrounding forest of Port Jackson willow. To our side, a path led away from the aperture to a narrow, puddled alleyway between the shanties. We followed it, counting off the unit numbers, which were spray-painted in orange on the zinc walls of each shack. The original structures had been free-standing, but the spaces between them had subsequently been claimed with makeshift walls, ceilings and fences, turning each block of units into a virtual fortress.

'*Oya vipi*,' said Sudi, knocking on the pine door of the only free-standing shack in sight.

'*Mambo vipi*,' came a muffled voice from inside and we heard a key being turned, a deadbolt shifting.

'It's dangerous here, especially at night, so the brothers keep the doors locked if their numbers are only a few,' Sudi explained.

A slight man with a long and sallow face – a human version of the central African masks on sale on Greenmarket Square – opened the door.

'Mege!' Sudi shouted, looping an arm around the man's neck and hugging him side-on. 'This is Mege JoJo, he got TB.'

The sick Beachboy smiled sheepishly, as if Sudi had exposed a personal failing. He was alone in the structure, which was furnished with a single armchair, a decent carpet and two double mattresses on good bases. WWE wrestlers were body-slamming each other on the screen of a television, which rested atop a low table. Next to this, a pot of *ugali* bubbled away on an electric hob and, although the atmosphere was dense with steam, the place was clean and otherwise dry – a true haven, measured against the dank Beachboy middens of the Foreshore.

'Is this your place?' I asked.

Mege shook his head vigorously from side to side.

'Who owns it?'

'All Beachboys.'

Sudi picked up the story. 'It used to belong to this guy called Juto, but Juto caught a ship and after that he stayed home in Ubungo in Dar es Salaam. He phoned to tell us that this house could be used by any Beachboy, so we made it our place for the sick. Every week someone walks around the Beachboy areas with the book. That's what we call it: the book. He takes a small donation from the Beachboys he meets. It can be anything, as small as fifty cents, and he writes it down. When he has the money, this person buys things for the house: food, medicine, even electricity, so that the boys can watch TV. Everyone is happy to pay something because they know that their turn for sick will come.'

It had been Barak's intention to return to the city with me, but he changed his mind on finding the sick house so quiet.

'Will you find your way?' he asked, seeing me off at the end of the sandy lane.

I glanced over the sheet-metal rooftops towards the cloudy face of Devil's Peak.

'I think so.'

◆

Back to Blikkiesdorp to check on Sudi and Barak, only to discover that the pair had returned to the bridges the day before, Sudi's chest having healed. It's just as well, because the sick house has become crowded and filthy.

'The boy with the gashes on his face got hit by a car near The Freezer,' Mege explained. 'He's lucky. He's the first one to survive something like that.'

Another youngster, face-down on a pillow, had untreated TB. Mege clearly resented his presence.

'It's dangerous; he's putting everyone else at risk. He should be in hospital but he won't go.'

On the far side of the structure, alone on the second double bed, a skin-and-bone Beachboy was lying with his hand over his eyes, tears running from under his fingers into a patchy beard. A freshly stitched cut ran across his lower abdomen.

'This boy was operated on yesterday, and they discharged him this morning,' said Mege. 'Maybe you can read his letter, so that you can help him to understand what has been done to him. He doesn't know, not really.'

I opened the envelope embossed with the Western Cape Department of Health's coat of arms, and read the Relevant History notes.

> 24 YEAR OLD FRED GIDION MNGINI PREVIOUSLY WELL 1 YEAR HISTORY OF LEFT SCROTAL SWELLING BECOMING PROGRESSIVELY MORE OMENTUM HERNIATING LEFT WITH COMPLICATED LEFT HYDROCELE PLUS FIRM THICKENING/MASS CORD SWELLING TAKEN FOR HISTOLOGY

The medical language and absence of punctuation made this locked prose. I shrugged my shoulders.

Mege put it more simply. 'He used to have balls like an elephant.'

'Who, Fred?'

'His real name is Chid. He got no documents so he borrowed the passport of Fred Mngini, another Tanzanian guy who has been in the country for one week. If Chid didn't do that they might not have given him the operation. Or they would have asked for money first, and he has nothing.'

'What was wrong with his balls?'

'We don't know, but it started one year back. The doctors told Chid he needed an operation but he was too afraid to go, so he left it, and they got bigger and bigger, until he could hardly walk. Two days ago the pain was too much and his friend Suleiman took him to Groote Schuur Hospital. They saw how big his balls were and operated on him straight. Now he looks empty there.'

'*Wa Kuchomwa* [puncture],' sniggered the youth with the cut-up face.

Mege admonished him with a cluck of his tongue.

'Chid says he wishes he was dead but the boys are telling him the pain is good, because it means he can try and stow another ship soon. Before the operation his balls were so big he couldn't run or climb fences.'

Mege escorted me down the lane. Since it was drizzling lightly when we reached the Conquest, he climbed into it. I noticed the words 'Memory Card' tattooed on his neck.

'Are you good friends with Adam?'

'I only met him in Johannesburg in 2010,' said Mege, 'but he's like my brother.'

The story of their friendship is a touching one. When Adam had arrived in South Africa for the FIFA World Cup, he had found Mege running errands for Tanzanians ten years his junior.

'He told me I should stand up for myself,' said Mege, 'but some of those Joburg guys are mad. If you argue with them they just hit you. "I am not a big person," I told him, "so it is better to just listen to what they say." Adam said. "Follow me, we going to fix this." He went to this tattoo guy and said, "Put this boy's name here."' Mege JoJo clapped his neck with his palm. 'After it was done, he said, "People gonna know now that they can't fuck with Mege JoJo, because they will have to fight me."'

Just as Adam had predicted, the bullying had ended there. When Adam had moved on to Cape Town, Mege, now established in Johannesburg, had chosen to remain. The friends had been reunited a few months ago, when Adam had journeyed down from Dar es Salaam after having been deported from St Petersburg. This time, Mege had felt ready for a change. He had packed his things and walked with Adam to the Kroonvaal Engen garage on the N1 highway, where they had bought space in a Cape Town-bound truck. The journey had been comfortable enough, although the trucker had coughed incessantly; with hindsight, Mege believes that this is how he had contracted tuberculosis.

'I was coughing two weeks after I got to Cape Town.'

The shift doctor at Somerset Hospital had referred Mege to the Brooklyn Chest Hospital, just a few hundred metres from the harbour. Here, he'd been informed that he had XDR TB – extensively drug-resistant tuberculosis – and told it would be months before he would be cured and able to leave. Three days later, he had taken a day pass and returned to the Foreshore. For a wet and windy fortnight, he had coughed himself almost to death in his *mchondolo*. When Adam had learnt of this, he had been furious.

'He asked, "What happened? Why did you leave?" I told him foreigners were being kept in that hospital until death. I told him it was better I die outside.'

Mege was referring to a specific patient in his ward, a senile old-timer from Somaliland who had been living in the hospital for three years, even though he had been clear of TB for two of those. A nurse had explained that since the old man was unable to walk, and had no family or friends, the doctors did not feel able to discharge him.

'Some leaders in the Somali community had tried to find his people, but they returned with bad news. They said the old man had been living alone on the streets of Cape Town for so long that his clan members had forgotten him. So they left him there,' said Mege.

The nurse had said that there were others like him in other parts of the compound: Angolans, Burundians and, yes, even Tanzanians, men with nothing and nowhere left to go. Some had been moved into halfway houses; others had died in their beds. When these patients died, the nurse had explained, their bodies were burned that very same day or buried in an unmarked grave somewhere in Milnerton.

'Adam told me I was not going to die. He said the beach would always be there, waiting for me. He called the ambulance and we went together.'

Adam had listened carefully while a doctor at the chest hospital had outlined the treatment options, which Mege had not understood when they had first been explained to him.

'Memory said, "Okay, this is what is going to happen. They will send your file to the clinic in Delft, and you gonna stay in the sick house and only go to the clinic once a week for your medicine. It doesn't matter if it takes the TB two years to go, nobody gonna mind. That is what Blikkiesdorp is for."'

It has been six months, and Mege says he has not yet missed an appointment to pick up his pills and have his sputum tested. He no longer coughs himself awake at night, and believes Allah means for him to live.

◆

A powerful storm, the kind that brings trees down and turns the Cape roads into parking lots.

It started yesterday morning with wind off Table Mountain, scooping up every loose plastic bag in the city and sending it down to the Foreshore where it snagged in the perimeter fence of the Culemborg industrial area. By the middle of the afternoon, tendrils of ripped plastic were reaching through the metal strands like the arms of raving spirits.

The rain arrived early this morning: clouds like giant box jellyfish dragging skirts of water across Table Bay. Stuck in traffic on Nelson Mandela Boulevard this evening, I couldn't help thinking about the Beachboys below, huddled around their fires – and of Adam, now presumed dead by some of his friends. I realise I miss him very much – miss being able to see the world as he does.

Thanks to Adam, the whole seaward view is permanently changed for me. Whereas before, the light playing off the Atlantic tended to turn the flyovers, cranes and ships into an oil painting, now I see only cracks and chinks: the bent palisade struts, tunnels, portals and hatches not just flaws in a postcard-perfect view, but rents in the great system of human controls.

◆

A fortnight in which my ability to move around the Foreshore has been curtailed by a series of mishaps and misjudgements.

To begin with, Daniel Peter called to say that he had been picked up by the border police, who sent him 1 500 kilometres to the north, to Lindela Repatriation Centre outside Pretoria. He said he was working on a plan to get himself out, and hung up. When he called back, it was to say that a guard named Salim Hassan had assured him he would be released upon payment of a R1 000 'donation'. I told him to go back with an offer of R500. He called back with the details of the guard's post office account.

The next day, he called to say that he had stood for hours at the side of the N1 southbound, hoping to catch a lift to Cape Town. Having had no success he was now in Hillbrow, Johannesburg, staying with some small-time dealers he knows there. It will be weeks before he has earned enough from hustling to enable his return to Cape Town, if this is his wish.

More worryingly, Barak and Sudi are no longer taking my calls. Last week, they were verbally attacked by several Beachboys for leading me through the railway reserve to Maskani. It could be that they have decided my friendship is not worth the trouble.

In an attempt to stay connected, I reached out to individuals whom I have met only fleetingly, but who have always seemed friendly. One such was Suleiman Wadfha, whom the Beachboys call P Diddy. Diddy's Dinka-dark skin contrasts memorably with the bright-yellow polo shirt he wears all week and somehow manages to keep clean. He is a natural jester with a square head and free-standing teeth, always feigning hurt or anger and then flashing his comical grin moments later. He speaks very little English, though, and with my Swahili still restricted to pleasantries we had scarcely spoken until ten days ago when he approached me in the company of a young man who looked like he might, if I talked too loudly, withdraw his head and limbs into his grubby, cerise-pink jacket.

'This is Feisal,' said Diddy.

Feisal's eyes were wet at the corners. When he extended a limp hand, they scanned the area behind me, as if to establish whether we were being watched.

His first words were, 'I speak English, German and Swahili, and I'm a qualified tourism operator. I want to ask you if you can help me to put an advertisement for my skills on the Internet. Please, I need your help.'

I asked Feisal whether he had any substantiating documents. He slipped two laminated A4 certificates out from under his ski jacket, one headed with the logo of the Tanzania Utalii College and the other professing to be the resume of one Msafiri Tungawaza Masaga. He explained that this was his birth name.

'My father was Christian, but he changed his faith in 2009 and we, his children, changed faith as well. Now my official name is Feisal Al-Amin Masaga, though my friends mostly call me Mussa.'

I saw Diddy and Feisal the next day, and the day after that. Each time they insisted that I meet them away from the Beachboy areas and it soon became clear that neither of them had much in common with the others. Diddy initially tried to pretend otherwise, claiming, through Feisal, that he had come to the Beachboy life years ago, after his parents had died.

'They left behind five children, four of which were girls. Diddy came to South Africa in order to support them,' Feisal explained.

I knew this to be untrue. Anyone you meet on the steps of Edward VII will tell you that Diddy's father works for the Tanzanian government, and that Diddy gave up a comfortable home to win back the affections of a former girlfriend, who had left him for a recently returned Beachboy. Diddy clucked his tongue in surprise when I mentioned this second narrative, but then grinned and authorised Feisal to make his confession.

'This is true. Diddy lost his girl to a guy who came back from Dubai with a lot of money. Diddy came here because he thought he would be able to get the same kind of opportunities as this other man.' Feisal giggled nervously. 'Diddy loved her very much, I can tell you this for sure.'

Feisal had come from a relatively stable family background, too. He was born in 1989, the third child of a nurse, Sarah Idd Kaya, and a doctor, Tangaraza Masaga. Growing up, he had been close to his older siblings, Farida and Haroum, and loved his two younger brothers very much when they were alive.

In 1997, Feisal had just started at Mtendeni Primary School when his father had 'divorced my lovely mother', who had then 'decided to disappear'. His father had moved the family to the island of Zanzibar, where they had all witnessed, first hand, the Tanzanian military's brutal suppression of political protests in the run-up to the 2002 elections. Feisal's father had treated victims in the hospital, and the experience had sent him into a depression so debilitating that he had quit medicine.

In 2005, Feisal learnt that his mother had died without having remarried. His father had remarried almost instantly – a woman from Kondoa District, where Feisal's mother had come from. Feisal and his stepmother had clashed; to get away from her, he had registered at a hotel school on the mainland, interning in the Serena, Kiwengwa Beach and Tembo hotels. The pay had been terrible, though, and ultimately he had pleaded with his father for a final loan with which he had bought a series of bus rides to South Africa.

Nothing had gone to plan since his arrival in Johannesburg Park Station in March this year. Within hours he had been both robbed and ripped off. The friend with whom he had intended staying took two days to respond to his many messages and, when he had, it was to say that he had moved to Port Elizabeth. When Feisal had travelled to Port Elizabeth, the friend had stopped answering his phone altogether. Some youths he had met in a KFC had said he could rent a bed in their city-centre apartment. He had used the last of his funds to pay upfront for two months' lodgings, and had set about looking for work. Some of the tourism companies he approached had said they would hire him if he returned with a work permit. When Feisal had told an official in the Home Affairs office what he needed, he'd been laughed at. Go home, the official had said. You do not belong here.

On the pavement, he had been approached by a woman who had claimed she could get him the required documents for a fee of R5 000. Feisal had asked his housemates to lend him the amount, but instead of helping they had hassled him for his next rent instalment. When he'd said he needed time to come up with the money, they'd given him two days, at the end of which they had thrown his clothes into the hallway.

He'd called his father, pleaded for more money. His father had sent US$100 via Western Union, and said there would be no more. This had enabled Feisal to take the bus to Cape Town, where he had bumped into Diddy. He had been living the Beachboy life for three weeks now, and already the conditions had taken a visible toll. The smoke from the cooking fires had gunked up his eyes, and his right cheek had become a sandpaper of little red bumps. The culture of communal eating, he confided, revolted him. The pots were never washed. Hands were never washed. The stews of rice, chicken and beans were eaten off ripped plastic bags placed on the ground.

All of this information had been written down in the journal I had given Feisal a week ago, and which he handed back to me today. Diddy shook his head sorrowfully as this transaction took place.

'That one no good,' he said, and Feisal explained that they had both been challenged under the flyovers the night before after Feisal had been spotted writing in it.

'They accused us of giving away Beachboy secrets to the *mzungus*,' said Feisal.

This was unfair. Comprising neat cursive, switching between upright and forward-leaning and beginning at the back of the notebook and moving from right to left, the story Feisal told about his life was interspersed with rambling passages about the history of Tanzania

Bara (Mainland), notes on the cultivation of cloves on the highlands of Pemba Island and, finally, a comprehensive list of the country's national parks, after which he had written 'TO BE CONTINEU ...'

But, of course, there is no convincing the others of this, and I can only hope that the misunderstanding will cause no further trouble.

◆

An SMS from Feisal at 5 a.m. yesterday.

> THANK YOU FOR YOUR SUPPORT FREAND, MAY GOD HELP YOU FOR YOUR KINDNESS. WE NEED YOUR IDEAS BECAUSE WE ARE GIVEN TWO DAYS TO LEAVE THE BEACHBOY AREAS. WE ARE BANISHED. WE ARE SCARED. WE DON'T KNOW WHAT TO DO. PLEASE WE NEED YOUR HOPE.

My mind went fuzzy while reading it. A dread message. Surely not, I kept thinking. A misunderstanding. There must be another way ...

I realise now just how much Adam meant to me, in terms of my ability to mingle with the Beachboys. If he were here, I would be able to ask him how to fix this situation. I would be able to establish whether Diddy and Feisal's plight is as serious as they claim. They could be in real danger, or it could be that I'm being played – I just don't know. I've gone out of my depth without realising it, and now that I know it I want to retreat and forget that this happened, wait for Adam to return before starting again.

But, of course, I'd be finished if I dropped Feisal and Diddy now, and not just on the Foreshore.

A social worker friend with whom I shared my predicament suggested that I convince both Feisal and Diddy to enter one of The Haven night shelters until a longer-term solution could be found. I suggested to the pair that we meet outside the Napier Street facility in Green Point to make the arrangements. This was a mistake on my part. The Napier Street shelter is just a kilometre from the Grand Parade, but for the pedestrian it lies over several multi-lane arterials and then under the Western Boulevard flyovers. To make matters more confusing, the roadways that pass beneath the bridges are only open at certain times to keep Cape Town's rough sleepers from straying into the upmarket Victoria & Alfred Waterfront precinct at night. The upshot was two hours spent trying to locate Diddy and Feisal, guided only by Feisal's maddeningly general upper-case messages.

WE NEAR TO BEACH AREAS

WE NEAR TO PARKING

WE NEAR TO CHINESE BOAT CALLED LING CHANG

And so on.

Eventually, I spotted the *Ling Chang* in a dry dock off South Arm Road, where pedestrian life is an odd blend of drifters, dockworkers and camera-wielding tourists. Diddy climbed in the back of the car and shrank into silence while Feisal explained that they had been summoned before a Beachboy 'court' the previous night, accused again of 'sharing the secrets of the beach'. Diddy had spoken up for Feisal, insisting that no such exchange had taken place. He was asked to present the notebook, but of course they could not, having already returned it to me.

'One guy took some wood and hit Diddy on the head,' said Feisal. Diddy rubbed his closely shaven scalp and looked out the window. 'They said we have been living nicely with them, peace and love you know, and so they would not give us a hard punishment like a beating with rocks or worse. They just asked that we leave the beach areas in 48 hours.'

The judgment is irreversible, apparently.

'It is just for Cape Town, not Port Elizabeth or Durban. But even if we go to these other cities the Beachboys there will get our report,' said Feisal.

We left that environment of canal-side hotels and singing yacht halyards and, just a few hundred metres inland, stopped at the end of Napier Street, in the shadow of the Western Boulevard flyover. The underpass had once sheltered such a large community of homeless men, women and children that the newspapers had dubbed it The Bridge Hotel. The area had been ruthlessly cleared in 2001 by the hirelings of a new public–private security initiative and, to discourage resettlement, large rocks had been cemented into the traffic islands, like giant teeth in a fossilised jawbone.

'It's formally known as defensive architecture,' said the woman who met us at the entrance to the shelter. 'This particular forest of rocks was inspired by the pigeon spikes you see in places like the Central Station. Nice, hey? My name's Edna, by the way.'

Edna explained that the shelter was full for the weekend, and that the Tanzanians would have to wait until Monday before registering as clients. Feisal outlined the seriousness of their situation and Edna made some more calls, eventually returning to say that Moira Henderson House on Chapel Street in Woodstock still had free beds.

'It's a halfway house for people who have some form of employment already, but speak to Laetitia. If you tell her that this *mzungu* is your employer for the next two weeks, she might be able to help.'

'This *mzungu* could kiss you,' I said.

Edna laughed and looked a little embarrassed. 'No, you're most welcome. Speak to Laetitia. She will work something out.'

Within minutes of arriving at Moira Henderson, Feisal and Diddy were handed clean towels rolled around pairs of hessian slippers. When I returned later in the afternoon to pay their board and lodging, they had both showered and were standing outside on the pavement in fresh clothes, smelling of soap. They excitedly showed me around their separate dormitories (the house policy being to separate friends), and also the shower block, which smelled of drain cleaner.

When I made to leave, Feisal drew me away from Diddy.

'Diddy had a dream about his home,' he said. 'Actually, it was more like a bad dream. He felt that something was wrong. What I want to tell you now is that Diddy's parents are both dead already. They died at least six months ago, but he doesn't know this. I did not know how to tell him, because life is already so difficult, you know. What do you think I should do?'

'What do you think is best?'

'I think he needs to return home.'

'And you?'

'I will stay. I came here to work, not to be a Beachboy.'

Eager to be done with this difficult situation, I withdrew and handed over R4 000, half of my earnings for the month.

'It's all I can afford,' I said, 'so you and Diddy must decide how to split it.'

◆

Feisal called from the Moira Henderson call box this morning with a sorry tale. Diddy, he said, had borrowed his cellphone at 6 a.m., saying he wanted to call his family in Dar es Salaam.

'I'm sorry, I lied to you,' Feisal confessed. 'Diddy's parents are alive, actually, but he was very homesick, so he told me to tell you that his parents are dead.'

Feisal had handed Diddy the phone and gone back to bed. He had woken to find Diddy gone with the money and the phone.

Surprisingly, Diddy picked up when I called Feisal's number. He complained that he had skipped out because Feisal had betrayed their friendship. It had to do with the only other Tanzanian client in Moira Henderson – a young man called Anwar, who shared Feisal's dormitory. When Anwar had learnt that Diddy intended returning to Dar es Salaam, he had proposed giving Diddy R1 000 so that Diddy could buy a stack of brightly coloured *khangas*, which he said they would be able to sell on Greenmarket Square for three times the original purchase price. Feisal knew that Diddy had no intention of returning to Cape Town. When he had secretly tipped Anwar off, the deal had collapsed. Diddy had guessed at the reasons.

'It was a mistake to warn Anwar,' said Feisal, 'so actually I am happy he took the money. But he was wrong to take my phone. Diddy knows that my brother's number is on that phone. Without it I can never talk to him.'

As bad is the fact that Diddy took the phone knowing that it contained the number of a man who had offered Feisal a job in his barbershop in the township of Nyanga. The offer had stemmed from a chance encounter, and Feisal will almost certainly never see this person again.

◆

Only a couple of days, now, before Barack Obama and his family are due in Cape Town, and what with the shuddering of Chinook rotors on test runs to the city from the US destroyer at anchor in False Bay, and the constant wailing of VIP cavalcades on the city's highways, even documented, paid-up citizens are starting to feel a little hunted, ring-fenced.

I ventured down to the Grand Parade and found it unusually devoid of Beachboys, no doubt because the place was crawling with cops and security guards. At the Golden Arrow bus shelters at the northern end I spied a young friend of Daniel Peter's, a Dar es Salaam Beachboy called Ditto. He was hurrying away from the fixed food stalls, looking concerned.

'The police are arresting everybody. There are fifty or sixty boys in Cape Town Central already,' he said, not stopping to talk.

I walked with him to the Foreshore underpasses, but they were deserted, too. The charcoal from the cooking fires had been swept away and all clothes had been removed from the trees, leaving behind a hundred eerie, home-made, string-and-stick hangers.

'The bridges are no good, the police have been here already. I'm going to The Kitchen, nobody comes there.'

'I'll drive you,' I offered. We took Table Bay Boulevard outbound and doubled back over the R27 bridge to the Beachboy Office, where we left the vehicle and continued on foot alongside the railway lines. Rounding the wall of the marble and granite business we confronted the railway tunnels under the N1, running to the Duncan Dock. The graffiti on the tunnel walls was so dense it looked several inches thick. Smoke was billowing out of the nearest mouth.

'Wait here,' said Ditto when we were twenty metres out. He went on alone as a Chinook thundered overhead, followed by another. When my eyes refocused, Ditto was walking towards me with a slender, lighter-skinned man, who raised a hand in greeting.

'Haiyo Sean,' he said, grinning his golden grin.

'Haiyo Adam,' I yelled back.

◆

When Adam had worked out from overheard conversations that the *Blue Sky* was bound for Cameroon, he had turned himself in to the first crew member he'd encountered and, later, begged the captain to put him off at the next port, Walvis Bay in Namibia. The captain, said Adam, had taken a shine to him. He'd been given his own cabin and had breakfasts delivered every morning, although he had eaten very little since his body had been wracked by the 'shitting, sweating and feeling cold' that comes of sudden heroin withdrawal.

In the evenings, he had been permitted to watch movies with the Filipino crew.

'If there was a scene where a woman takes her clothes off the crew would say to me, "*Spanana*," and make like they were wanking, and I'd say, "Oh yeah, *spanana*," and do the same thing and everyone would laugh and then go back to watching the movie,' he said.

The microtactics of cross-cultural endearment.

Before he'd been disembarked on Namibian soil, Adam claimed the captain had handed him a gift of US$1 600, which he had duly wrapped in plastic and stowed in his 'Beachboy wallet', being his arse. He had spent some days in a police station with some other Tanzanians who had been disembarked from another ship some time earlier. The week before, this group had embarked upon a hunger strike, and a story about it had appeared in the pages of *The Namibian*.

'They were dirty and hungry and it looked like they were dragged through a greasy machine', the journalist had reported. 'The seven are sharing a cell at the Narraville Police Station. According to Chief Inspector Johannes Hamman [...] "They refused to eat the food that we gave them, swearing at us and saying that it was not even fit for a dog to eat"'.

Pushed on the subject of the captain's 'gift', Adam admitted that it had, in fact, been a bribe.

It used to be, he explained, that the primary Beachboy objective was to leave the African continent for good. Success had depended on the willingness of the captain and the crew to allow stowaways to slip off unseen at the next port of call, and for decades this had happened more often than not. Now, said Adam, the consequences for seafarers who were caught aiding and abetting stowaways were serious – instant dismissal, in most cases. This had changed the game, and shipmasters had begun adhering to the International Maritime Organization guidelines on dealing with stowaways. These stipulate that a stowaway be returned either to his home country or to his port of embarkation in cases where nationality cannot be established. In reality, though, few countries will take a stowaway back, putting all responsibility for the handling of stowaways on the ship's crew and its agents.

'It is not as simple as them just buying us a ticket,' said Adam. 'The agent must first get the stowaway's name and then check that this is correct with the Tanzanian embassy in Pretoria. This is where we start to play our game.'

The hustle is fairly straightforward. The stowaways understand that time costs a great deal of money in the world of shipping, and that their chances of being offered a bribe rise if they drag out the processes of deportation.

'We lie and say we are from Somalia or Burundi, anywhere where there is bad suffering, and then we pretend we understand nothing else and keep quiet. If we do that, the ship company has to make an asylum application for us, and this takes a long time.'

The shipping agent will take pictures of the stowaway for sending on to the Tanzanian embassy in Pretoria, because, although the South African government tries to insist otherwise, it is generally presumed that any stowaway originating from a South African port is likely to be Tanzanian by birth.

'The agent hopes the embassy will recognise us from their computers, because if that happens they can send us home. If the embassy does not know us, or if the ship is in a big hurry, the captain will start offering money for us to say, "Yes, my name is Adam Bashili, and I am from Tanzania."'

Adam said he has worked the bribe up as high as US$3 000 in the past, though he usually settles for a lower amount, mindful of the fact that his details have been archived in a number of official databases and that it is only ever a matter of time before his true identity is uncovered.

'If that happens you get nothing,' he said, and explained that he had settled for a particularly low amount from the *Blue Sky* out of respect for the friendly Greek captain.

Back in Dar es Salaam, Adam had been charged with leaving the country illegally and taken to a holding cell at Julius Nyerere Airport, only to be released an hour later after payment of a TSh200 000 (approximately US$100) fine. He had stayed for five days with his delighted mother (who'd cried when he had handed her five somewhat worn US$100 notes), in her house on the south shore of the harbour. On day six, he'd struck out for South Africa for the fifth time in his life.

Adam related this account of modern stowaway dynamics casually, like it was nothing – just the way things are for Beachboys now. But I sensed some negativity in the background.

'It's not really the Sea Power way,' he admitted. 'If I'm honest, these days some of the younger boys only stow away so that they can take money and go home. Others have no hope of getting anywhere different, so they have dedicated their lives to *unga* and tik. It's sad, man. I try to remind them that every day a new baby is born – you never know what is going to happen tomorrow, and you will never know if you don't try.'

I recently purchased Karel Schoeman's *Early Slavery at the Cape of Good Hope, 1652–1717* and, last night, read his contention that the first slave in the Cape was a stowaway, a man known only as Abraham, who had boarded a ship named the *Malacca* in Batavia. The ship was Europe-bound but Abraham had been discovered, and on 2 March 1653 he was disembarked at the Cape of Good Hope with orders that he be sent back to his master. Three years passed before this happened, during which time Abraham was put to work by Jan van Riebeeck, who recorded that 'in consequence of ill health the man was unable to earn half his food'. In 1655, two more runaway slaves were disembarked at the Cape. Thereafter, the trend in stowaway traffic was of slaves attempting to leave Africa's southernmost port, usually in the VOC fleet bound for Europe. In 1685, records Schoeman, nine slaves who went missing were immediately suspected of having taken refuge on a French ship then at anchor in the bay.

'This may have occurred quite frequently without being detected', he writes, and reproduces the following note from Cape of Good Hope archivist HCV Leibbrandt:

> *Slaves often missed. Supposed that they escape in the return fleet. Two again gone. Fugitives write to the slaves here about the vast difference between liberty and slavery, and about the Fatherland, making them also anxious to escape. This should be stopped; and we therefore beg you to have all the ships examined before the men leave them, and also to see whether the two runaways are on board and send them back in irons to be punished, to deter others. This is a matter seriously affecting the Company and the people.*

Since my first encounters with the Beachboys, I have resisted making connections with Cape history, although they occur to me all the time. When I lifted up that ship-shaped rock on the highway ledge, for example – the one under which Kham'si Swaleh Kigomba had hidden his emergency travel papers – I was instantly reminded of the *padrão* (stone cross) that the Portuguese mariner Bartolomeu Dias had erected on these shores on 12 March 1488 to mark his 'discovery' of the Cape of Good Hope. It seemed a nice echo, but what was the connection, really? The one functioned as an imperial land claim, the other as nothing more than a homeless immigrant's valuables locker.

I have also felt tempted to connect the desires of the early Cape slaves with those of the Tanzanian Beachboys.

Escape the cape. Today Africa tomorrow yurope

Abraham, Adam – Abram. It seemed too neat, too clever.

But Adam, of course, found these details fascinating.

'Yow, what you telling me?' he said when I read out Schoeman's assertion that the earliest stowaways tended to be lighter-coloured slaves, because they were able to engage the sympathies of the coloured seamen working aboard the VOC ships. Slaves looking to escape the continent also tended to favour the first three months of the year, because this was the busiest time in the harbour, with ships coming and going in great numbers ahead of the Indian Ocean monsoons.

'It is the same for us,' said Adam. 'We mostly stow ships in winter, because the bad weather makes the guards go inside. When the weather is worst here in Cape Town we don't mind, we like it.'

I suppose the continuum is real enough. Desperation, discovery, oppression, emancipation, entrapment.

The weather, and its infinite effects.

◆

Usually, when he wants to meet or talk, Adam sends a Please Call Me and I call back as soon as I can, knowing that his phone battery may not last long and that it could be days before he recharges it. A month or so ago, he broke with tradition and called three times while I was occupied. I knew it meant that something unusual had happened.

When I called back, he said, 'I have something to show you.'

'What is it?'

'Something beautiful.'

'Okay. I'll meet you after work, 5 p.m. outside the KFC on Darling.'

(After a lengthy period of unemployment, I have taken a job as a copywriter with an advertising agency, based in Paarden Eiland. I work on the supermarket accounts, mainly, but was recently entrusted with a pilot campaign for Snus, a Swedish smokeless tobacco product. The only upside is the view from my desk of the breakwater, and the fact that my route to work goes through the Beachboy areas, allowing me to take my lunches with Adam at The Kitchen, or to meet him on the Grand Parade on my way home.)

At 5 p.m., with me double-parked in the usual place, Adam managed to make it to the passenger door before I spotted him. He jumped in. I wound down the windows.

'Do I smell bad?'

'Like a dead dog.'

He giggled. 'Go around the corner,' he said, glancing left and right. I slipped up Plein Street, came to a stop outside the display windows of Fashion Express. Adam fished a tall, narrow paper bag out of his pants, the kind dispensed in pharmacies. It was all scrunched up, but the necklace he extracted from it hung neat as a snake from his fingers.

'White gold,' said Adam.

I glanced left and right. 'It's a nice-looking chain.'

'You want it?'

'No.'

'Can you keep it for me?'

'Why?'

'I want to send it to Aniya. It's her birthday soon.'

Since being deported from England, Adam has remained in contact with Rochelle and Aniya, albeit erratically. Whenever he takes a ship, months of no contact pass. The same lapses occur when he's in Cape Town and smoking particularly hard, from morning till night. In the grip of these binges, he divests himself of all responsibility, sells his phone, stops washing. Since returning to Cape Town this last time, however, he has been both dissolute and determinedly in touch with his daughter.

'She has her own phone now,' he tells me. 'I can call her anytime I want.'

In this way, he is, for the first time, establishing a relationship with Aniya.

'She talks to me like I'm there with her,' he says. 'She talks until my airtime runs out.'

A day after he showed me the necklace, and in spite my misgivings about its provenance (a tourist's handbag on a Long Street pavement), I helped Adam to post the gift to Birmingham. We tucked it inside a small leather bag he had bought on Greenmarket Square, and added a postcard of Robben Island, which he did not write on. He called Rochelle ten days later, on Aniya's birthday, expecting to hear how delighted they both were with the chain. We were seated in the Conquest, and I couldn't help noticing his wince of disappointment on learning that his plan had misfired. I pointed out the window at a *Cape Times* news poster tied to a streetlight. *Post Office Strike Deepens*.

'Yow, Rochelle, you know what, fucking post office is on strike here. I think that is why Aniya's present is late.'

The conversation moved on to other things – Rochelle had just watched *Iron Man 3*, and thought Adam might enjoy it – but he was distracted now, crestfallen. He told Rochelle I needed my phone back, shouted *mwah mwah mwah* into the device, and ended the call.

'You think they gonna get it?'

'I'm not sure.'

'I hope so.'

The strike broke a few days later and shortly afterwards Rochelle sent Adam a message to say that the package had arrived.

'Aniya got it. She love it, man. I'm so happy right now. I wish I could have seen her face,' he said.

'When was the last time you actually saw her face?'

'When she was a baby, in England.'

'You should Skype her, Adam. We can do it right now, from my computer.'

'Okay.'

'Call Rochelle, ask her for her Skype details.'

'Okay.'

Adam called Rochelle's number.

'Hello.'

'Yow Rochelle, it's me. I'm with Sean. We want to call Aniya over the Internet.'

'Do you have Tango? Aniya uses Tango to make free calls over the Internet.'

'Tang … yow Sean?'

I shook my head.

'Sean never heard of Tango.'

'We can download it,' I whispered.

'We gonna get it,' Adam said. 'We gonna call you again.'

We raced back to my computer and downloaded the Tango app, but I couldn't get it to work. Adam consulted with Rochelle.

'She says Aniya has gone to her friend now anyway. She is going to try to get Skype. We can call them again next Saturday.'

We called Rochelle's new Skype account a week later, without success. Adam called her cell from the landline, but the number rang and rang.

'Can we try again next Saturday?'

'Sure. Anytime.'

This went on weekend after weekend. An arrangement would be made, and something would go wrong. In most cases, something had come up on their side and, since Adam had no phone, Rochelle was unable to inform him. I began to feel put upon. Each failure cost several hours and left me feeling anxious and unhappy. I worried that these failures to connect were somehow deliberate, that Rochelle might be dodging Adam – us. No, it is the *us* that bothers me. When Adam makes contact, it's always and inevitably us. If I'm not seated next to him in the car, then I'm in the 24-hour pharmacy on Darling Street, buying toiletries I don't really need. I can't go far, because if my phone locks my help will be needed to unlock it. He remembers a dozen phone numbers, but can never remember my four-digit phone code.

As the week went by without a single call or message from Adam, I started to feel a building relief. For the first time in months, a Saturday lay open before me. No deadlines, no commitments, no reason to leave the house at all. By now, I should know better than to allow a situation like this to develop, but I couldn't bring myself to intervene, to give up the rare and delicious gift of time. And so the inevitable happened. I squandered it in the old way, starting up shortly after lunch, so that I would be sober in time for dinner with my wife. When she had gone to bed, I picked up where I had left off. I lay down for a few hours in the early morning, but did not sleep. I counted off my wife's waking routine – run with the dog, shower, blow-dry, make-up – and stood up to see her off to work. I was about to kick out again – to take it to hell and down – when Adam called.

'Rochelle says Aniya is going to be ready at 10. It's going to happen this time.'

I closed my eyes, allowed purple and yellow figments to build up and swirl behind my eyelids. 'Sure. I'll leave now. I'll pick you up at the Beachboy Office in 15 minutes.'

I reckon I could do the rest with my eyes closed; it may even be safer that way. There's a lonely inexorability to the familiar routine, especially on weekends. If the Conquest is facing downslope, I simply release the handbrake and let gravity pull us away from the gate. I run well-known intersections for want of traffic, only slowing out of necessity. I drift over De Waal Drive and into the lonely, open fields of what was once District Six. I send the car under Nelson Mandela Boulevard at the Chapel Street circle, the lazy screech of the balding tyres amplified by the bridge mouth. This morning, residents of the Chapel Street night shelter were smoking on crates they had pulled out onto the sunbathed pavement. On Main Road, working down to Albert, anyone not fixed to their own front yard and family seemed to be going about chores with an intensity that glorifies families and stoeps in general. Finally, I pulled up outside the marble and granite business, and took my pick of the bays. The guard, who knows my car by now, waved. I killed the engine and reclined the seat. Normally I leave the car and walk alongside the freeway on the Beachboys' towpath, then dip down to The

Kitchen to greet Sudi, Barak and the others. Today, I closed my eyes and waited for Adam to come to me.

Walking back into my office I received a shock, as if I'd stumbled into a crime scene. Shoes and papers were scattered around the floor, empty mugs and glasses and oat-begrimed bowls crowded the tables. I'd left the paraphernalia of my binge next to the keyboard, a business card curled in on itself.

Sean Christie – Foreign Policy Correspondent

I groaned.

'You okay?' asked Adam. I shook my head.

'I thought you stopped, but actually I knew it. You look red, like a balloon.'

'I've felt better.'

'I understand.'

'I know.'

I clicked the green telephone icon on Skype. Dialling sounds from the machine resolved with a crackle of feedback into two faces, a mother and her child, eyes flickering in our direction but not yet focused on anything in particular.

'Aniya!' Adam shouted. 'Can you hear me, Aniya?'

'Yeah.'

'Amazing. Did you just wake up? What time did you wake up?'

Too many questions; the little girl shrank towards her mother.

'Aniya?'

'Yeah?'

'I love you.'

'I love you too.'

'I always loved you. Oh my god,' said Adam, his voice cracking. 'So, did you have breakfast?'

'Ummm.'

'Are you shy? Don't be shy. It's your daddy. Fucking amazing. I can't believe it. Aniya?'

'Yeah?'

'Everything gonna be okay. I love you.'

Rochelle cut in. 'She looks just like you.'

'You think?' said Adam, blowing kisses to the screen. *Mwah, mwah, mwah.* 'Aniya, you look just like your mum. Beautiful. You have her nose and everything. I wish I was there with you. A weekend like this, we're supposed to watch a football match.'

'She don't like football, she's a girl,' said Rochelle.

'But I'd like to take her. I don't know why I had that thought.'

I made to leave.

'Sean, come here a second.'

I picked up my Airedale terrier and walked into view.

'You see the dog, Aniya?' said Adam. 'His name is Barkly, he looks like a teddy bear.'

'Yeah.'

I put the dog's big wet nose up to the screen, eclipsing the room view, then retreated. The dog licked my face and convulsed out of my grip.

'He didn't like it when you did that,' Aniya scolded, her forehead creased. Now she looked like Adam – uncannily so, with her fierce dark eyes and eyebrows, her high cheekbones and caramel skin.

'This is my friend Sean, you hear me Aniya. This is his place. His wife's name is Andret. They're trying to have a baby. She was pregnant already but they lost it. I know they gonna get their baby though. Inshallah. That is what we say, inshallah.'

I waved and fled the room, unable to stand the unexpected scrutiny a second longer. But, no matter where I went in the house, I could still hear Adam talking, asking Aniya about school, telling her she should behave, listen to her mother. I stepped outside, felt uneasy in the sun. The dog let rip at a pedestrian so I dragged him inside and shut the door, then walked to the far side of the house, to the bathroom, which was cave-dark. I put the lid of the toilet down, and sat back. *You've got to make those changes*, I mumbled. Over and over.

Then Adam laughed – a clean, joyful sound, with none of life's scum on it. I stood up.

Okay. Everything gonna be okay.

◆

Lovely, sunny afternoon.

I called Sudi and Adam and said I knew a place where we could go and enjoy the sunshine. They climbed into the Conquest outside the Grand Parade KFC and we hauled up to Deer Park, on the mountain slopes above the city. The Platteklip River runs through it, so named because the early Cape slaves used to wash laundry on the flat rocks above the weir. Today, the waters attract the sack Rastas who bathe under a secret waterfall upslope, and also a constant stream of Pentecostalists who take away bottles of the stuff for use in ritual cleansing ceremonies. Dog walkers come and go, and some drug smokers.

Here and there on the banks, under a mix of indigenous trees, pines and eucalypts, are some concrete tables and benches and, at a specific point where the riverside trees have knitted, some inspired crew has placed a table in the river. If you get there first at this time of year, you can enjoy water around your ankles while you eat and drink.

'Beautiful place,' said Adam, removing a pair of paint-flecked work boots. 'In Tanzania, somebody would make you pay to come to a place like this.'

Sudi mumbled something in Swahili.

'Sudi say he thought black people are not allowed on the mountain.'

'Really?'

'Yeah. In Tanzania there are too many places only white people can go. Or you need to have money to be there, but most Tanzanians got no money. It is the same here in Cape Town. If we go into the city from the Parade the CCID follow us, and they never leave. If you try to go into a bar they tell you no, sorry, this place is not for you.'

The range of the Beachboys has been successfully confined to the freeway bridges, highway culverts and railway reserve, where the city has little jurisdiction (the railway reserve is the property of the state transport parastatal, Transnet). Only Transnet can initiate and drive eviction proceedings in these areas, but the repeated demands for it to do so seem to fall on deaf ears. But, even here, movement is restricted.

'We got our own politics, and not every Beachboy is free to go wherever he wants,' said Adam.

The revelation came as a surprise.

'You seem to go where you like.'

'Memory can go anywhere,' said Sudi, 'but not others.'

It has to do with Adam's stowaway record, Sudi explained. By his reckoning, Adam is currently Cape Town's most effective stowaway. In the past 12 months alone he has made it to sea three times, an extraordinary feat in this time of heightened port and ship security.

'Many Beachboys have been trying to stow away for five years and more, without success,' said Sudi.

And then, of course, there is the matter of Adam's years in England. In all the Beachboy community here, which I estimate at between one hundred and fifty and three hundred individuals (based on the number of subscriptions that are paid whenever a Beachboy dies), no more than a handful have actually made it through the western world's immigration nets and spent time living abroad. For those who have, the achievement is worth more than Olympic gold. It allows them to cross effortlessly over community faultlines. Adam walks where he wishes, and is never far from being asked to join a meal or share a joint. The younger Beachboys want to hear his stories and ask for his advice. They would queue up to accompany him to the docks – pay him for the privilege, even – if it weren't well known that he prefers to go it alone.

But Sudi was quick to add that admiration often masks jealousy down on the Foreshore.

'After Memory went the last time, some guys came and said, "Sudi, show us where Memory keeps his *mkoba* [medicine bag]." They think he must be witches [a witchdoctor] to do everything he done.'

Adam was hearing this for the first time, and he looked concerned. He interrogated Sudi furiously in Swahili, and exited this exchange saying, 'Nah, that's bullshit, man. They might think they were making a joke but saying that I have a *mkoba* is no fucking joke. It could get me killed.'

I was lost, and must have looked it. Adam explained.

'There are too many evil witches in Tanzania. If a Tanzanian person is jealous of somebody, he can go and see an *uchawi* [witchdoctor] and pay the *uchawi* to make a spell. After that you can be sure something will happen to the person he was jealous of. That person might have an accident, or somebody might put his eye out in a fight. Sometimes there will be nothing wrong with him, and an hour later he will be dead.'

'You really believe that?'

'Of course, Sean, of course. One of our boys was killed by witches just the other day. His name was Chandiraya, an old guy, experienced guy. He went to the Stones during low tide, and he was walking on the other side in water this deep,' said Adam, sloshing his feet around in the river.

'Some other guys saw him walking like that, but when they looked again Chandiraya was gone. He drowned, in water up to his socks. We call a death like this a *chanous*. Somebody put witches on Chandiraya, no doubt about it. Maybe it was one of us. Or it could have been somebody in Tanzania. It doesn't matter how far away you are, because witches fly around at night, they can get you anywhere.'

I studied Adam closely. He had slipped into his theatrical mode, but seemed to believe everything he was saying.

'You sound like you're afraid of witchdoctors?'

'I am afraid, I can't lie. I can go to any ghetto, California or anywhere, I won't be scared. I can explain myself to those niggers and we will understand each other. But this witches stuff scares me. You don't know when they want you. You don't know what they think of you. You can see an old woman every day and she says, "I love you," but actually she might have a different plan for you, an evil plan. If I ever get money I will never let anyone in Tanzania know. I will pretend I got *fokol*, because what witches like is somebody with nothing – somebody who don't think of a better life. If a witch thinks you're going to get a better future, they will destroy you. If you're clever, making good business, they hate that, I don't know why. These African witches ...'

Adam's eyes were ablaze. He sucked his cheeks in and let his words trail away.

'They're all poor, and they deserve to be poor. If you give them money, they will take it and say thank you, *asante sana*, but at night they will take out their *mkoba* and curse that money, and you will never get a penny again.'

The Beachboys, Adam and Sudi agreed, were somewhat buffered from the scourge of witchcraft by the fact that powers of *uchawi* are generally matrilineal and there are no female Tanzanians living among the Beachboys. There are exceptions, though, said Adam.

'A boy can get his mummy's power if there is no daughter. But if this has happened to any Beachboy he would never tell nobody, not even his *achoose*, because he knows people will be proper frightened. They might even try do something to him before he can put witches on anyone. That's why it was no joke for those boys to say what they said about me. Somebody might hear it the wrong way, and tell another guy. In one week everybody will be saying, "Ah Memory Card, that guy is *uchawi*, see how many ships he already got." And they might try to take me down.'

Adam said some Beachboys feared witchcraft more than others – and that those who truly believed in it tended to be the ones who had grown up in rural villages.

'I grew up in the bush, and there were witches everywhere. I knew this one boy from the village, name of Mohamed, who disappeared one day and nobody saw him again. His family called a big witchdoctor, because sometimes a big witchdoctor can save a person, bring him back. But this guy said it was too late, because the witches had already cut Mohamed's tongue out. This guy said they put Mohamed inside a tree, a big tree in a big forest. Mohamed had been sitting there so long his bum had become like a big wound, all the skin coming off and dying. He said there's nothing nobody can do to save that boy. And you know who done it? The people knew; it was his father-in-law's sister.'

When Adam stopped talking, the sounds of the forest came up, the gurgle of water and the creaking of the nearby stone pines in a gentle breeze. Some red-winged starlings whistled to one another, somewhere out of sight.

And, behind it all, the now-reassuring drone of city traffic.

◆

Daniel Peter, the young boxer from Keko, has a new friend called Aisha, a 21-year-old coloured man of the *sakman* order of Rastafarians, so called for their ethic of wearing clothes fashioned entirely from jute. For months, since Daniel Peter's return from Johannesburg, the oddly matched youths have shared a section of the Lower Plein Street pavement. Each morning, the Rastafarian sets out a flax mat and populates it with 'bush medicines' from the slopes of Table Mountain – mainly *imphepho* at this time of the year, alongside some bunches of lemony confetti bush and sprigs of *bloublomsalie*. Daniel Peter stands beside him from noon onwards and hustles marijuana.

They could hardly be less alike. Daniel Peter, like many other Beachboys, has embraced the low-slung jeans and jewellery of American hip hop culture. Aisha goes about barefoot and wears nothing but a sack cilice fashioned from a Finca el Retiro coffee bag, the brand name upside down across his abdomen. Following the rules of his order the dreadlocked youth washes at least once a day, eats no meat and smokes only Jah's sacred herb. Daniel Peter smokes *unga*, relishes boiled cow head and, like most other Beachboys, can go for weeks without washing, especially in winter.

There is a more fundamental difference. The sack Rastas see themselves as the true indigenes of this place, tracing their ancestry all the way back to the Goringhaicona people who lived in the valleys of Table Mountain in precolonial times. They will tell you about Autshumao, the Goringhaicona leader who received the Dutch settler Jan van Riebeeck when he and his men sailed into Table Bay in 1652, and will claim Krotoa, Autshumao's niece and later Van Riebeeck's interpreter, as one of his progenitor grandmothers. They will always call Table Mountain by its Khoe name: Hoerikwaggo, the mountain in the sea.

Daniel Peter knows nothing of the Cape's social history, precolonial or otherwise, and scarcely acknowledges the presence of the mountain, except when a ship chugs left out of the harbour and disappears in a southerly direction. If a Beachboy happens to have stowed away on a south-bound ship he is said to have gone *nyuma mlima*, behind the mountain. It is considered something of a disaster, since the ship will soon round Cape Point and set course either for one of the East African ports (of no interest to Tanzanian stowaways), or for the positively dreaded ports of the Far East.

Aisha and Daniel Peter are also twins in some ways, the Romulus and Remus of the Cape underworld. They both live at odds with the law (wild harvesting on the slopes of Table Mountain is illegal), and enjoy smoking marijuana and drawing pictures. Both come from broken homes in impoverished communities, which they have been able to escape by taking on new identities.

After weeks of deflection, Aisha told me today that he grew up in gang-ruled Lavender Hill, on the southern side of the Cape Flats. His mother still lives there; when he visits, which is not so often any more, he dresses in normal clothes, stays indoors and goes by his birth name, which is Brandon.

◆

Memories of my first encounter with another notable 'sea tramp', whose time in the Cape changed the course of this country's history. It took place in the early 2000s, when I had little better to do with my time than haunt the old city library, which was housed on the second floor of the City Hall, overlooking the Grand Parade. It was among the shrieking children who used the place as an after-school playroom that I first read *A Mouthful of Glass*, Henk van Woerden's story about the life of Dimitri Tsafendas, the Mozambique-born drifter who fatally stabbed Prime Minister Hendrik Verwoerd in 1966.

Rereading certain passages now, I am struck by the parallels with Adam's story. Tsafendas, like Adam, was born of a Greek father and an African mother. Being of mixed blood, writes Van Woerden, Tsafendas was unable to follow his Cretan father legally when he moved to supremacist South Africa in the thirties, but decided to follow him anyway: 'He knew the borders were porous and poorly controlled. In the autumn [...] he concealed himself among some machinery packed in a railway goods-wagon, and crossed the border at Komatipoort with no difficulty. Then on to Pretoria.'

It was the first of many border crossings, literal and otherwise. The documentary trail left by Tsafendas at the time of his arrest stretched across 25 countries, 13 ships and 12 hospitals. On his travel permits and deportation orders, he was referred to variously as Tsafendas, Tsafendis, Tsafandis, Tsafendos, Tsafandakis, Tsafantakis, Tsafendikas, Stifanos and Chipendis. Adam, who goes by Bashili, Brazili, Chazili and Swalehe, could similarly be tracked via a series of charge sheets stretching from Cape Town to Birmingham and from Walvis Bay to St Petersburg.

Tsafendas spent so much time away from the country of his birth, and made so much trouble wherever he went, that his home government ultimately adjudged him *persona non grata*.

'He was a rogue *que tem una vida sempre instavel e de aventuras* – "constantly drawn to an unstable and adventurous way of life"', writes Van Woerden, words that would not be out of place on any Beachboy headstone.

Above all else, Tsafendas loved the sea.

'During the two decades Tsafendas spent outside South Africa, the sea was the only constant presence in his life', Van Woerden writes. 'He remained almost exclusively on the coastline of the countries he lived in, in cities where the docks beckoned him and where the sounds of winches, seagulls and engines rose above the hiss and roar of the ocean. Piraeus, Oporto, Lisbon, Marseilles, London, Hamburg – he was most himself amid the restless, provisional lives of people who did not know where they might be the next day or the day after it.'

In the weeks before he stabbed Verwoerd four times – with a knife bought on Cape Town's Long Street and at the urging, he later told state psychiatrists, of a talking tapeworm inside his own gut – Tsafendas had spent most of his free time aboard ships berthed in the port, sharing the crews' meals and generally hanging out. It is tempting to imagine that, had his life continued to follow this course, he may have lived out his winter years under Nelson Mandela Boulevard, or Eastern Boulevard as it would have been called then.

◆

For all of Adam's talents and achievements, if the local Beachboy community has a superstar, he would have to be David Mndolwa.

Mndolwa was born in Dar es Salaam in 1988, in Magomeni, Sudi's home district. In 2009 he had travelled to South Africa, making it to Cape Town in 2010. Not long afterwards, Mndolwa and a Beachboy called Jocktan Kobelo had boarded a reefer named the *Dona Liberta*. They had hidden in the ship's engine room and remained there for nine days before being discovered and set adrift on a raft off the coast of Liberia. Kobelo, who could not swim, had drowned after slipping into the stormy ocean, but Mndolwa had managed to hang on and was washed ashore. He had reported the incident: the *Dona Liberta*'s predominantly Filipino crew had been arrested and ultimately convicted of murder, entirely on the strength of Mndolwa's testimony.

After his ordeal, Mndolwa had been returned to Dar es Salaam, only to find that he was not welcome back in his mother's house. His survival tale had travelled the Beachboy networks, though, and doors were opened for him all over the city. Sudi, recently deported from South Africa, had hosted him for weeks, and the two had become friends. They had travelled back to Cape Town before the end of that year, and today Mndolwa lives in a makeshift den built among the drooping fronds of a portside palm tree.

It is to this bivouac that some well-known international journalists have recently beaten a path. Some months ago, Adam called to inform me that a man with a noticeable limp had been wandering the Foreshore, asking about Mndolwa's whereabouts. This person claimed to have been on the spoor of the *Dona Liberta* incident for months, even travelling to Dar es Salaam to visit the grave of Jocktan Kobelo.

'He gave me this,' Adam said, producing a simple business card embossed with contact details for João Silva, the legendary South African war photographer who lost both his legs in 2010 when he stepped on a landmine in Afghanistan.

More recently, Mndolwa had been visited by an investigative team from the *New York Times*. In the first of several features about lawlessness at sea, the journalists exposed a litany of crimes committed by various crews of the *Dona Liberta* over a period of several years. Finding Mndolwa, one of the authors said in an online podcast, 'was a huge coup. We didn't know his name and we certainly didn't know where he was [but] through lots of scramble and gum-shoe and luck we found that guy, and amazingly he was in a stowaway shanty town twenty feet from where he had originally boarded the ship'.

The *Times* team got bogged down, however, when two videographers named Ed Ou and Ben Solomon travelled to Cape Town to chronicle Mndolwa's life.

'One afternoon', the story ran, 'Ed went alone to meet some of these stowaways, and several of them jumped him. After punching and kicking him, they made off with thousands of dollars worth of film equipment. Ed was left with a black eye and bruised ribs.'

When I mentioned this to Sudi and Adam, they became very angry. The alleged attack, they said, could never have happened.

'How can we beat and rob an international journalist, and still be here today?' Sudi asked.

It is a reasonable question. The Beachboys remain in their living areas under tenuous licence, constantly monitored by the railway police unit and dozens of CCID guards. For quite a time, SAPS Woodstock has been under pressure from the business community to 'do something' about the Beachboy encampments in the railway reserve. The Beachboys are well aware of these dynamics, and practise a degree of self-regulation. It is forbidden, for example, for any Beachboy to commit serious crime in the Beachboy living areas. Contravention of this code is punishable with violence, said Adam, and offered an example. Three weeks ago, two young Beachboys thought it would be a good idea, after a night of drinking in the Seaman Bar off Draklow Street, to rob the Burundian night guard who works for the AfriSam cement plant on Beach Road. The AfriSam factory overlooks The Kitchen, and when Adam, Sudi and Barak heard of the robbery they found and severely beat the young perpetrators. The guard's phone was returned to him with a community apology, in the hope that he would take the matter no further.

The Kitchen would not exist, in fact, were it not for the verbal deal between the Beachboys and the owner of WOMAG, the adjoining marble and granite business. Before the Beachboys settled outside the walls of this property, the business had experienced a terrific problem with theft. When the Beachboy tents started appearing, CEO Oren Sachs told the Beachboys that he would leave them be as long as they saw to it that his property was not touched. His business has not experienced a single case of theft since.

There is also the story of a young Cape Town journalist called Kimon de Greef, who sat down on the steps of Edward VII one afternoon. While he listened to a series of stowaway tales, Adam rifled his bag, stealing what felt like a cellphone. Back under Nelson Mandela Boulevard, Adam was surprised to find that he had, in fact, stolen the journalist's digital recorder. Stored on this, to Adam's delight, was an interview that De Greef had just completed with the US rapper formerly known as Mos Def. A group of Beachboys had gathered around to listen, and used the device afterwards to record a series of spirited Swahili raps. Meanwhile De Greef, who had not yet written up his interview, returned to the Parade to try to recoup his device, offering rewards willy-nilly. Adam came to hear of this and invited the journalist down to the flyovers, where he returned the recorder. This story was corroborated in all its details by De Greef, who has since become a friend.

What, then, to make of the *Times*'s accusations?

The issue has bugged me for days, to the extent that I called Ed Ou, the Canadian videographer from the story, and begged him for a more detailed account of the mugging. He surprised me by saying that the attack had not, in fact, occurred in the Beachboy living areas, but on a street in lower Woodstock. This is territory controlled by the Hard Livings gang, and Ou's description of the attack (his attackers made off in a car seconds after robbing him) makes it almost certain that his attackers were not Beachboys.

'I guess we don't know who attacked me and we'll never know,' said Ou.

The editorial error was acknowledged and the online version of the story was duly altered.

'Tha's good,' said Adam when I told him, practically radiating smug satisfaction. 'But you know, Sean, I since heard that David is working with a housebreaking gang in Woodstock. Local guys. HL [Hard Livings], I think.'

◆

At a point last night, sitting around the cooking fire at The Kitchen, Adam ran out of weed. We duly collected my car, which was parked under the nearby Integrated Rapid Transit flyover, and drove around to the pedestrian bridge that leads to Maskani.

Adam went up the staircase to the pedestrian bridge alone, leaving me in the panhandle, watching junkies spill out of a bank of nearby rushes. I heard the engine of a sports car fire up outside eKapa Tavern. Seconds later, a black Chrysler Crossfire had boxed my Conquest in. The driver looked the archetypal tycoon with his silver hair, crisp white shirt, and jacket. He was talking on his phone and gesturing furiously. He showed no intention of wanting to leave his vehicle, so I walked over.

'Can I help you?'

'He's here now, Commissioner. Come quickly, please,' the man said into his phone, and then pressed it to his chest and looked up angrily.

'What's your name? What are you doing here?'

'I'm dropping off some friends.'

'Oh, so you condone this,' he said and, putting the phone back to his ear, yelled, 'Commissioner, he says he's dropping off some friends. Come quickly, please.'

'Condone what?'

'I saw someone leave your car and go over the bridge.' He put the phone back against his chest.

'It isn't any of your business,' I said.

'He says it's none of my business, Commissioner, come quick, come quick.'

I presented one of my impressive foreign policy correspondent cards. 'Here, take my details if you like.'

The Crossfire's window scrolled down an inch and I smelled the booze.

'What's *your* name, mister?'

'He's asking me for my name, Commissioner. Come quick please.'

Adam, who had returned and was watching the exchange with some amusement, shouted encouragement in a mocking falsetto: 'Come quick, Commissioner, come quick.'

'Now hang on,' the man said, changing tack, 'let's try to work together. It's terrible to be on the streets, I know that. I am someone who cares for the homeless, even to the extent of providing some of them with temporary shelter in my residence. We all need to try to be more understanding. But do you know that there are two kinds of homeless people? There are those who are homeless because they have nothing in the world, and nobody to support them, and there are those who are homeless by choice. Do you know that? Because most people don't.'

We left the businessman like that, his phony phone call quite forgotten, though he kept his phone pressed to his chest like a sapphire amulet.

To my surprise I received an e-mail this morning from one André Pienaar, the director of a company that operates several new hospitality businesses in Woodstock – eKapa Tavern being one. He apologised for confronting me and explained that his reaction had been fuelled by months of complaints from his customers, who often returned to their vehicles to find that their hubcaps had been stolen or their windows smashed. He went on to propose 'an exchange of Letters on the Homeless between Sean and André', which he said he would publish in the monthly magazine of the Woodstock Improvement District.

'I envision something similar to the letters between George Orwell and CS Lewis', he wrote, 'not a pro- or anti-homeless debate, but a frank exchange of views. Please consider it favourably.'

I have considered it all morning, and can't keep from grinning. Just imagine, in this decolonising milieu: *Letters on Homelessness, by Sean and André.*

◆

In the late nineties, an elderly relative had spent a great deal of time inside the Port of Cape Town sketching oil rigs. She used to arrive with her charcoal sticks and set up her easel on the lip of A Berth without encountering any resistance. The rather impressive results hang in frames on the walls of her retirement village cottage, huge black-and-red semi-submersibles from up the west coast crested with cranes and drill towers.

'Then those terrorists flew those planes into the Twin Towers and it was suddenly impossible to get anywhere near the rigs,' she explained, when asked to recap her experiences.

After the September 11, 2001 attacks, the US government fast-tracked the finalisation of the International Ship and Port Facility Security (ISPS) Code, which had been in development for years. The international ratification of the code was expedited by a US stipulation that ships docking in countries that were not signatories would be denied access to US ports. All ships dock in America sooner or later; so, everyone signed, and set about meeting, the new security provisions, which included the establishment of perimeter fencing, CCTV surveillance, 24-hour security patrols, and so forth.

For a deeper sense of the impact that the ISPS Code has had on life in and around Cape Town harbour, I went in search of the Ship Society building in Duncan Road, where the road markings are rendered irrational by security cones, randomly scattered dolosse and railway tracks. Previously housed in the much roomier Clock Tower in the Victoria & Alfred Waterfront, the society's maritime artefacts practically swarm on the walls of the new premises: framed photographs and posters depicting bygone vessels, medallions and model ships, a life ring from the *Reina del Mar*. In the sagging library, which was furnace hot, a man called George was meddling with a curtain rod, grasping it between his knees with the wooden finial jutting outwards in a suggestive manner.

'When I was a boy, I could cycle around the docks without a problem. I went on countless ships,' he said. 'Bill, there you are, just the man,' he said when a gent of similar age hobbled in. 'You'll back me up. We'd walk right up the gangplanks and introduce ourselves to the crew, wouldn't we?'

Bill, hair as white as guano, put down the pile of donated books he'd been carrying. He held a copy of Andrew Feinstein's *After the Party* aloft and said, 'Make no mistake, George, the ANC is rotten to the core,' then launched into a series of jokes about the electrical power outages that had been occurring countrywide.

'President Jacob Zuma wants to bring back the death penalty,' said Bill, 'but advises that use of the electric chair would result in unmanageable backlogs.'

George had meanwhile become absorbed in his cellphone.

'Ah, it's deigned to work,' he said, and then, 'No! No, what's happening now?'

'The red button cancels your call,' said Bill, looking over George's shoulder.

A woman wearing bright-red lipstick came in with a plate of sausage rolls. 'Thanks, Sally,' said the men. Pastry flakes on their lips, they started again on issues of access.

'My gripe with the present security set-up has to do with the anomalies,' said George, drawing the last word out in a gravid way. 'The breakwater, for example – why restrict access to the breakwater? It's still possible to access the breakwater in Durban and, if you allow it there, why not here? And then there's the Royal Cape Yacht Club and the fisherman's dock, smack bang among all the shipping. These little boats can come and go as they please. A fisherman can pick his pal up in Saldanha Bay and drop him at the Cape Town docks, no problem.'

'Don't forget about the cruise ships that enter the V&A,' added Bill. 'Their noses loom over the concrete, almost near enough to touch. Anybody can gain access to the hulls of these ships.'

Coincidentally, the early edition of the *Cape Times* had carried a story about two Tanzanian teens who had been discovered in Port Elizabeth on the small platform above the rudder of a bulk carrier. The paper said the youths had stowed away in the port of Cape Town.

'The funny thing about that article was the response those boys gave the journalist. After being rescued from almost certain death, they claimed they were bitterly disappointed. They had been trying for Europe!' exclaimed Bill.

The short article was eclipsed on the front page by a far bigger and bolder story about a near-disastrous Boeing 777 landing. The landing gear had come off, requiring all passengers to evacuate via the emergency exit slides.

'It's a sign of the times,' said George. 'Shipping matters simply do not capture the public imagination the way they once did. Like when the *Apollo Sea* went down near Dassen Island in '94. The first sign that anything was wrong was when the public started complaining about oil washing up on Camps Bay beach. When the oil was analysed it was found to be engine oil, and word went out to shipping companies that were expecting one of their fleet in port. Sure enough, the *Apollo* was missing. The entire crew of 34 drowned, but all the public could think about were the fucking penguins.'

'George!' gasped Sally.

'It's true. The Port of Cape Town is here, an enormous physical reality at the foot of the city, yet as far as most Capetonians are concerned it might as well not exist.'

'It's all back to front,' Bill agreed.

Our conversation was interrupted by a cabin bell signalling the start of the evening's screening: a documentary about the Union-Castle Line, which had ferried passengers between Europe and Africa for much of the 20th century before being discontinued in 1977.

'You should stay and watch,' said George. 'It's narrated by Laurens van der Post.'

◆

Surprisingly little has been written about stowaways. The term elicits no pings from the world's major online research databases, and hardly any in the physical libraries I visit.

Then again, I have never been much of a sleuth. I was employed as a researcher by an internationally renowned academic, once, and given her latest edited version of Olive Schreiner's *Dream Life and Real Life* to proofread and set. '*Do not* introduce any new errors,' she had warned at the outset. Evidently I had introduced a bunch, and thereafter had found myself transporting boxes of her academic papers between her office and her home, or on secondment to her colleagues as a box lifter.

I was excited, therefore, to receive a call a month or so back from Amaha Senu, an Ethiopian PhD candidate at the Seafarers International Research Centre at the University of Cardiff. In a gentle voice, Senu explained that he had been looking into seafarers' experiences of stowaways for some time and was now keen to meet some real-life stowaways to get a sense of their experiences of captains and crews.

'It appears that we have been exploring the same territory, but from different angles,' he said, and proposed an exchange of favours. If I could facilitate introductions to a few stowaways, he would happily share his textual resources with me. Amaha arrived and spent more than a month interacting with Adam, Barak, Sudi and others. Once a week during this time we would meet for lunch, usually at Addis restaurant on the corner of Long and Church streets and, over *injera* and *doro wot*, we'd compare notes. As promised, Amaha presented me with a succession of his resources.

The first out of his briefcase was Robert Louis Stevenson's travel memoir, *The Amateur Emigrant*, which includes a chapter describing Stevenson's encounter at sea with an experienced stowaway called Alick, who impresses with his storytelling abilities. 'I wish you could have heard him tell his own stories,' he writes. 'They were so swingingly set forth, in such dramatic language, and illustrated here and there by such luminous bits of acting, that they could only lose in any reproduction.'

For Stevenson, stowaways are 'sea-tramps', drawn to an adventurous path through life and likely as not to be 'poisoned by coal-gas, or die by starvation in their places of concealment; or when found they may be clapped at once and ignominiously into irons, thus to be carried to their promised land, the port of their destination, and alas! brought back in the same way to that from which they started, and there delivered over to the magistrates and the seclusion of a county jail.' The neo-romantic writer's instinctive sympathy for this way of life is tempered by his actual experience of meeting and interacting with Alick, who, he decides, is lazy, 'his character [...] degenerated like his face, and become pulpy and pretentious'. The chapter ends on a compensatory note, though, with a description of a woman he deems 'remarkable among her fellows for a pleasing and interesting air'. As the journey progresses, a rumour circulates among the passengers that she, too, is a stowaway.

'The ship's officers discouraged the story', he writes, 'but it was believed in the steerage, and the poor girl had to encounter many curious eyes from that day forth.'

During a subsequent exchange Amaha wanted to know, 'Are there female stowaways among the Beachboys?' I started to reply that there were not, but realised that this was an assumption. I put the question to Adam, who surprised me by saying that yes, there had been several female Beachboys. The best known of these, he said, is a woman called Mwatum, the aunt of Ayoub Omary, a friend of his. Mwatum had travelled to Durban in the mid nineties and stowed away with several others on a ship bound for Brazil. She had ended up 'being' with the captain, who said he would drop the others off in Brazil, but would take Mwatum and her brother Mwamotto to Italy. Adam says that the two now live in Italy's Caserta province, where she apparently makes a living as a drug dealer. He added, though, that female stowaways are 'very rare' and that they would have to be 'pure ghetto' to survive in the Beachboy areas. They would have to be brought in by a male Beachboy – and not just anyone, but a big, respected character.

Next out of Amaha's library was *The Stowaways and Other Sea Sketches* by John Donald. The setting is again the Scottish coastline, though Donald's stowaways are Scots boys from the port and harbour towns on the River Clyde who grow up in thrall to the 'beauty and mystery of ships and the magic of the sea'. The objective, more often than not, is less to get somewhere different than to win over the captain, be put to work aboard his ship and, in this way, enter manhood and earn a living. The book is a trove of mid-19th-century seafarer diction ('if I can mak' my wye to the fo'c'scle, an' thaers naebody aboot I'll lift the hatch an' ye can come up') and reveals much about the strategies of 19th-century stowaways:

> *The stowaways' modus operandi was to conceal themselves onboard (often with the connivance of one or more members of the crew) before the vessel hauled out of the harbour, and remain in hiding until the tugboat, after towing her charge sufficiently far down the channel, had left for home, when they would crawl up on deck and be hauled before the 'old man' (the captain), who, according to his disposition, would give them either a 'lecture', or a 'rope's ending', or both, and send them forward to work.*

In a note, Amaha explained that the practice of putting stowaways to work faded out in the mid 20th century, and went hand in hand with the modernisation and corporatisation of shipping (the first shipping containers were loaded onto a ship in Newark in 1956) and the increasing attention paid to human rights. The distance between stowaways and seamen has been widening ever since, amplified by the often-stark cultural differences between crew members on the one hand, and crew members and stowaways on the other. In one sense, a rationale that had applied for centuries has fallen away: the chance of a life at sea. It has been replaced by another: the chance to get somewhere different, away from home, out of poverty. But this, too, has more or less fallen away as port and ship security tightens.

The business of stowing away, once considered reckless in a romantic sort of way, has been rendered desperate, irrational.

The last book that Amaha lent me makes the difference very clear. Titled *Benyam*, the book recounts the experiences of a young Ethiopian stowaway called Benyam Bouyalew, as told to the Spanish writer Fernando Sorribes. Unlike that of Stevenson and Donald, there is no romantic tint to this tale, which begins with the death of Bouyalew's father, a relatively well-to-do businessman from the Ethiopian town of Dese. When the family's fortunes begin to slide, Bouyalew leaves home for the port of Djibouti, intending to stow away on a ship bound for Europe.

He soon discovers, however, that the port is 'a world apart, a world unto itself'. In a city filled with starving people, including tens of thousands of Somali and Ethiopian refugees, only the most desperate filter down to the water's edge, where port authorities resort to vicious tactics to keep them from reaching the ships.

'The French had recently been given operative control, which put an end to loose security', recounts Bouyalew. 'At night a battery of lights looking out to sea would sweep the coast in search of swimmers heading for their boat and freedom. The entire port was surrounded by walls and fences with extra-sharp razor wire of a particularly terrifying French design.'

Bouyalew sneaks in all the same, and finds no fewer than two hundred men living among the bric-a-brac of the harbour. He recalls that '[a]lmost all were covered in scars or had limbs missing, from fights amongst themselves with machetes, from beatings by the guards or from injuries sustained in their failed attempts to get to sea'.

Two rival gangs dominate the scene: the Aseb boys, hailing from the Eritrean port city of Aseb, and the Oromos, comprising Oromo Ethiopians. Many of the Aseb boys, says Bouyalew, 'were toughened fighters with no compassion' – veterans of the last war between Ethiopia and Eritrea, which redrew the region's borders. These men controlled the supply of khat into the port, which ensured a measure of influence with security guards and police.

'Around one o'clock in the afternoon was when the khat was handed out', writes Bouyalew. 'It has an effect similar to that of amphetamines; chewing khat leaves produces a euphoric high and feelings of mental sharpness. Everyone used it in the port, particularly the security guards and patrolmen. At that point, everything would come to a standstill. People would sit down, begin chewing together and talk endlessly. After a few hours they would be out of control, or on a come-down.'

The Aseb boys were cruel; the Oromos could be just as vicious, though they were not nearly as organised or well trained in violence. Bouyalew spends his first months in the port being bullied, first by the Oromos and later by the Aseb boys. He is seen as unwanted competition for the boats, his inexperience viewed as a threat to all, since failed stowaway attempts tended to focus the attentions of the port's security forces. One afternoon, seemingly without reason, Bouyalew is stabbed by a well-known stowaway and left for dead. He is rescued by some passing Ethiopians, who encourage him to take his life in a new direction. Bouyalew's mind is made up, however, and he returns to the port. Again and again he makes it onto ships, only to be caught and deported back to Ethiopia, usually after being viciously beaten by crew members; as if in a trance, Bouyalew returns to Djibouti three, four, five times, where he finds the Aseb boys and the Oromos waiting with new tortures. The life of a stowaway, Bouyalew realises, is 'like a board game, where you always land on the square that sends you to jail'.

As the months grow into years, the young Ethiopian comes to understand that 'time as a measurement is a concept that gets lost in this place. Days pass, and more days pass, and yet more days pass. The khat has a lot to do with it, that damned drug that has people completely hooked.'

After 'two long years', Bouyalew finally goes free. He swims out to a container ship, climbs aboard using the anchor chain as his ladder and, ultimately, hides in the cabin of a luxury yacht that is being transported atop a stack of containers. In this surreal eyrie he makes it to the port of Valencia in Spain, and here slips out into Europe, black with grime and so starved that he imagines he looks 'like an eel with human features'.

Today Bouyalew lives in Madrid, where he sells a device that captures the 'signature-wave information' of fresh human hair samples and automatically sends this information to Germany for an analysis that takes fifteen minutes to come back. 'This information', Bouyalew explained in the course of our short correspondence, 'assists professionals of the nutritional, dietary and supplement industry to advise customers about making changes in their environment and lifestyle that would be suitable, from a health perspective.'

E-mail has little in the way of tone, but I like to think that Bouyalew, the former stowaway from Dese in the north-east of Ethiopia, was grinning while he wrote this.

◆

Benyam Bouyalew's top stowaway tips

1. Drinking water is everything for a stowaway. It will give you strength when you think you can no longer carry on. Make sure you have a good supply of it.

ለስቶአዌ የሚጠጣ ውሃ ከምንም ነገር በላይ አስፈላጊ ነው። አቅምህን አሟጠህ የጨረስክ ሲመስልህ ውሃ አቅም ይሰጥሃል። ስቶአዌ ከማድረግህ በፊት በቂ ውሃ እንደያዝክ እርግጠኛ ሁን።

2. It pays to work out when the port's surveillance is at its weakest. In the port of Djibouti, this was after the khat was handed out at 1 p.m. For most of the afternoon, the guards would be sitting down, talking madly or coming down.

የወደብ ጥበቃ በሚዳከምበት ወቅት መሞከር የተሻለ ነው። በጅቡቲ ወደብ ይህ የሚሆነው ከቀኑ ሰባት ሰዓት ላይ ሁሉም ጫት በሚይዝበት ጊዜ ነው። የወደቡ ጠባቂዎች ከዚህ በሁዋላ ያለውን ጊዜ ተቀምጠው በመለፍለፍ ወይም ምርቃናቸውን በማብረድ ነው የሚያሳልፉት።

3. Ships flying the Panamanian flag are likely to be from anywhere except Panama. Panamanians pay fewer taxes and a lot of ships use their flag to save port fees. A ship with a Panamanian flag is a good option for getting to Europe or America.

የፓናማን ባንዲራ የሚያውለበልቡ መርከቦች በአብዛኛው ከፓናማ ሀገር አይደሉም። መርከቦች ለፓናማ የሚከፍሉት ግብር አነስተኛ ነው። ስለዚህ ብዙ መርከቦች አነስተኛ ክፍያ ለመክፈል ሲሉ በፓናማ ባንዲራ ስር ይመዘገባሉ። የፓናማን ባንዲራ የሚያውለበልብ መርከብ አውሮፓ ወይም አሜሪካ ለመሄድ ጥሩ አማራጭ ነው።

4. Do not take a Chinese ship. Even a Russian ship is dangerous. The Koreans can be cruel but Filipinos are mostly kind.

የቻይና መርከብ ላይ ስቶአዌ አታድርግ። የራሽያ መርከብ ራሱ አደገኛ ነው። ኮሪያኖች አንዳንዴ ጨካኝ ናቸው። ፊሊፒኖች ግን በአብዛኛው ደግ ናቸው።

5. Hide your possessions well and never reveal what you have with you. In port and aboard ships, you can trust nobody.

የአንተ የሆኑ ነገሮችን ለማንም አታሳይ፤ ደብቃቸው። ወደብ ውስጥ እና መርከብ ላይ ማንንም ማመን አትችልም።

6. It is important to have faith. There are eternal laws in this life, and one of them is this: if you wish for something strongly enough, the effect will occur.

እምነት ይኑርህ። በህይወት ውስጥ ካሉ ዘላለማዊ ህጎች መሃል አንዱ አንድን ነገር አጥብቀህ ከፈለከው ይፈፀማል የሚለው ነው።

7. Look for ships that sit high in the water. Ships that sit low in the water are full of cargo, and can sit in port for a long time. If you stow away on a ship like this, your food and water might run out before you leave shore. A ship that sits high has already offloaded and is likely to leave at any moment. [The opposite is true in Cape Town, and other ports from which goods are exported.]

ከውሃው መስመር ወደላይ ከፍ ብለው የሚንሳፈፉ መርከቦችን ፈልግ። ውሃው ውስጥ ሰመጥ ብለው የሚንሳፈፉት መርከቦች ገና ጭነታቸውን ያላራገፉት ናቸው። እነዚህ ወደብ ውስጥ ብዙ ጊዜ ሊቆዩ ይችላሉ። እነዚህ መርከቦች ላይ ከወጣህ ገና መርከቡ ከወደብ ሳይወጣ ምግብ እና ውሃህን ልትጨርስ ትችላለህ። ወደላይ ከፍ ብሎ የሚንሳፈፍ መርከብ ግን ጭነቱን አራግፎ የጨረሰ ሲሆን በማንኛውም ሰዓት ወደቡን ለቆ ሊወጣ ይችላል። [ጭነት ወደውጭ ለሚላክባቸው እንደ ኬፕታውን ላሉ ወደቦች ግን በተቃራኒው ነው።]

8. Try to learn from the stowaways who have already made it overseas. They can teach you what you want to know. Unfortunately, the experienced stowaways are often the cruellest, and the ones most likely to betray you if they feel you are holding them back.

በመርከብ ወደሌላ ሀገር ሄደው ከሚያውቁ ስቶአዌዎች ልምድ ትምህርት ውሰድ። ማወቅ ያለብህን ነገሮች ሊያስተምሩህ ይችላሉ። ችግሩ ልምድ ያላቸው ስቶአዌዎች ብዙውን ጊዜ ጨካኞች ናቸው። ለጉዟቸው እንቅፋት መስለህ ከታየሃቸው ሊክዱህ ይችላሉ።

9. The anchor chain locker is the most dangerous place on the ship. You can hide there when it is empty but when the anchor comes up

the room fills very quickly, and you could be crushed. If the anchor is already in, and it goes out, you could be pulled apart.

የመልህቅ ሰንሰለት የሚቀመጥበት ቦታ መርከብ ላይ ካሉ ቦታዎች ሁሉ አደገኛ ነው። መልህቁ ዉሃው ውስጥ በተጣለበት ሰዓት ይህ ቦታ ባዶ ነው። ያንጊዜ እዚህ ቦታ ውስጥ መደበቅ ይቻላል። ሆኖም መልህቁ በሚሳብበት ጊዜ ሰንሰለቱ ቦታውን በፍጥነት ስለሚሞላው ውስጥ የተደበቀውን ሰው ሊጨፈልቀው ይችላል። ሰንሰለቱ ውስጥ ተከማችቶ ባለበት ጊዜ ከሆነ የተደበከው መርከቡ መልህቁን በምትጥልበት ጊዜ ሰንሰለቱ በከፍተኛ ፍጥነት ሲወጣ ሊበጣጥስህ ይችላል።

10. A big ship is like a small city. It is very easy to get lost. At night, you may be able to move around, but to find your way back to your hiding place it is a good idea to find something with which you can mark the places you pass.

ትልቅ መርከብ እንደአንድ ትንሽ ከተማ ማለት ነው፤ አቅጣጫ ለመሳት ቀላል ነው። ማታ ማታ ላይ ማንም ሳያይህ መርከቡ ላይ መዟዟር ትችላለህ። ሆኖም መንገድህን ላለመሳት እና የመደበቂያ ቦታህ ጋር በቀላሉ ለመመለስ ያለፍካቸው ቦታዎች አካባቢ የሚገኙ ነገሮችን ማስተዋል እና እነሱን እንደምልክት መጠቀም ጥሩ ነው።

11. If a crew of a ship are Muslims, they will not allow the ship to be searched by dogs. So, study the crew carefully, if you can, because dogs will locate your smell and you will be found.

መርከቡ ላይ ያሉ ባህረኞች ሙስሊም ከሆኑ አነፍናፊ ውሾች መርከቡ ላይ እንዲወጡ አይፈቅዱም። ስለዚህ በተቻለህ መጠን ባህረኞቹን አጥናቸው። ምክንያቱም ውሾቹ በጠረንህ አነፍንፈው ያሲዙሃል።

12. Do not cross your legs when talking to Asian seamen, especially Koreans. They see it a sign of disrespect.

ከእስያ የመጡ ባህረኞችን በተለይም ኮሪያዎችን ስታናግር እግርህን አጣምረህ አትቀመጥ። እንደንቀት ነው የሚመለከቱት።

13. The anchor chain is a good way to access a ship. The links are huge, and provide excellent footholds for climbing.

የመልህቁ ሰንሰለት መርከብ ላይ ለመዉጣት ጥሩ መንገድ ነው። የሰንሰለቱ ቀለበቶች ትላልቅ ስለሆ' እንደእግር መወጣጫ ያገለግላሉ።

14. On board you must be methodical and calculating, swift and efficient. These are the true qualities of a stowaway.

መርከብ ላይ ዘዴኛ፣ አስተዋይ እና ፈጣን መሆን አለብህ። እነዚህ እውነተኛ የስቶአዌ ባህሪያት ናቸው።

15. Try not to eat anything with salt in it, as this will just make you

thirsty. Do not drink Coca-Cola: it will drive you crazy with thirst.

መርከብ ላይ ስትሆን ጨው ያለበት ምግብ ፈፅሞ አትብላ፤ ኮካኮላም አትጠጣ። ጥማትህን ያስብሱብሃል።

16. Learn the flags of the nations. This way, you will be able to tell where the ship you are boarding is from. You will also be able to tell which port you are coming to.

የሀረጋትን ባንዲራዎች ለይተህ አወቅ። የምትወጣበት መርከብ ከየት ሀገር እንደሆነና ወደዬትኛው ወደብ እንደሚሄድ ለማወቅ ይረዳሃል።

17. You must try not to think about your family at home. You may be trying to help them, but you must not think of them. This will disturb your mind, and a stowaway with a disturbed mind is not likely to succeed.

በተቻለህ አቅም ስለቤተሰብህ አታስብ። ልትረዳቸው እየሞከርክ ይሆናል። ሃሳብህን ወደእነሱ እንዲሄድ ልትፈቅድለት ግን አይገባም። ምክንያቱም ጭንቅላትህን ይበጠብጠዋል። ሀሳቡ የተበጠበጠ ስቶአዌ ደግሞ ስኬታማ አይሆንም።

18. Be prepared to suffer great disappointment. Being a stowaway can feel like a game in which you always land on the square that sends you back to the start.

እጅግ የሚያስከፉ ነገሮችን ለመጋፈጥ ዝግጁ መሆን አለብህ። ስቶአዌ መሆን ማለት ሁሌም መጀመሪያ ወደተነሳህበት ቦታ እየተመለስክ እራስህን እንደምታገኝበት ጨዋታ መስሎ ሊሰማ ይችላል።

19. You need to view your life as an adventure. That will help you to remain detached from the terrible things through which stowaways all suffer. It will help to keep you hopeful.

ህይወትህን እንደጀብድ ጉዞ አድርገህ ልትመለከተው ይገባል። ይህ ስቶአዌዎች በሙሉ የሚያልፉባቸውን አስከፊ ነገሮች እንዳታስብ ይረዳሃል። ተስፋ እንዳትቆርጥ ያግዝሃል።

◆

Although winter is generally held to be the best season for boarding ships, Adam and Sudi have been plotting to do something that the Beachboys call 'going the Stones'. It's a strategy that entails hiking out to the northern end of the breakwater and then crawling back through the dolosse towards the container terminal. The breakwater's giant concrete knuckles lock together in such a way that they leave spaces large enough for a body to scramble through, enabling Beachboys to get within thirty metres of certain ships without once having to surface.

To progress through this maze, however, the human body must constantly bridge bulbous shapes that are permanently slick with sea-spray. If a foot or hand slips, you clatter down to the next level of concrete limbs – and sometimes all the way down to the roiling sea. Feet and ankles can become wedged in unyielding joins and, in the icy waters of Table Bay, hypothermia can set in within minutes. The breakwater being entirely unguarded, it would be some time before help could be fetched.

'You need to be strong for this one,' Sudi said this evening. We were sitting on camping chairs outside Barak's *mchondolo*, and he wanted to be sure I understood that many Beachboys younger than me had hurt themselves badly doing what we were about to do. I nodded.

'Hand me the Green Eagle,' I demanded, using the Beachboy term for Gleneagles whisky (R95 a bottle). We set off across Table Bay Boulevard after dark and joined the R27, which follows the curve of Table Bay into the Paarden Eiland industrial zone. Within a kilometre we reached the Salt River canal, which slips under the port fence on its way out to sea.

Adam went through a hole in the roadside fence.

'Your shoes are going to get wet,' he said, lowering himself over the edge of the canal wall. He let go and landed with a splash. 'Shit, the water is high.'

I lowered my body over the edge and felt the sucking of water on my ankles. By the time I felt the concrete beneath my feet I was up to my thighs in icy water, which was flowing up the canal instead of down, and with a force that pulled our pants tight around our shins.

'Bad conditions,' said Sudi as the water deepened. At low tide, he explained, the ocean often withdrew from the dolosse, making it possible to walk towards the container terminal on the far side, on beach sand. Now, simply to reach the mouth of the canal, we were having to swim.

'Watch out for the stones under the water,' Adam hissed, as we reached the mouth. 'You can't see them but they're there, and you can bump yourself badly when the waves come in.'

Our bodies were numb by the time we struck the line of submerged dolosse and slowly pulled ourselves out of the foamy water. Being this cold so early on in the mission had not been part of the plan.

It was a hot, windless night, though, and our blood quickly warmed when we started through the hard, rimy maze. We kept as high above the churning sea as we could, trying our best to dodge the chutes of spray that exploded all down the line when the bigger swells came rolling in. Light from the railway fixtures penetrated here and there, illuminating inscriptions on the vast concrete knuckles.

'Do you understand what we mean when we say tunnel life?' Adam whispered, pointing to where TANAL LIFE had been written in permanent marker on a flat bit of dolos. 'It means this life of small, dark places. On the ships we move in the tunnels, crawling in the dark like worms. This is also the tunnel life right here, what we are doing now. I dream about tunnels, I swear, it doesn't matter where I am.'

I had the oddest recollection, then, of standing with an intellectual aunt in some woods outside London many years ago, in early adolescence. The property, a small farm, belonged to her aunt, who had lived in the farmhouse alone since her husband's death in the nineties. She was the loveliest woman, apple-cheeked and gentle, like a Disney godmother, though sadly her own children had stopped speaking to her not long after her husband's death. This was their way of punishing their mother, my aunt speculated, for her failure to stand up to her husband's brutality in life. Her son still lived on the property, in a cabin to which no road led. We had come upon it on a rambling walk. We stood staring at it.

'Curious,' she said. 'When you look at his chalet, what do you see?'

'An A shape,' I said confidently.

'It's a womb,' said my aunt, turning to leave.

I laughed out loud at the memory, and wondered what my aunt would make of this scene: three men in their thirties, crawling about in a forbidden, uterine maze.

Sudi put a finger to my lips.

'Sorry. I'm thinking crazy thoughts.'

'Drink some of this,' said Adam, passing me a two-litre bottle of Jive Orange.

Over the waters of Table Bay, we could see the signal lights of several ships – reds, greens and whites in different combinations. The water seemed oddly luminescent, so much so that Adam risked a look over the top of the breakwater.

'No way!'

Sudi and I scrambled up to join him. To the north, rising above the Tygerberg Hills, was the upper dome of a full moon. It was a third revealed, but already projecting vivid shadows in the rail yard.

'Not good,' said Sudi.

Shivering, and with the cover of darkness now lost, the Beachboys decided to backtrack. We walked openly in the port, confident that we could make it back to the canal if it came to a chase. The black hull of a container ship reared up behind us, mocking.

'We're going to try again for that ship tomorrow,' said Adam, when we parted ways in the parking area of the Beachboy Office.

'You want to come again?'

'No.'

SUMMER

And should you follow these footpaths really not
that much further, they soon become streets,
granite kerbs, electric lights. These streets soon
grow to highways, to dockyards, shipping-lanes.
You'll see how it is—how these paths were only
an older version of streets; that the latter, in turn,
continue the highways, and the quays of the harbour,
and even, eventually, the whale-roads of the sea.

You'll see how it is—it's still that kind of city—
here where one thing leads, shades into another;
where footpath becomes road, road a roadstead,
where the stone of the mountain runs to street-stone,
and you'd almost believe the one were the other,
and that where it all leads, the sole place it could end,
over refinery, cooling towers, a freeway in the sunset,
is where it ends now—in that other freeway overhead:

The skies of these evenings, and their clear foreheads.

– Stephen Watson, 'Definitions of a City'

'See you in Africa.'

These words have been turning around inside me since my return from a six-week stay in the KwaZulu-Natal Midlands where, having left my job at the ad agency, I reported on a story about a triple homicide on a dairy farm outside Rosetta. Three of those weeks were spent in the Pietermaritzburg High Court, covering the trial of Mzwandile Magubane and Nhlanhla Dladla, two young Zulu men charged with the murders. I have reported on violent crimes before, but this one was different, strangely personal. A friend, Brian Jones, had been among the first respondents; as a policeman turned private security specialist, he continued providing support to the victims' families, working closely with the investigators assigned to the case. The families trusted him because they needed to trust someone and, since I was with Brian at all times, I was accepted into their circle of pain, confusion and fury.

When the trial started we were all seated in the same row, holding hands as the farm owner, Neville Karg, gave his testimony.

'It was an ordinary day on the farm,' he began. 'We had just begun supper when I received a telephone call from my son, saying the manager had reported a fire in the corner of the property, amongst the new hay bales. I told my son I would investigate and then called him back and asked him to send more workers to help extinguish the fire. I also phoned my wife and asked her to bring some workers. A few minutes later I phoned back to ask her to bring bush knives so the beaters could cut branches to fight the fire.'

When his wife, Lorraine, failed to arrive, Neville had returned to the farmhouse to see what the problem was. He entered the yard and parked his bakkie next to the house. When he opened the laundry door, he saw two people on the floor. One was motionless, and the other indicated with hand movements that he should leave, as there were many strange men about. The farmer waited for the police to arrive before re-entering the yard, and when he did he found his wife's car with its doors open. Next to a tree in the yard he found his wife's body. According to the forensic pathologist who conducted the post-mortem, Lorraine Karg had a large laceration from centre to right of her neck, which had severed the carotid artery and jugular vein. He estimated that she had bled to death over a period of fifteen to twenty minutes. A few metres away the police found the body of Zakeue Mhlongo, an elderly Zulu man who had tended the farmhouse garden. His throat had also been cut. The third victim was the still figure from the laundry, Hilda Linyane – a Zimbabwean woman in her thirties who had been working as a domestic servant. She had been shot.

The victims had all been good, peaceful people – there was no doubt about this. They had interrupted a robbery in progress. Wrong time, wrong place. But why had the robbers killed them, and so viciously? The families were in court to hear the answers to these questions. More than justice, they wanted understanding. By the end of the first day, however, it was clear that there would be no satisfaction. The state witness – the brother of Mzwandile Magubane – had recanted on the stand, claiming that his testimony had been beaten out of him. Since this was the only evidence connecting the second accused to the crime, the state prosecutor was left with no choice but to drop the charges against Nhlanhla Dladla.

As he left the dock, Dladla – who had a broad nose, drooping eyes and buttery skin criss-crossed with small scars – had flashed Neville Karg and his adult children a winning smile. To the children of Hilda Linyane and Zakeue Mhlongo he had whispered: 'See you in Africa.'

There was no doubt about his intended meaning. The heads of the Linyane kids immediately went down into their arms, while the Mhlongo boys stared daggers. Dladla's Africa was not the courthouse, the Nando's up the road, or even the sprawling farm near Rosetta. It was in the distances between, the walk from the Mooi River taxi rank to the Absa ATM, the stretch of district road between the farm school and the farm gate. Africa was the region's latticework of pedestrian paths, and the entire world outdoors after nightfall. You are enisled by Africa, is what Dladla effectively told the children of his victims, and your islands will not sustain you forever. You must, at some point, venture out.

A week before the start of the trial I had travelled to Bulawayo in

Zimbabwe, to Pumula township off to the east of the city. I had stopped outside a box-shaped house, the façade of which was almost entirely covered by the branches of a large avocado tree. This was the home that Hilda Linyane, the Zimbabwean victim, had built with the money she had earned in South Africa. Her son, Innocent, had returned with her remains to Pumula, and he was now preparing to go back for the trial, to take the stand and add his testimony to the prosecution's case. He had not mentioned to the prosecutor the fact that he was not in possession of a valid passport, because he did not want this to stand in the way of his contribution.

To get around border control, his plan was to wade across the crocodile-infested Limpopo River, then hitchhike the thousand or so kilometres to the farm to reunite with his sister, Priscilla, before facing their mother's killers. I had become emotional when I had seen him sitting in court on the first morning, knowing what he had gone through to be there; when Dladla had uttered those words, reducing Priscilla Linyane to tears, I had experienced a strange loss of self-control. Like a robot I had followed Dladla out of the courtroom, through the antechamber and into the streets. He had been wearing a white windbreaker and, the moment he had got outside, he had flipped the hood over his head, turning himself into a beacon on the busy pavements of Pietermaritzburg. Having no better weapon, I had grasped my car's key like a shank. I had known exactly what I was going to do, but before I could catch up with him two members of the murder and robbery unit had overtaken me and grabbed his arms.

'You're under arrest,' said the one. 'Possession of a firearm.'

I had wished Innocent had been there to see the Dladla's face, how his mouth had popped open in abject shock. One of the officers had jerked back the hood of his windbreaker. I had walked over and stood next to the policemen, picturing my fist slamming into his gut, again and again, while they held him upright.

Once I had calmed down, I turned to face some difficult questions.

Have I been guilty of overlooking the fact that many of the Beachboys I call friends were once the Magubanes and Dladlas of their home communities? I know there is blood in Sudi's past, and that certain others are only in South Africa because the alternative was life in a Dar es Salaam prison for the worst crime there is.

See you in Africa: it is exactly the sort of pointed threat I can imagine Adam addressing to a CCID guard, or a policeman.

And yet, I sit around the fire at The Kitchen, fascinated by their tales and impressed by their ingenuity, their forbearance. I don't see their crimes stacked up behind them, the motherless and fatherless children of Magomeni and Mburahati. I don't think: if all people were Beachboys, the world would be hell.

I have been grappling with these questions, and I am still grappling with them.

◆

Maskani is an unsettling corner of the city – a place where people pass through fences and walls like ghosts, and touch hands instead of speaking. When they do this it is almost always to transfer a quarter gram of heroin, or *katte*, and receive the required R20 in notes that are more often than not veined and scaled like moth wings.

Martingale gambling areas abound between drifts of litter and small hills of discarded railway ties. The principal gamblers squat, forming an inner circle over which a secondary ring of punters nod in and out to place their bets. Enterprising traders display oranges at the foot of the railway bridge, and the junkies stand about, peeling the skins off with their sharp *kisus*. It is not a safe place, by any standard. There are as many coloured gangsters here as Beachboys, as many prostitutes as drug dealers, as many tik users as *unga* smokers. More than anything, it is this – the intermingling of these two very different highs, the opiate and the methamphetamine – that gives this place its jumpy air.

Today, Adam, Sudi and Barak were smoking cocktails in one of the area's many ruined buildings when the air was suddenly ionised with the word *polisi polisi polisi*, not yelled but whispered. The gambling circles unravelled at the sound of four pairs of boots on the pedestrian bridge. In the smokehouse there was a general break for the doorway – Sudi up and away first, as always, followed by Barak and a young but unusually rotund Beachboy called Juma.

By the time the policemen reached ground level, most of the Maskani wide boys had made it to the far side of the railway reserve and were heading for the innumerable exits onto Table Bay Boulevard. Sudi was haring off in the direction of The Kitchen, followed by Barak and the fat youngster. Adam was not with them, though; as soon as they realised this, they turned to see whether he had been caught.

He had not even left the ruin. When Juma realised this, he began declaiming loudly. In his panic he had abandoned a pharmaceutical bag containing 120 *kattes*, and was now convinced that Adam had seen him do this and stayed behind to steal the stash. Sudi warned the young dealer to shut his mouth, but six or seven of Juma's allies had gathered around. When the policemen moved off, they all rushed towards the ruin, Sudi and Barak in hot pursuit. Adam emerged nonchalantly from the building to face his accusers, telling them that the police must have found the drugs.

'What did you think would happen? You shouldn't throw things away if you don't want them to disappear.'

Juma pulled a *kisu* from his pocket and called Adam a liar.

'You showing me a knife? Come then, and your friends. You can kill me but I will take one of you with me today I swear.'

Sudi tried to calm the situation, but there was no stopping Adam now: 'You young boys don't know anything. You dropped your stash, R3 000 of *unga*, and you ran away. Now you show me a fucking knife and call me a thief! If I had wanted to take your drugs I would have taken them, but I didn't, I took the risk and buried them before the police came. If they caught me with that much *unga* I would get three years in Pollsmoor. I took the risk. You ran away.'

Heads nodded in understanding as Juma rushed into the ruin to dig up the bag. The contents were counted and Barak, ever the diplomat, stepped in to recommend that Adam be given a quantity of *unga* for saving the stash and for having endured the accusations and threats. Juma grudgingly counted out seven *kattes* and walked off with his friends, his arms swinging around his thick hips.

'*Mwiba mwitu* fuckers,' Adam called after them, though not so loudly that they could hear. Sudi and Barak chuckled nervously.

'What does that mean?'

'It means wild dogs. That's what these Mbagala boys call themselves.'

Seated around the fire at The Kitchen, they explained how the Beachboy scene was changing again, and not in a good way. From the start, said Adam, Cape Town's Beachboys had been divided along lines of origin. The largest number of Beachboys had always been from Dar es Salaam – Bongomen – with the balance made up of men from Tanga, Tanzania's most northerly seaport. Being in the minority, the Tanga Boys had always been more tightly knit and, over time, they had drifted away from the main Beachboy living area under Nelson

Mandela Boulevard into the Woodstock railway reserve, where they had become integrated into Woodstock's underworld.

'The Tanga guys hardly try for the ships any more. Many of them work with South Africans in Woodstock, selling scrap metal or breaking into houses. If you closed your eyes and listened to some of them speaking Afrikaans, you would think they were coloureds,' said Adam.

In 2009, the Bongomen and the Tanga Boys had gone to war. The spark had been the rape, by several Beachboys, of a young Tanga Boy called Mohammed, after he had been accused of stealing a single *katte*. The Tanga Boys were outraged, as were many of the Bongomen, but the rapists had been part of a sub-group of men from Mburahati, a particularly lawless part of Dar es Salaam, and had refused to acknowledge the will of the broader community.

'They had a gang in Dar es Salaam called Komando Yosso, which used to go out at night to other areas, like Magomeni and Temeke,' said Adam. 'If they found a party they would surround it with their pangas, and make everyone empty their pockets. If they killed someone, they took the body back to Mburahati, because they knew that even the police would not come looking there.'

To end Komando Yosso's reign of terror the police had unleashed their own, arresting all known members and killing any who resisted. Most of those who escaped the dragnets fled to South Africa.

'The ones who came to Cape Town formed another gang called Al-Qaeda, and they started bullying other Beachboys. Three guys died after they raped that Tanga Boy, and eventually the older Beachboys from both sides came together and broke Al-Qaeda together. They made a rule that there must be no more gangs,' said Adam.

The Bongomen had also needed the Tanga Boys at this time. With the bridges being cleared in anticipation of the World Cup, the only safe territory had been in the railway reserve, which was Tanga territory. Permission to enter was granted only to older, established Beachboys, like Barak, Sudi and Adam, who founded The Kitchen. Maskani also falls within Tanga territory, and access to this area is also conditional.

'I can't go to Maskani and say anything I like. It's their place and we have to respect that,' said Adam.

For three years the peace between the two major Beachboy factions has held, but trouble is back in the air. The problem, again, is of Bongo provenance.

'At the moment there are too many Dar es Salaam guys coming

to Cape Town, a different generation. They have no respect, not even for each other. Our generation came from old Dar es Salaam communities like Sinza, Magomeni and Temeke. In these places you must show respect, or the police will kill you. These new boys come from a place called Mbagala, outside the city on the road to Mtwara. Ten years ago it was just bush and rivers, but now there are thousands of people living there in *mchondolos*, without any electricity, without any proper toilets and no police station.'

Sudi, who is better acquainted with Dar es Salaam's social undercurrents than Adam, said that the youth of Mbagala had earned a reputation for pack violence. 'They do something called ten-in-ten-out,' he said. 'This is when twenty boys come to a street carrying pangas. Ten guard the street while the other ten rob the houses. If anyone tries to leave or fight he will be killed. That is why they are called *mwiba mwitu*, because they move together like wild dogs.'

When it came, the police response had been savage; for months, now, the scatterlings of the Mbagala underworld have been crossing into South Africa and bleeding into the Beachboy communities. Use of the term *mwiba mwitu* has been outlawed in Cape Town's Beachboy areas, which was why Adam had uttered it under his breath earlier. But this has not stopped the *mwiba mwitu* from reforming in sub-groups. Their refusal to acknowledge the Sea Power code has set them at odds with the older generation of Bongo Beachboys, and has pushed the Bongo–Tanga peace accord to the limits.

'We're thinking of getting out, y'know, me and Sudi,' said Adam. 'Summer's a bad time for stowing ships but me and Sudi are gonna stop smoking *unga* and try anyway.'

◆

A series of Please Call Me messages from Adam late at night. I clambered out of bed, walked to the most distant point of the house and called back, fearing the worst.

'Haiyo Sean, we're going to meet the prophet tomorrow.'

'Eh?'

'The prophet in the cave above Woodstock. You heard of 'im?'

I have often heard singing from the mountain crags above Woodstock, especially when the fog rolls in. I had tried to get nearer once or twice, but could never find the trailhead that might lead me to the source. The voices have remained disembodied, eerily beyond reach.

'Sudi heard about the prophet in Pollsmoor. Some of the prisoners have gone to see him after serving their time, and they say he has big power, this guy. People come all the way from the Congo to visit him in that cave, that's what I hear. Sudi wants to pray with the prophet tomorrow, so that we can have good luck and take a ship.'

At 9 a.m. I found the two friends smoking a cocktail around The Kitchen's near-dead fire. Smoking heroin is not a thing Beachboys like to rush, and Adam slowed the process further by winding loops of spittle behind the cherry of the joint.

'The *unga* burns slower than the weed, so we wet the ganja this way and everything burns at the same speed.'

When the last of the vinegary smoke had been exhaled, we crossed the railway tracks into Woodstock and walked directly upslope on Mountain Road, passing under Nelson Mandela Boulevard. From the edge of De Waal Drive, which divides the city from the Table Mountain National Park, we caught our first sight of the Woodstock Cave: a broad, thin-lipped mouth halfway up Devil's Peak. The speeding traffic proved a perceptual challenge for the stoned Beachboys, but we made it safely across and clumped through the mountain fynbos to a eucalyptus copse that enclosed an abandoned quarry. Metal cutouts of rams, turkeys, pigs and chickens had been set up at different distances within the quarry, targets in a shooting range.

Sudi turned to Adam. 'There's a lot of metal here.'

'About R500,' Adam agreed, and I felt a little sad knowing the members of this silhouette shooting club would arrive at their next meet to find that their animals had all been poached for scrap metal.

Zigzagging up on Fire Services roads we reached the highest point of the ridge, where a contour path leads below the cliffs of Devil's Peak. We could not see the cave, the gradient being too steep, but adjudged it directly upslope, where a stream crossed the path. Turning up the narrow watercourse we began to push through dense, combustible scrub, red-winged starlings whistling at us from rocky ledges. Pushing through a last thicket we came to a spill of boulders below the cave, on which several containers had been positioned to catch the water wafting over the mouth. Aside from the tok, tok, tok of water into tin, the kloof was silent. We approached quietly, and slowly pulled our bodies up over the lip.

There was no doubt that this was the place. The cave floor had been worn glassy by feet, and parts of it had been carpeted with mountain grasses. In one corner, a grid of low stone walls had been built, from which mattresses protruded. On one of the walls, a small clock – the type that folds into its own casement – rested on a book. The dorsal end of the book was afforested with torn strips of magazine paper, almost one to a page, as if this was the only book ever written and every page was equally important.

'The prophet's not in,' said Adam, lying back in one of the little cells and staring up at the 'Jesus is Lord' graffiti on the cave ceiling.

'Maybe he went to buy airtime,' said Sudi, who had pulled a packed bin liner from a cranny and was rifling through the twist of blankets and shirts inside. He tossed a green woollen beanie over to Adam.

'Some Beachboy will enjoy this.'

'It could mean bad luck to steal something from the prophet.'

'It's just clothes,' said Sudi.

He pulled one of the mattresses out onto the ledge and we sat on it and worked the cityscape with our fingers, identifying the Grand Parade, the Foreshore flyovers, The Freezer, The Kitchen, Wa Tony, Maskani.

'Look how many metal poles there are,' said Adam, passing a hand over the Foreshore's streetlights, cranes and railway semaphores. In the container dock, an MCC ship was being tugged away from its berth; we wondered which of the ships out in Table Bay would be coming in to replace it.

'There could be some Beachboys inside that ship right now, going to England, Italy or Brazil. You never know,' said Adam. 'I don't think so, but they could be there, inside the life raft, or maybe locked inside the storage hatches. Strange to think.'

'You boys still going make du'a?'

Sudi shook his head and stood up. 'We can make du'a anywhere, anytime.'

His disappointment verged on anger. Even if the prophet had been in, this was clearly a place of Christian worship. He exited the cave on a well-trodden path at the southern edge – the path I'd never been able to find. Adam was last out. Looking back, I saw him pull the prophet's green beanie out of his pants and toss it back towards the mattresses and blankets.

◆

A call from Adam to say that the police were preparing a major raid of the railway reserve.

When I arrived at the Lower Church Street bridge I could see that the policemen, alongside officials from the city's land unit, had already swept into the railway reserve, where they were overseeing the destruction of Beachboy *mchondolos*. When this happens, and it happens a few times a year, the officers occupy the high ground at the top of the highway embankment and watch others of the city's homeless do the dirty work of pulling the tents apart. The lackeys – coloured people, mostly – work on the understanding that they will be allowed to take ownership of anything they find inside the tents, be it money, drugs or shoes. It is an explosive underworld dynamic, especially since the lackeys tend to abuse the Beachboys both physically and verbally while going about their work, knowing that the police will arrest anyone who fights back.

Adam shouted a single statement of defiance – 'You will find our houses here tomorrow again' – and took out his phone to call Barak, whose tent was just then being pulled apart. Barak came running down the railway service road from the direction of Maskani.

'We must quickly go to the shipyard,' he panted, 'before the plastic is all gone.'

Groups of Beachboys were already crossing the railway tracks, heading for the Robertson and Caine catamaran factory on the corner of Beach and Railway. The dumpsters behind this facility are always stuffed with sail offcuts and large sheets of plastic, which make excellent roofing materials. By the time we made it over, approximately thirty Beachboys were jostling for the last materials, shouting abuse at each other and pulling their fists back in mock punches. Two men pulled at opposite ends of a blue blow-up mattress, eventually ripping it in two. Adam shook his head and said he would try again in the week, when the dumpsters would be full and uncontested. Until then, he would bunk in a friend's tent beside the Christiaan Barnard bridge.

Barak, who values his privacy, waded into the fray.

◆

A stabbing last night outside the Seaman Bar. By the time I arrived there was no body, just a shiny disc of blood on the tarmac. A police cruiser parked outside the pool hall's entrance washed the walls with its blue lights. Adam was listening in on the conversation between the bar owner and the police officers. I'd never seen him so animated.

'They already take him to Somerset Hospital, guy by the name of Aubadeeleh Juma Saloum. He was a real Cape Town Beachboy, an' he been stabbed by a young boy of just four months in the city. I think this means war y'know Sean. Somebody gonna die for this, I'm telling you.'

Adam said he had been in the bar earlier, watching the CAF Super Cup Final between Al-Ahly and AC Léopards. He had put R150 on the Congolese team, but Egyptian winger Mohamed Barakat had scored in the 71st minute to put the game out of reach and Adam had wandered back to The Kitchen to sleep before the final whistle. Sudi had stayed behind, and had intervened when the fight had broken out between Aubadeeleh and the young Beachboy, whom everyone calls Chawa Suga. When the fighters had been parted, the owner had kicked them both out. Sudi had returned to his bar stool, feeling that this was the end of it. Only some time later, when he had heard the ambulance siren, had he realised that something terrible must have happened out on the streets. He had grown up with Aubadeeleh, playing countless football matches with him in Magomeni East.

'To be honest I'm nervous,' said Adam. 'That guy was like Sudi's brother and now Sudi has to step forward or people will think he is a coward. Me and Barak can't let him step alone because he is our brother, too, but that guy Chawa Suga is a Mbagala boy – *mwiba mwitu* – and he got his own boys who will step for him. Anything can happen now.

I can't tell you if it will finish this way or another.'

We drove to Somerset Hospital where we found Sudi on the entrance stairs, punching his left hand with his right.

'*Wafu*.' Dead.

Adam clapped his hand over his mouth.

'No fucking way. Sudi, sorry man. We gonna get that boy I swear. Come, we must start looking now, before he has time to run too far.'

The V&A Waterfront sidewalks were still fairly busy with revellers as we exited, the faux-vintage streetlights illuminating Sudi in the back seat where he was still punching his hands like some sort of cinematic menace. In furious bursts of Swahili, he told what he knew of the incident.

Chawa Suga and his friends had been drinking Klipdrift brandy all day, and had arrived at the Seaman Bar very drunk. Aubadeeleh had been there, watching the football, sober as always.

'Aubadeeleh only smoke weed, he never drinks,' Adam explained.

Chawa Suga had taunted Aubadeeleh for much of the first half, and the older Beachboy had finally snapped and knocked Chawa Suga to the floor. Chawa Suga's friends had pounced on Aubadeeleh, punching and kicking him until Sudi had intervened, pushing Aubadeeleh's attackers back. He had been joined by the owner and a well-known Nigerian drug dealer, who had also been in for the football. The young Beachboys had launched a verbal attack on Sudi. Why was he getting involved in somebody else's fight? Was he looking for trouble, too? Sudi had countered that it was not their fight, either, and that the two men should be left to sort the matter out between themselves. 'A fair fight, Bongo to Bongo.'

At that point, Aubadeeleh had made for the door. The bar owner had ordered the young Beachboys down the stairs as well, and as they had jostled through the exit a Beachboy called Temba, who had not been involved in the fight, had handed Chawa Suga a *kisu*. Sudi was told as much by the Nigerian, who had seen it happen.

'Allah never gave me the idea to follow them,' he said, over and over.

When he heard the ambulance, he had run out into the road, where he'd found Aubadeeleh moaning on the ground, the lower half of his shirt soaked with blood.

Adam knew more about the stabbing, having talked to several of the witnesses who had hung around the scene after the ambulance had left.

'Aubadeeleh was walking away when Chawa Suga came out. Someone shouted that he had a knife, so Aubadeeleh started to run away but he fell. He was shouting [falsetto], "Sorry, I'm really sorry, please, I'll never fight with you again," but Chawa Suga said [forte], "You didn't know me, now you know me," and he started stabbing him in the back. The Nigerian guy tried to push Chawa Suga. He said, "Why you want to kill your brother, eh? Why?" But one of Chawa Suga's friends pushed the Nigerian, and the Nigerian said, "Okay, if you want to kill your brother, then kill your brother." Chawa Suga stabbed Aubadeeleh three more times before running away, followed by his friends.'

'The doctor told me that if Aubadeeleh had survived he could never have walked again,' said Sudi. 'The knife cut his *mgongo*, somewhere at the back here.'

To get the car as close to The Kitchen as possible, I parked on the traffic island formed by the Lower Church Street on-ramp and the outer lanes of the Table Bay Boulevard incoming. Leaving it with the hazards flashing, we skirted the highway on foot for a few hundred metres before dropping down the highway embankment to the tents. Barak emerged from the dark beside his *mchondolo*. He held a rusty fence pole with a lump of concrete fixed to one end. He had been waiting like this, he said, since hearing the news.

The friends began talking – quietly at first, and then in angry voices as the disagreements racked up. Sudi was in favour of immediate retribution, whereas Barak argued that it would be better to call a meeting of all Beachboys in the morning, to hit on a group solution and prevent the Beachboy community from splitting into factions. Adam seemed to be in two minds.

'What would you do if it was me or Sudi?' he asked Barak. To Sudi, he made the point that they could not be certain how much support Chawa Suga had under the flyovers. If they went there now, they might find themselves greatly outnumbered.

I left when it seemed they would wait out the night and take stock in the morning. Adam walked me back to the car, which had attracted the attention of a fat tow-truck driver, who said he had just called the cops.

'I saw a bag inside the car, and I know the area is bad for crime,' he said, eyeing Adam.

'There's no problem.'

'We must still wait for the cops, man.'

'You just waiting because you want to tow this car,' Adam said.

The policeman who arrived wanted nothing to do with the curious situation. We were together for just a minute – the constable, the tow-truck driver, the writer and the stowaway – before engines were fired up again and, one by one, the vehicles slipped back onto the highway, leaving Adam behind in a pool of street light.

◆

The fight that led to the death of Aubadeeleh Saloum had its origins two weeks ago, in a Maskani gambling circle. This is unsurprising. The only game going in Maskani is simple but open to abuse, and easily the biggest cause of fights between Beachboys. It works like this.

Punters buy in for R10 and squat around a dealer, each nominating a card – five of diamonds, jack of spades, whichever. Behind them a row of secondary punters choose a bet to double up on, and add their R10 to the pot, taking it to between R100 and R200 a round, depending on the size of the game. The person whose card comes out of the deck first scoops up all the money, dividing it between his seconds. The trouble usually starts in the late afternoon, when a high percentage of the punters is likely to be stoned. A dealer could gradually increase the speed at which he slaps cards down, knowing that it will be difficult for pie-eyed betters to follow the action in the fading light. In this way, a friend's bet could be favoured and the spoils shared that night. Chawa Suga had accused Aubadeeleh of exactly this trickery two weeks before he had murdered him. Aubadeeleh had been dealing and, when Chawa Suga asked to be shown through the dealt cards, the older Beachboy refused. The ensuing scuffle ended quickly because Aubadeeleh had been in the company of friends.

Chawa Suga was no ordinary youngster, though.

'You know that *chawa* means?' said Adam. He had asked to meet in the Company's Garden alongside Parliament, to be sure that we would encounter no *mwiba mwitu*.

'No.'

'It means "rice".'

'Rice?'

'Not eating rice. I'm talking about a kind of *dunkhas* that lives in your clothes and your hair.'

'Lice?'

'Yeah. We call that thing *chawa*. *Suga* means you can't kill it. So *chawa suga* means the lice that won't ever die. The boy took that name in

Durban after some sailors tried to dash him in the sea, a Chinese crew. He survived and now he wears his new name like a badge of respect.'

Chawa Suga had left Durban to link up with some friends in Cape Town after his major ally in the Durban community had become implicated in a drug deal gone bad, forcing him to flee to Maputo. It had been Chawa Suga's intention to try for the ships in the Port of Cape Town, but his reputation had preceded him and he was soon a major dealer under the Foreshore bridges, hustling *kattes* for a middleweight Tanzanian dealer called Hassani Abdul and Adam's old friend Mas Bato.

I'd met Bato. I visited his apartment in Walmer Estate about a year ago in Adam's company. He'd been pleasant, but had seemed too flaky for his occupation – more interested in partying with tourists in The Dubliner on Long Street than growing his drug business. His passion, he'd informed me, was hip hop, and he had the face for it: a strong nose, sharp dreads and a soft chin à la Puff Daddy. He had played us his latest recording, a track called 'Short of perfect', composed in Sotho by one of his musician friends.

In setting up his heroin business, Bato had originally played to his strengths, using his charm to cultivate friendships with as many Beachboys – his customers and his hustlers – as possible. Owing to the regularity with which they moved between Dar es Salaam and Cape Town, they were also his primary mules. Freshly deported Beachboys tended to invest a portion of their bribe monies in *unga* for smuggling back to South Africa when the time came to return. Not many Cape Town dealers were interested in chasing after such small quantities, but Bato had discovered that these regular infusions – anywhere between 10 and 250 grams per traveller – ensured consistency of supply all year round, whereas the bigger dealers, who relied on larger but more infrequent deliveries, were often short of stock.

By all accounts, Bato's relationships with his Beachboy friends waxed and waned according to how hard they were trying to stow away. Any Beachboy who looked to have become comfortable in Cape Town was of little use to him. And, since the younger Beachboys tried for the ships most persistently, it was increasingly the relative newcomers to Cape Town whom Bato sought out on his visits to the Grand Parade. Adam, who had once considered Bato a friend, warned him that such fluctuations in sincerity ran against the Sea Power code, and that he risked making enemies at a faster rate than new friends.

It has come to light that, after stabbing Aubadeeleh, Chawa Suga had fled directly to Bato's apartment. Bato had sheltered him; in the morning, when the news broke that Aubadeeleh had not survived, Bato and his business partner, Hussen, had handed Chawa Suga enough money to flee the country. By the time this had leaked, the murderer was in the wind. Some said Maputo, others Maseru or Mbabane. Everyone had a theory.

For Sudi and Adam, Bato's intervention was intolerable.

'I know what Mas was thinking,' said Adam. 'He thinks by supporting Chawa Suga these other young boys will become loyal to him. But Mas don't know nothing about loyal.'

Sudi has done little to alleviate the tension in the beach areas by declaring that he will kill Bato if he sees him. The bad blood between the two dates back to an incident last year. Sudi had used Bato's phone to send some WhatsApp messages to Sauda, his wife in Dar es Salaam. Bato had continued sending messages to her for weeks afterwards – from the comfort of his apartment, while Sudi had been camped out beside the highway, metres away from the icy, stinking Atlantic, trying for ships every other night in the hope, one day, of providing a better life for his family.

Adam deems the situation the most dangerous he has known.

◆

Barak had gone ahead and called a meeting of all Beachboys, to which Bato and Hussen had been summoned so that they might answer the allegation that they had aided a Beachboy killer. The meeting had been scheduled for noon yesterday in Maskani, but it had never taken place. A group of *mwiba mwitu* had come storming in over the railway bridge. They had gone straight for Sudi and Adam, accusing them of stirring up unnecessary trouble and warning them to 'stop talking shit about the dealers'. The gathering had instantly broken up into several vociferous factions; the meeting had been abandoned before it could be called to order.

'The dealers beat us, I have to say,' Adam admitted. 'They bought the support of these young guys, and divided the Sea Power.'

I had never seen him look so grim. Both he and Sudi now walked around armed, and never strayed more than a few metres from each other. It is easier for Barak, who has been altogether less jingoistic. He clearly makes his decisions based on a very different set of considerations. Cape Town is his chosen home – he has no other – and this means making peace, ultimately, with whatever happens in the beach areas.

It was suddenly apparent just how unlikely the notion of a community comprising stowaways is, with its own set of codes and practices, distinct from the grubby laws of the street. The sub-culture's strongest defenders – men like Adam and Sudi – keep vanishing over the oceans, leaving the meek, the uncommitted, the inept, behind.

As anyone who has spent time on the street knows, the underworld has no regard for transients.

◆

A further twist.

A little while back, the story goes, a jovial Beachboy called Ally had stolen eight kilograms of uncut heroin from the storehouse of a Tanzanian heroin syndicate based in Delft. He had approached Mas Bato with his score; Bato had foolishly chosen to raise the US$100 000 asking price from Cape Town's informal credit system. The uncommonly large loan amounts had created ripples that the syndicate members had followed back to Bato's flat. A few days back the genial, self-absorbed dealer had returned from the gym to find the syndicate members in his living room, the remainder of their heroin on the coffee table. Bato had pleaded that he had known nothing of the robbery, but they had broken his shapely nose anyway, knocking him out cold. They had then taken turns raping him in his own home; when they were done, they had dropped him outside the Departures terminal at Cape Town International Airport.

When I asked Adam why the gang had used rape as a punishment, he initially said it was 'because some Tanzanians are pure evil, brother'. Later, he reckoned it probably had something to do with attitudes towards homosexuality in Tanzania, where sex acts between men carry a maximum sentence of life imprisonment.

'In Tanzania it is better to be known as a killer than a gay. It is the same here in Cape Town. The guys who raped Bato knew that Mas would be too ashamed to tell anyone what happened. They also knew that most of the Beachboys would think that, if Mas didn't tell anyone, then he must secretly be gay. So they released this information, and now Mas don't want to show his face. It sounds crazy but it's the truth.'

To back this up, Adam told a chilling story about a nineties-era Beachboy called Obadia who has a reputation for preying on the young methamphetamine addicts within the Beachboy community.

'He watches for boys who have been smoking tik for days, and follows them around until they finally pass out. When a tik addict sleeps, nothing can wake him. Obadia was caught last week in the tent of this one boy. He had pulled his pants down and his dick was out, but lucky for the guy who was sleeping somebody noticed what was going on and chased Obadia away. We had a meeting about it. Some of us were saying we need to punish this guy so that he will never do it to anyone again. But some of the others said, "No, we must leave him, because he teaches us which Beachboys are gay."'

Given the events of the past fortnight, Adam feels little sympathy for Bato.

'I know he used the money from the stolen heroin to play politics and propaganda with us after Chawa Suga stabbed Aubadeeleh. But in the end snitch get stitched, that's how it is. Now Mas has run away, I don't know where. Hussen is in Johannesburg. Chawa Suga is gone, and the dealers caught Ally in Zanzibar. I'm not sure what happened there but I don't think he is alive now. That's where it is left. Allah knows best, he spreads the punishment.'

◆

An SMS from Adam at 11 p.m.

Memory card 2 c agen.

I debated whether to call, worrying that he may not have switched his phone to silent, but couldn't help myself.

Adam answered in a whisper. 'Yow Sean, how are you?'

'Good.'

'How is your wife?'

'Good.'

'How is Barkly?'

'Where are you?'

'I dunno, man. Big fucking ship. Sudi was with me, we didn't see the name. I don't know if he made it but I think so. The ship is leaving now, I can see Cape Town. It looks beautiful.'

I told him I'd check the Vessels Departing list on the Port of Cape Town website and call him back. Under the Ship Movements tab, eight vessels were listed. I went to the MarineTraffic website and, one by one, fed the names on the list into site's live tracking facility. A figurative map of Table Bay appeared, the vessels underway represented by spade-shaped counters and those at anchor by diamonds. Only three of the vessels on my list were moving away from the harbour. I clicked on their symbols, and their recent movements appeared on the map as streams of green arrows. Two were bound for Lagos, Nigeria. The other was going *nyuma mlima*, bound for India. When I called back to give Adam this sobering information, I reached the phone's answering service.

I tried again. And again. He was gone.

I looked back at the bay on the screen, where the distance between the ships had already grown. One click and the site would inform me where each ship had been yesterday, and where it would be tomorrow, in which country it had been registered and at which speed it was travelling.

But no resource on earth would inform me whether my friends are headed north or south.

AUTUMN

In the street, the citizens, men as well as women, rich and poor, known or unknown, waved at me as I left in the car. In response, I raised my fez. I was neither a leader, nor a legal man nor a council member. I was an ordinary man who lived in peace with them. This farewell was one of my finest hours. Even if this brief burst of fame were to be my last, I would not complain because I would have had my share.

– *Shaaban bin Robert,* Maisha Yangu na Baada ya Miaka Hamsini

The customs official who took my passport at Julius Nyerere International was called Happiness.

'Are you here for a holiday?' she asked.

'Yes.'

'Then why do you have two, two, two?' She swept her hands over the electronic hardware I had been asked to unpack from my luggage: two laptops, two cellphones, two cameras. This was Adam's doing. He had asked me to meet a friend of his before I flew. This friend, he explained, had been keeping his prize possession safe: a 2013 West Brom football jersey with the number 1 on the back under the arch of his nickname, Memory Card. He had asked me to bring it to Dar es Salaam, but it wasn't in the drawstring bag his friend handed me, which contained only the electronic items. There had been no accompanying charger cables. Happiness looked as if she had noticed the same discrepancy.

'I might do some work while I'm here,' I said, feebly.

'Then what you are telling me is that you are here on business? This means you are applying for the wrong visa. You must go back to immigration and get a business visa.'

My holiday visa had cost US$50. A business visa would set me back US$250.

'*Hakuna*, no, no,' a shrill voice interceded, which I recognised as belonging to Francis, the middle-aged man who had sat next to me on the plane. He repacked my bag.

'She is just trying to take your money. Come, you have done nothing wrong, let's go.'

The official glared but made no move to stop him. We moved off, pushing through taxi touts.

'Here in Tanzania you must pay the equivalent of a year of your salary in advance if you want to be a government employee. Police, soldiers, customs officials – they have all paid dearly for their employment. You can imagine the corruption this causes as they try to win back their losses.'

With Dar es Salaam harbour in view through the plane windows Francis had struck up a late-flight conversation, saying that he was just returning from a stay of several months in South Africa, where he had received navigational training from the South African navy. He was employed, he said, as a second mate on an anti-piracy patrol boat, and would be shipping out in the morning. The thump of the landing gear on the runway saved me from having to say anything about my own credentials and movements.

But now, in the relative quiet of the airport parking lot, Francis picked up where we had left off.

'What brings you to Dar es Salaam?'

I contemplated telling him the truth: about my years-old gentleman's agreement with Adam, the stowaway from Tanzania, which I had forgotten about until he had called from Dar es Salaam last week. Being interested in his life I had promised Adam I would follow him to Dar es Salaam when next he was deported, so that I could meet the surviving members of his family and visit the significant sites of his childhood. Afterwards we would hitchhike back to South Africa, jumping national borders if need be. It was a fairly simple story to relate, but instead I said, 'I'm visiting relatives,' and marvelled at the economy of this lie. 'Actually,' I added, using one of Adam's counterintuitive charm tactics, 'I'm lying to you. I have no relatives here. It's a long story.'

He gave me an interested look.

'Where are you going? I'll call you a taxi.'

Waking up my phone I scrolled to 'Adam Tanzania', pressed 'Call' and handed it over.

'Please, if you don't mind getting the directions from my friend?'

After talking with Adam, Francis relayed the directions to a taxi driver. '*Enda kwa* Sheikilango Road *katika* Sinza, Kinyume Camel Oil Petrol Station.'

Turning to me he said, 'Your friend speaks a very interesting dialect of Swahili. Is he from the islands? Pemba, perhaps?'

'I don't have a clue, to be honest.'

'Okay. Well, take care while you're here. The city isn't as safe as it once was. There are good parts and bad parts, and the bad parts are multiplying and the good parts are becoming extinct.'

'Is the place I'm going to now good or bad?'

The navigator pursed his lips and waggled a palm from side to side. 'Half half, I think we can say.'

In the taxi, I opened my notebook with the objective of writing down what I knew about Tanzania. I soon closed it, though, realising that my pre-knowledge wasn't worth the dust billowing in from the air vents. My insight into the underpinnings of the modern state consisted of a slippery, schoolboy's sense of the aims embodied in the 1967 Arusha Declaration.

The Dar es Salaam of the Beachboys' stories was equally out of focus. My notebooks were full of local place names – Sinza, Temeke, Magomeni, Mburahati, Kigamboni, Ukonga, Mbagala – but these might as well have been slums in Mombasa or Lagos, for all the specificity I had to hand. In the accounts of the Beachboys these townships figured mainly as departure points, places it had been necessary to leave. Daniel Peter had come closest to providing me with a distinct image by saying that returned Beachboys tended to draw ships on the walls of the houses they stayed in. I had conjured entire residential quarters given over to the commemoration of stowaway histories: doors daubed with dripping container ships, like talismanic blood marks.

Being so completely ignorant I would, in the coming weeks, depend on Adam in a way I had not depended on anyone since childhood. Where he went, I would have to follow, because I had not arrived with enough money to exist in that other Dar es Salaam of multi-star hotels and revolving restaurants with harbour views. This was not some deliberate immersion strategy, but an inescapable imposition of my bank balance. Adam and Sudi's sudden deportation, after being caught aboard a ship called the *Warnow Moon*, had caught me in a lull between paying work and, after purchasing my plane ticket, I had been left with just a few hundred dollars in ready cash. Adam was fully aware of my position, and had been nothing but encouraging.

'There's always a way,' he had said. 'Just get yourself here.'

My confidence in his assurances was not shared by all of the family members and friends I'd told about my impending trip.

'Can you trust him?' was the most commonly expressed concern.

My stock answer was equally testy: 'Yes, of course. We're friends.'

Most took the hint and dropped the matter there, but with expressions bursting with supplementary questions. Is friendship even possible when the terms are so unequal? I mean, does he visit your house? Would you go out to a bar with him?

My wife, who knows the answers to these questions – yes, yes and yes – needed little convincing. 'Just make sure you're back in time for Marcia's wedding, please.'

Her feigned indifference has become a habit, almost an art. Our preparatory discussions follow similar lines: How long will you be away? Where's the money coming from? Who can I call if I can't reach you on your cellphone? Three days is the allowed period for zero contact, unless I submit that I will be out of range for longer and, in these cases, I provide as much information as I can about my projected movements: the names of towns I will almost certainly pass through, border crossings I intend making. When she is asked how she puts up with it all – and, being a hairdresser, in the tabernacle of frank talk that is her hair salon she is asked this all the time – her stock response (I'm told) is to tell her clients that this type of work, and these journeys, helped deliver the two of us from a troubled and often painful relationship into a happy and enriching marriage. Before, I had been impossible, squandering my energies in the same fixed position, like a Catherine wheel nailed to a post.

And, she knows Adam. They have met a handful of times, and although his gangster appearance and street stink initially repelled her, his politeness and charm (How are you today, mama? How is the business? Amazing what you done, mama, amazing ...) soon won through. She cried the first time he told her about Aniya and, although I've repeatedly explained that Adam's motivations for stowing away are manifold and complex, her mind is made up: he does what he does because it's the only way he will be reunited with his daughter.

She has never questioned my trust in Adam. She understands enough of the Cape Town's underworld dynamics to know what Adam has done for me, already – that, without him, the bridges, the railway reserve, this extraordinary world at the foot of the city would be closed to me.

But now, stuck in what the airport taxi driver described as a *foleni* (a traffic jam comprising four unmoving lanes of traffic on a two-lane road), I wondered about the limits of the friendship I have claimed. Would it survive the transposition to a new environment, and the added dynamic of my total dependence? If not, what then? In the short term, I'd be stuck with the problem of how to get home. In the longer term I would have to re-evaluate an array of personal and professional suppositions, and that was likely to be shattering. I felt a little queasy as the taxi turned into the Camel Oil Petrol Station off Sheikilango Road. Adam appeared at the passenger window as I was paying the driver. He was wearing baggy jeans, with a tail of red bandana hanging from a back pocket. He peered in from under a Chicago Bulls cap.

'Wha's he charging?'

'TSh100 000.'

'That's bullshit,' said Adam, and blasted the driver until he threw up his hands and said, 'Okay, thirty thousand, thirty thousand.'

'That's the last car you gonna take in Dar es Salaam. From now we only take buses, maybe some trucks. How are you anyway, Sean? *Mambo vipi?* It's hot, innit? You don't need to worry about nothing any more, this is our place.'

Shouldering my backpack he headed down a lane of light-coloured dirt, flanked by seamless rows of single-storey houses. By and large these were plastered with concrete and unpainted and, although most seemed to be homes, every third structure accommodated a service hatch of chicken wire behind which life's essentials were on sale: soap, candles, soft oils, cigarettes and airtime. A buzz saw whined in one structure, sawdust billowing out of the doorway.

The only multistorey building on the block was still under construction, and being watched over by a group of young Maasai askaris, proud in their *National Geographic* reds, blues and purples. They greeted me – '*Karibu, Mzungu*' – but did not acknowledge Adam.

'Bush-y people,' he said, as we passed by. 'In the rural areas they used to stand around all day looking after cows, but now they stand around all day looking after rich people's houses.' There was no scorn in his tone. 'Everyone needs to eat,' he said, ducking off the lane into a doorless building split down the middle by a passage leading to a small, barren yard in which a few chickens pecked at rice grains. There were three small rooms on either side of the passage, the doorways covered by lengths of fabric. Only one of the rooms had a lockable wooden door. Adam banged his fist on it.

'*Vipi* Baba Esau,' Adam called out, like he owned the place. The door was opened by a grinning and shirtless Sudi Brando, a white, diamond-patterned *kofia* on his head. He grabbed my hand and gave it the thumb-snap shake.

'Mr Sean-y, we have been waiting for you, brother.'

I peered into the room, an eggshell-green box with a single window in the facing wall, small and situated peculiarly near to the ceiling.

'In Dar es Salaam we build our windows up there because there's too much stealing,' Sudi explained.

A mattress with pink roses on it occupied a third of the floor space, with much of the rest of the room taken up by shoeboxes, packets and plastic laundry baskets crammed with clothes. These were Sudi's possessions, which remained in the room no matter who happened to be renting it. In Cape Town everything Sudi had owned – his *kisu*, his *kofia* and a few items of clothing – had fitted into a small, navy backpack. It was strangely reassuring to know that that he'd had this material anchorage all along, in a room six thousand kilometres away.

When Sudi left to buy beer from a nearby tavern, Adam said, 'You won't believe it, but Sudi owns this whole building. He's had it since his daddy died in the nineties, 'im and his sister.'

We dragged some beer crates out into the yard and made a three-legged plastic chair usable by propping the problematic corner up on the steps. Sudi returned with five Safari quarts and, as per Adam's ritual, we all poured a libation into the yard dust. Sudi took up the story of the building.

'My uncle built it for my father a long time ago. It was 1991 I think. Or 1992 … no, wait, I need to fetch somebody who can tell this story nicely. I was too young, I don't remember.'

He ran down the corridor and out into the street, and we could hear him asking after someone a few doors down. When he returned it was with a fit-looking greybeard, shirtless under the straps of his dungarees. His forearms were covered in sawdust, and it struck me that the neighbourhood buzz saw had fallen silent. Adam rose deferentially and shook the man's hand.

'This man is a Beachboy,' he whispered. 'Early generation. He worked overseas with Sudi's daddy in Switzerland.'

'Sweden,' the man corrected, and introduced himself. 'Kidagaa.'

Sudi directed him to the three-legged chair.

In unfaltering English, Kidagaa explained that Sudi's father Kabiru (whom everyone had called Marlon Brando) had sneaked aboard a freighter moored in Dar es Salaam harbour in 1977. This quite possibly made him the first of the Beachboys.

'No way,' said Adam.

'It's true. We heard that some people used to stow away on ships after the Second World War, because things were very difficult then. But these stowaways found the ships in places like Mombasa, or Djibouti. Dar es Salaam was still a small port at this time, not many ships called here.'

The harbour had been expanded in the post-war years, and the city's population had started to grow very rapidly.

'You know who the real father of all Beachboys is?' Kidagaa asked.

'No.'

'Julius Nyerere.'

Adam and Sudi nodded, the statement requiring no explanation for them. I was lost and only made the ground up much later. In Kidagaa's view, the growth of Dar es Salaam had gone hand in hand with a Nyerere-era act of social engineering called Operation Vijiji, which aimed to relocate – forcibly, in the end – all rural Tanzanians to collective villages, supposedly to facilitate agricultural production and make it easier for the government to supply communal services. The relocations began in 1973, but agricultural production soon declined to the point of mass starvation.

'Many rural families migrated to the cities, where things were not much better,' said Kidagaa. 'Marlon Brando's parents settled in Magomeni, which at the time was on the edge of the city. There were no schools, no churches, no *dukas* [shops].'

As youths, said Kidagaa, he and Marlon Brando had worked as *machingas*, hawking cigarettes and sweets around the newly opened Kariakoo market. 'Sometimes, if it was too hot, we used to walk to the harbour for a swim. We became very good swimmers. Me and your father could go across the harbour mouth to Kigamboni and back without thinking about it.'

'Yooo,' Sudi and Adam interjected, 'that's too far, daddy.'

'All the stevedores who worked in the harbour used to know us. They used to call us the beachboys because we were always out on Posta beach, or in the water. The younger generation doesn't know about stevedores, I don't think.'

'We know about stevedores, daddy,' Sudi insisted.

'Well, we used to always ask the stevedores, "Where is this ship coming from? Where is that one going? What is this one transporting?" And they would tell us. Every time a nice ship came in we would say, "I'm going to take this one to Europe, I'm going to take that one to America," but we never did it.

'One day this big ship came in, a really nice ship. Kabiru told us he was going to stow away on that ship. Nobody believed he could do it but he walked into the port and disappeared. A few hours later the tug came around for the ship and pulled it out to sea. We could not believe that your daddy was inside, but we knew he must be. I was not happy, because I thought I would never see him again. I knew that his mother – your grandmother – was going to ask me: "Where is Kabiru?" I did not want to tell her the truth, so I told your uncle, and he told your grandmother. For maybe a year we heard nothing, and then one day a stevedore came to find us on Posta beach. "Your friend Marlon Brando is in Sweden," he said. I asked him, "Who is this Marlon Brando?" and the man said, "He is your friend, the one who took the ship. Now he calls himself Marlon Brando. Come, he has sent something for his family." I went with him to the docks and I met this sailor. He gave me a small package, and told me that Marlon Brando was working on a construction site in Sweden. Inside were some things for his family.

'He told me that Marlon Brando wanted me to join him. I said, "No, how is this possible?" And he said that the ship was sailing that night. He said if I came back to the harbour he would try to hide me. I ran all the way back to Magomeni, straight to your grandmother's house, and I gave her the package. Inside was money, Swedish krona, about two hundred. In Tanzanian shillings this was about four hundred, which was a lot for that time. Your grandmother could not believe this luck. After that I ran back to the harbour and waited by that ship. That sailor came down and said I must wait until night, when he would give one sound' – the old Beachboy gave a low catcall – 'and that was my sign to run up the plank. When I was up, he said he would show me a good place to hide. After two days I was supposed to come out to meet the captain. He said the captain would ask me if any of the crew helped me to hide, and I must say no. If I kept quiet like that, the captain would take me to Sweden.'

'Big story, daddy. Respect,' said Adam.

'We stayed in Sweden for the whole of the 1980s. The government gave us a residence permit, but we did not want to leave because we did not trust that we could make it back. Your father used to send money to your uncle from time to time with instructions for him to build a house. This is the house that your uncle built for your father.'

'My uncle stole my father's money,' Sudi interjected furiously. 'He was supposed to build a big house with that money.'

Kidagaa tried to reason with him in paternal Swahili, which Adam translated for my benefit.

'He says that Sudi's daddy was dreaming of a very big house of many levels, near to the sea in one of the rich areas, like Mikocheni, or even Oyster Bay. He's trying to tell Sudi that the money was never enough for that. He says that Marlon Brando did not understand how expensive it was to build a house in Dar es Salaam at this time. Everything for building a big house had to come from overseas – roof, pipes, tiles, everything. So the cost was too much.'

Sudi refused to accept this. Turning to me he said, 'This man was a friend of my uncle, so he can't say anything bad about him. But I know what really happened. When my father came back from Europe and saw this little place – this small shit place – he became sick, and after just a few months he died. My mother told me it was because he was too shocked. He never recovered himself. I was just a small boy, but I wanted to kill that uncle. If he was alive today, I would kill him.'

The old Beachboy shrugged, drained his Safari and left. A minute later, the buzz saw's whine resumed.

Sudi conceded that Marlon Brando had not been a good father. He had missed much of Sudi's childhood and, when back home, he had regularly beaten Sudi, his sister and their mother. He had not mourned his father's death for too long, particularly since the rent from the rooms now came directly to him and his sister.

This sister, he said, had recently betrayed him. Their long-standing agreement was that, whenever he was away chasing ships – and he had been away for seven of the last ten years – his share should go to Sauda. The last payment had not been made, however.

'That is a big deal,' said Adam, 'because, here in Dar es Salaam, tenants pay for six months at a time, and they pay before, not after. So Sudi's sister stole six months' rent, and for this whole time Sudi's boy could not attend school because his mummy had no money. It was driving Sudi crazy in Cape Town, he never showed it but it was. Now his sister is hiding because she is scared what will happen if Sudi finds her. She moved house, and never told anyone where she moved to.'

For all this time, a neighbour had been busy with the evening meal, which was brought over by her daughter, sagging in two black rubbish bags: rice (*wali*) and red kidney beans (*maharage*). Sudi placed the bags on the ground and tore at the sides until the rice and the beans were accessible. He fetched a container of water and a bucket to pour it into, and helped us to wash our hands. When the last glutinous fistful had been eaten we retired to the room, and lay down in the stuffy darkness on the double mattress on the floor.

'Sleep nicely,' said Adam. 'Tomorrow we have a full programme.'

◆

To get to Adam's mother's place – the first objective of our programme – we walked to where the auto-rickshaw taxis clustered like bright sheep under the flame trees at the corner of Sheikilango and Morogoro Connect.

Adam played tour guide as we weaved through the morning traffic jam, riding mostly among the pedestrians on the pavements.

'You see that street vendor, we call 'im a *machinga*. This one is selling peanut toffee. We call it *kashata*.' Auto-rickshaws like the one we were in were called *Bajajis*, motorbike taxis were *bodabodas* and minibus taxis were *daladalas*. The little shops set well back from the road were *dukas*, and the tricycle carts being pushed in the space between the *dukas* and the road were *mkokotenis*.

As someone who has become accustomed to navigating his home city by its iconic mountain, I sensed that I would leave Dar es Salaam with a poor sense of how I had moved from one place to the next. The coastline, I had noted from the air, is very flat for dozens of kilometres inland and, rather than climb upwards, the city has sprawled outwards along eventless radials, all of which feature potholed, two-lane road surfaces flanked by open stormwater drains and facing lines of *dukas*. There is no dominant architectural vernacular, just endlessly recurring shapes and textures: waves of corrugated roofing, gritty breeze blocks, metal doors. Here and there the verges looked lush, but the plants always turned out to be potted rather than rooted: roadside nurseries. If you peered through the fronds, you could almost always spot the business owner asleep in a wheelbarrow. There were no street names, and all depressions in the earth were choked with litter – so much so that it seemed as if plastic was welling up from the ground instead of collecting in it. There seemed to be several open-air beer halls to every block, advertising beer brands drawn from the lexicon of the colonial safari: Tusker, Savannah, Kilimanjaro, Serengeti. The all-purpose *dukas*, elsewhere in Africa fronted with Coca-Cola signage, were here wrapped in cellular network branding: Airtel, Vodacom, M-Pesa. Billboard advertising was clearly at a zenith.

On Morogoro, the city's major arterial, we pushed our way onto a *daladala*, coloured red for Kariakoo.

'Kariakoo was where all the black people lived back in the day,' said Adam. 'Any place where just black people live we call *Uswahilini*. The places where the white people live, like Sea View and Masaki, we call *Uzunguni*, and the places where the Indian people stay we call *Uhindini*.'

The road was in the process of being widened, so the line of *daladalas* bound for the city centre careened on and off a broad shoulder of earthen detours, the vehicles ahead of us dipping and cresting like ships on a stormy sea. In the distance, the city skyscrapers stuck up against dark clouds.

'We gonna introduce you to another *maskani* now,' said Adam, stepping off the bus onto Bibi Titi Mohamed Street and then setting off at pace through a crush of pedestrians and vehicles, slipping between the high-rise buildings until we reached Kivukoni Road, which runs along the northern edge of the harbour. Large holes in the port's perimeter fence provided access to grey dunes leading down to the beach. Adam and Sudi slipped through without any problems but when I tried to follow a polyphonic cry went up from the fruit traders lining the road. Then came a hard blast on a whistle.

'Police. They think we are going to rob you.'

'Talk to that man,' Adam shouted up to me. 'Tell him that everything is all right.'

A policeman in a white US navy-style uniform called me over to the coconut palm he was leaning against, one shiny boot up underneath his behind, heel hooked on the bole.

'If something happens down there I can't help you. Those are not good people. Is he really your friend? And that other one?'

'Yes,' I said, but the policeman wasn't interested. He had blown his whistle and calmed the fruit sellers. Whatever happened next would be my own fault.

The path I took led through the grey dunes to a series of makeshift tents, ranging in shape from gazebo to yurt and constructed from driftwood and multiple layers of plastic sheeting. In another context – a rubbish dump, say – these may easily have been mistaken for polymer outcrops, built by the prevailing wind. A smell of burning heroin wafted out of the nearest of them.

'*Karibu.*'

A large man whose red underpants reared clear of his frayed shorts appeared behind me. Adam made the introductions.

'His name is Hansopy, or Ans, The Bulldog. Ans sells the drugs down here – 'im and his beach wife, Ana.'

'We have been waiting for you. Sit here,' said Ans, kneeling at the tent opening and shouting at the ten or so men sitting inside. They shifted closer together, and a seat cushion was passed from hand to hand and put down in the space cleared for me. I sat and said my *Jambo, sijambos*, bumping fists with all but Ana, the only woman in the tent. If

The Bulldog was in his early thirties, Ana was over forty, and as sober and modest in her light-blue denim dress and multiple head wraps as her partner was drunk and naked. She was seated with her legs crossed, her knees brushing a plastic crate that had been placed over a paraffin lamp. A hole had been cut in the top of the crate and a large tile had been placed on top of this. Ana was using it as a mortar to crush a succession of *kattes*, grinding the hard pips of heroin down to dust with a short, thin piece of metal.

'This metal is used to tie things down inside ship containers,' said Adam, 'but, whenever you see it in Dar es Salaam, you will know that there are boys nearby smoking *unga*.'

Ana had pre-rolled several marijuana joints, leaving them open at the top. Now, taking these in her fingers one at a time, she sucked in the floury heroin, twisted the joints closed and left them cocked on a box of Puff matches, like miniature cannons. She offered one to me but Adam intercepted it.

'He never smoke before. He not gonna start now I don't think.'

Sudi nodded agreement. 'When you smoke for the first time you feel sick and vomit everywhere. Sometimes this happens the second time, too.'

'Drink,' said Ans, thrusting forward an unlabelled half-jack with clear liquid in it. I accepted the bottle and sipped. The taste wasn't unpleasant, like rice wine with hints of mango.

'*Gongo*,' he said, putting his shirt over the mouth of the bottle and downing the contents through it.

'Why did you cover the top?'

'It's dirty.'

'Usually it's made with fruit, but the worst *gongo* is made with old clothes,' added Adam.

'Oh. Okay.'

Smoking *unga* and drinking home-brewed *gongo* had long ago replaced stowing away as the daily aim of the Posta Beachboys. There was no consensus about why this had happened. Some took the view that too few ships entered the harbour these days, and that the shipping that did merely plied the continent's east coast or went to and from the ports of South East Asia or the Far East. Others said the practice had come to an end in the nineties, when courts started putting harbour trespassers into Keko Prison for six months.

'Keko is no joke,' said Adam. 'It makes Pollsmoor seem like a hotel. People die in there all the time.'

In his view, the men in the tent were not true Beachboys. 'Most of these are not even from Dar es Salaam, they're from the bush. They ran away from their families and ended up here because it is the only place they can stay.'

He pointed at a young man with a cheerful face. 'This boy here came to Dar es Salaam in 2010, for Eid. The city is packed at this time, and everyone dresses the same, so a lot of children lose their parents. That is what 'appened to this boy. He was young, 13 I think. He was walking around the streets crying because he didn't know anyone.'

Adam paused to make a few abject crying noises, rubbing his eyes to the delight of the others. 'He came to the beach, crying, crying, and some of these boys asked him, "What's wrong?" and he said, "Hooo, hooo, I lost mummy, I lost my daddy," and so they said, "Come with us, we gonna find your mummy and daddy," and when he got to the beach they took all his clothes and said, "Stupid boy, why do you believe anything anyone say?" and the boy walked away crying, but then he came back because he had no clothes and he knew nobody, and they let him sleep here.

'The next day he still couldn't find his family, and it went like that for the whole year. One day he was walking by the ferry terminal and someone recognised him and called his family. His family told that person to put the boy on a bus to the village but this boy ran away. You see, he had a new family now. He had already seen another life. I can understand his mind, to be honest. I grew up in the bush, just like 'im. Bullshit place that, full of stupid people.'

Adam wanted pictures taken, and strutted up and down the waterline in a proprietorial fashion, stopping occasionally to gaze out at the dhows sliding past container ships and gas carriers like olden-day toys. Beachboys spilled from a distant tent to howl abuse at me. Adam shouted back furiously and the objectors put their hands up in contrition.

'Nobody can tell me anything here. This is my place, I was born here. My daddy came on one of these ships. My mummy lives across there.' Adam pointed across the harbour waters at the palm-fringed shoreline of the Kigamboni Peninsula. In all the time we'd known one other, he had said very little about his mother or father. Now, stoned on *unga*, his mother waiting with lunch on the other side of the bay, he performed the story of his beginnings for the smokers who had spilled out onto the beach with us.

'My daddy was a Greek sailor, you know. He came here in 1981 and made my mummy pregnant, then he left. I never seen him till this day.'

'*Unajua nini kuhusu baba yako* [what do you know about your father]?' asked a man with pointy ears and good teeth. I had made the same mistake before, and braced for the inevitable.

'You know what is Greek style?' Adam asked pointy ears. 'When a Greek sailor comes home from the sea he fucks his woman's front, you know, the pussy. When it is time to go he fucks the arse. That is Greek style. My daddy must have been a confused Greek sailor, because he did it the wrong way round. That's all I know about my daddy – he made my mummy pregnant with me, an' then he left.'

Sudi was not impressed by the characterisation.

'Memory, you can't talk about your mother like that.'

'You right Sudi, sorry *mwanagwu*. I love my mother. She made me. She left me in the bush with fucked-up people but she made me. Everything's okay between us now, we made peace a long time ago. I love my daddy, too, even though I never met him. It's because of 'im that I love the sea.'

To quell the spreading concern about my presence on the beach, Ans took me between the tents, making introductions. While this was happening, a deal was being struck between Adam and a man fetched down from Kivukoni Road. The Sony camera and the Nokia phone I had brought from Cape Town went into his rucksack, and he handed over a fan of pink 10 000-shilling notes. After this Adam signalled it was time to leave, and moved off along the grey shoreline in the direction of the Kigamboni Ferry Terminal, cutting up through the food market below the Kilimanjaro Hotel.

Adam had been energised by the heroin and, in a switch I knew all too well, he became rowdy – first in the fish market that abuts the ferry terminal, then among the taxis at the head of Barack Obama Drive, which had been renamed from Ocean Road a few months previously. As always, it began with truly bad rapping. 'Yo, yo, fucken Dar es Salaam, city of peace, city of peace but ghetto youth never know no peace, mother fucka!' We progressed past the ticket booth, paid TSh30 each and entered the terminal's open-air waiting area just as the ferry was churning out into open water. It hardly mattered that we'd missed it, though, because another was already halfway across the narrow harbour mouth.

'This country is fucked up, you know. Look how close it is to the other side, less than five hundred metres, but the government never built any bridge like they promised so long ago, because the ferry owners are powerful people, and they want everyone to keep paying.'

Beggars with horrendous deformities worked the gathering crowd, jangling tins slung from their necks. An adolescent with hypermobility syndrome removed his hat from his head with his toes, his leg up along the side of his body.

'No fucking way,' said Adam.

Sudi took my backpack from me and wore it over his chest to ensure that no hands snaked in when the gates were lowered, which they soon were, causing the crowd to surge forwards down the slipway and up the ferry's tail ramp. Cars, *Bajajis* and *bodabodas* streamed out of a separate lane, wing mirrors duelling as they hooted their way aboard. Adam made for the prow, where he hopped over a boundary chain and took a roomy seat on the gunwale. The engines turned and the Kigamboni shoreline swung into view, an even line of palms broken here and there by single-storey houses, the beaches and shallows thick with small fishing boats.

'Soon everything gonna change,' said Adam. 'The government wants to build a new city on this land. They got a lot of money from rich countries to buy the houses of the people who 'ave lived in Kigamboni their whole lives, but people been stealing that money and what they ended up giving the people was not enough. When the government comes to make them move there is going to be a big fight, trust me.'

He stood and yelled out at the press of passengers.

'Fuck the government. Fuck the president.'

Sudi grabbed his arm. '*Nyamaza* Memory Card. *Kijinga*!'

'Sorry Sud, you're right. We don't need to worry about this government where we going.'

The ferry docked minutes later and we ran down the front ramp to avoid being trampled, ducking right into the village at the first opportunity. Adam hailed three young men he recognised and bought a cigar-shaped package of weed from them.

'I think my mother is the poorest person in the whole village. She got six other children, and some of her children got children, and she tries to support them all.'

Mama Suna's place, which was not far from the scrimmage of tourist stalls around the ferry terminal, was notable for the absence of a roof. Bright sheets of fabric covered the window apertures and a plastic sheet served as a front door. As we approached, the sheet was lifted and a woman in a red dress burst out and came running towards us. She planted several kisses on my cheeks. 'Sean-y, Sean-y, *karibu*,' she sang, taking my hand.

Adam laughed merrily. 'She says you're the first white man she's touched since my daddy.'

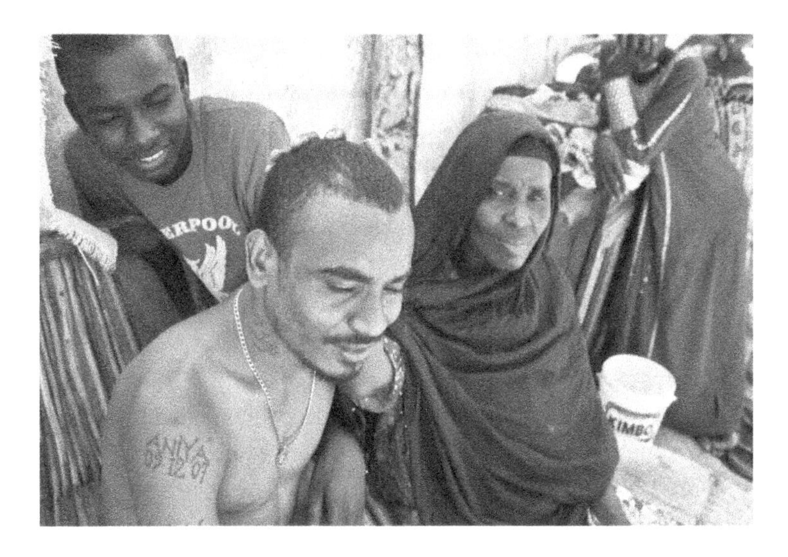

The brown scarf tied around Suna's head framed skin that was somehow both unlined and lived in. She hustled us inside the ruin of a home, where her daughters sat on reed mats with their legs out in front of them. They rose to their feet and shook hands while chiding their children, who were climbing on the crumbling interior walls. A smartly dressed teenage boy exited the only room in the building that had a roof on it, as if he had been awaiting his moment. He walked up to Adam and shook his hand solemnly, then turned to me and, just as solemnly, said, 'I am very pleased to meet you. You are welcome. My name is Mohamed. I love you.'

Adam laughed in delight. 'This is Suna's youngest child, Hamidi. He's still in school. A good boy. These are my younger half-sisters,' he said, indicating the three brightly dressed women who had retaken their places on the mats. 'There is an older brother and an older sister, but they are not here. I have not seen the older sister since 1998.'

Suna dashed into the room and came out with our lunch of squid tentacles and fish, which had been fried away from its bones. We ate quickly and, afterwards, Adam and Sudi smoked a procession of joints while Suna pressed Mohamed's Grade 7 English into the service of her life story.

She had been born, she said, in Mbeya, the youngest of eight children. She had married a man of her village at the age of 16, and had two daughters with him, the elder of whom had died at the age of five. She believed that she had been cursed – that one of her sisters-in-law had taken the child's faeces and buried them at the entrance to the house, and that the child had died as a result of this witchcraft.

Adam put his hand up. 'You need to understand something, Sean. The place my mother comes from is deep bush, they don't even speak Swahili there. It is a place of witches. In fact my grandmother, Halima, was one of the most powerful witches in Mbeya. That power passes from mother to daughter, so my mother's sisters got it, and the sisters of her husband also had it. She didn't stand a chance. When her baby died she never knew who cursed her but she knew it was witches that took the baby.'

Suna's husband was a successful trader in coconuts. To take care of his accommodation needs on his frequent trips to Dar es Salaam, he had bought a house in Temeke. After the death of their child Suna had insisted they move to the city, but they had quarrelled so incessantly in their cramped city quarters that she had left, and was soon living with a police officer, with whom she had had a son, Adam's older half-brother. While living under the police officer's roof, Suna had met a Greek fire watchman in a portside bar. His ship, the name of which she could not recall, had docked for just a week. When she gave birth on 1 March 1982, her policeman boyfriend had seen that the child was coloured and promptly barred Suna from returning to his home.

'Ask me mum about me dad,' Adam prompted.

'Ask her what?'

'Ask her how did they meet.'

'She said they met in a bar.'

'Ask her what he said to her.'

'You will have to ask her for me.'

Adam asked the question.

'She says my daddy couldn't speak any Swahili, and as you can see my mum speaks only Swahili, so they couldn't understand each other. But my daddy had an idea. He pointed at her and asked, "Are you Amina, or are you Anna?" She said Anna. He said, "Good, good."'

Are you Christian or Muslim? A pick-up line for the ages.

Mama Suna didn't have much more to add. Adam's father had been kind to her, she said. He had not been young: in his fifties, most likely, and quite fat, so there was little chance he was still alive. He had asked her to return with him to Greece, and the proposal had caused her to flee to Mafia Island, several hundred kilometres to the south-east, where she remained until well after the ship's departure. Unable to read or write, she only had the sound of her lover's name to go on when she registered her child's birth a year later. The first name was easy enough, but the second had been an unusual sound; so, it is perhaps unsurprising that on all of the Internet, Adam's patronymic connects only to a mountain range on an island in the South China Sea.

Suna stroked Adam's head as he smoked, and said he had been the clever one; that, had his education not been nixed by certain spiteful relatives, she would not be living in a home without a roof. Adam nodded slowly, deeply stoned. We picked the fishbones clean and tossed the skeletons into the empty *ugali* bowl. Afterwards, Suna walked us through the village to the edge of the main road, calling 'Sean-y, Sean-y, mwah, mwah,' as we moved away from her. Mohamed led us on to Mikadi Beach, following a litter-strewn path through some neem trees. A young Maasai askari had been posted on the invisible line between the free and the paying parts of the shoreline, but he knew better than to challenge Adam and Sudi, who looked particularly exotic with their shirts off, red bandanas trailing from their back pockets. The friends sat down and rolled up near a group of flak-jacketed tourists, who pretended not to notice the smell of burning ganja as they sipped their complimentary sundowners.

I stripped down and asked if I needed to worry about sharks.

'No,' said Adam.

'Yes, there are sharks,' Mohamed insisted, though he said they would not harm me if I kept my shoes on.

'Feet look like fish,' he explained, with youthful authority.

The sea was a sun-warmed bath for the entire five hundred metres of the beach shelf, beyond which I was swallowed by the Indian Ocean's blue chill. The coastline looked idyllic from this distance, the city centre and the harbour hidden by the peninsula's curve. I couldn't keep my imagination from raising skyscrapers above the palms – the skyline of New City – but only had to dive down a few feet to reset the current reality of evening strollers and pulled-up *ngalawas*.

◆

Adam's plan is for me to meet people in the order in which they had featured in his life, and to do this he has enlisted Suna's help, a process that could not have been easy for either of them.

Adam had only lived with Suna until the age of five, when she had dropped him in the village of Kiparang'anda, a day's journey from the city on the roads as they were then. Adam had never seen this village before, or any village, for that matter. He does not recall his mother leaving him there, only that she had, and that there had not been a single light to see by that first night in a house filled with people he had only met for the first time that day: his grandmother, three of his mother's older sisters and her brother, Uncle Mageni, the headmaster of the local primary school. He had seen his mother again at the age of ten, when she had returned for just a few days before taking off again, only returning when he was 14. She had taken him away with her then, and he had not returned to the village since.

When we boarded the bus for Mbagala at 8 a.m., Adam merely said that we were going to meet his grandmother in a district called Pwani ('which means near to the sea'), and that it would be a long day. When the *daladala* skirted the National Sports Stadium in Keko he added, 'She's old, you know, over one hundred years I think. You can work it out, because Suna is nearly sixty years now, and she's the youngest child out of eight my nanny had. People say she has survived so long because of her powers. She can't walk no more but you can be sure that she still flies around at night when everyone else is sleeping.'

Adam's belief in witchcraft is unshakeable, and possibly implicated in his need to believe that his mother had no choice but to leave him on his own.

'My aunts got it from my grandmother. That is why my mother could not stay in the village. She was too afraid they would put witches on her. It's a big decision for her to return with us today,' he said as we pulled into the Mbagala bus station. Suna, who had travelled ahead of us, was standing at the side of the road, a blue bucket on her head. She looked tense.

'*Njia hii*,' she shouted to us, running across the rank in a turquoise *khanga* to stop a minibus that was just leaving its bay. '*Haraka*,' she shouted, and climbed in.

'Fuck man, she's too stressed. It makes me stress myself, y'know. She needs to chill.'

We climbed in after her and seated ourselves on the ledge behind the front seats, facing the other passengers. Suna fished in her blue bucket and retrieved a black plastic packet, half-filled with *pepeta* – rice that has been cooked and then flattened and dried, and which tastes a bit like popcorn. We scooped out handfuls and crunched them between our teeth, splinters dusting our laps and the shoes of the facing passengers.

Dar es Salaam does not release vehicles quickly in any direction, but, when it does, it does so suddenly. One moment we were travelling between a dense press of shanties, with palm trees among them here and there, and the next we were shuttling between dense forests of palm trees, with just a few huts below them here and there. After an hour on this green sea, our *daladala* reached the end of its route and we disembarked and boarded another, which drove at frightening speeds for two hours before pulling into a sandy bay.

'Kiparang'anda,' Suna announced, taking a footpath that led into dense bush. This soon opened on a disc of foot-polished earth, on which two breeze-block buildings stood beneath giant avocado trees.

'Kiparang'anda Primary School,' said Adam, and pointed out the windows he had slipped out of whenever he wanted to bunk classes. Children streamed to the doorways to gawk at the odd procession. There was an irony to this return. Suna had brought her son to the village to keep him off Dar es Salaam's mean streets. Now here he was, an advertisement for those streets with his tattoos and glinting teeth, encouraging the schoolchildren with gang signs borrowed from music videos.

Suna, carrying a melon on one raised palm, increased the pace and we soon dipped out of sight into a valley in which spiky pineapple plants, sugar cane, cassava bushes and banana trees flourished. It was nearing midday, and several women were lying in the shade of some cashew trees, waiting for the air to cool before resuming their chores beside the well.

The compound in which Adam had grown up was on the valley's southern crest. It consisted of a large rectangular building with an open-air atrium at its centre, and a smaller two-room building a little way downslope, accessible through a fence of sticks. As we approached, a man lying on a reed mat on the veranda of the larger building sat up slowly and waved.

'That's my uncle,' Adam said, without enthusiasm. Suna returned her brother's wave but then ducked into the smaller building, pulling me into a gloomy, windowless room furnished with two beds at right angles along two of the walls.

'A baby,' Suna cried. 'Baby, baby, baby.'

Adam's grandmother was lying on the smaller of the two beds, being spoon-fed rice by her eldest daughter, Maria. Age had stripped the old woman of all musculature, leaving behind perhaps thirty kilograms of skin and bone, ending in toenails that had turned to vegetable ivory. She appeared not to notice the arrival of her youngest daughter, but when Adam walked in the creases on her face turned upwards. 'Kitenga,' she croaked, and raked the air with a hand, signalling that Adam should take over the feeding duties. Maria sniffed and stood to leave, and as soon as she was gone the old woman ordered Adam to eat what was left over on the plate. He did, explaining in a rice-slow whisper that, although he had been sent to live with his uncle, his grandmother had raised him.

'Sometimes my uncle and aunt wouldn't feed me for three days at a time, so me nan used to save her dinner and feed me late at night, when nobody was looking. Even now she doing it, you see. Nah man, I love me nanny too much. She raised me.'

Suna broke out a flask containing our lunch of sugary noodles. Since we had only our fingers to work with much of it ended up on the concrete floor, before being pulled under the beds by two emaciated kittens. Adam remained cradling his grandmother's head in his lap. She looked adoringly up at him.

'She say she feels ready for the end of life now. She's worried that if it don't come soon all her daughters will die first, because they are old women already.'

Halima closed her eyes and fell asleep, and quietly as we could we retreated from the dark room and shut the bamboo door.

Slowly, reluctantly, Suna and Adam walked over to the main house.

'Ah, Kitenga,' said Uncle Mageni, extending a hand from his prostrate position on the veranda. The two of them ground through some pleasantries and were spared further awkwardness when Adam's phone rang. He stalked away to the edge of the banana plantation, dribbling a deflated football as he talked.

'Please, sit.' The former headmaster patted the open space on his reed mat. He was dressed in shorts and sandals, and his legs were perfectly hairless. I sat down and we traded a few lies. He said Adam had been a good boy – 'Happy, no trouble' – and I said that Adam was doing well as a trader in Cape Town, that he lived under a roof, had many friends.

'Why does everyone call him Kitenga?'

'That is his name. A *kitenga* is a ... what can I say, like a basket, made of natural materials. We Tanzanians use them to carry coconuts. You tie the basket to the body, and fill it with coconuts. When Kitenga's mother was pregnant with him she reached 11 months, and he still was not born. Her stomach was out here, and we worried the child was dead inside her. She went to see a doctor who told her the child was alive, and that she must call him Kitenga after he is born, to remind herself of how big he made her, like a basket full of coconuts.'

Adam's aunt came out onto the veranda, her eyes made up with pink and green eyeshadow. For a few moments she watched Adam talking on his phone at the foot of the property, before turning and walking back inside the house. She did not return.

'Hey Kitenga,' I said, passing the football back and forth with Adam a few minutes later, 'are we staying the night here?'

Suna, who was watching us, chopped her fingers across her neck.

'No, no sleep.'

'You see what Suna say, Sean? These people are witches. I'm serious. If we stayed tonight you gonna hear them whistling to each other. You heard about the witch's whistle?'

'No.'

'Come on, you must have heard about it. Every witch keeps a whistle hidden somewhere, made out of a small boy's dick. At night they use this to call each other.'

'Where the fuck would I hear something like that?'

Adam giggled. 'We call it a *filimbi*. Just imagine.'

But witchcraft was not the problem, or at least not for Adam.

'What did my uncle say to you?'

'He said you were a good boy.'

'He's lying. I used to run away all the time. Sometimes I would hear him coming down the path and I would hide in the bushes, just to miss him.'

'What did his wife say?'

'Nothing.'

'That woman is evil, I'm telling you. You see this,' he said, tapping his gold-plated incisors with his pinky fingers.

'Look again.' He raised his head so that I could see his upper dentures from below. The gold plates did not sit over his incisors, which were well back from his front teeth, and badly stunted.

'That woman did this to me. She pushed me into a chair when I was a little boy and knocked my teeth out. Her own children used to fight, you see, but when their mother came they would tell her it was my fault, and she would always punish me, never them. My uncle saw this happening but he did nothing to defend me, even though I am his sister's blood. When it came time for me to go to high school he sent his other children but he never sent me. His friend said he would train me as a railway engineer but my uncle refused him because his plan was for me to stay and work on the farm. That's how my uncle saw me, like a slave boy. I don't hate him, you know, but I don't respect him either. I could have been different if he had been a kind man.'

These memories took the enjoyment out of our game, and Adam told Suna we were leaving.

'Call us when you are finished here,' he said, setting out on a different path to the one we'd come in on. We soon heard feet behind us and, turning, saw Uncle Mageni labouring up the hill.

'Please give this man TSh10 000, just so that he will go away. It's all he wants.'

I handed the former headmaster a pink *shillingi elfu kumi* bill, watermarked with Julius Nyerere's face. He took it, turned and shuffled downhill. Adam continued on through the palms and greeny-yellow grasses, seeming smaller to me than he ever had against the vast concrete haunches of Nelson Mandela Boulevard. It was so completely still that at first I struggled to place the sound of an approaching motorbike. The machine and its driver came up behind us at speed, forcing me to step off the path. The rider came to a halt a few metres beyond Adam. He lifted his helmet and gave a delighted shout.

'*Pedi pedi*!'

'No way,' said Adam, flicking his fingers. 'Sean, climb on the back of this brother's bike, we're going to meet some people.'

We were soon blasting down bush paths and through the yards of reed houses, where the cry went up again and again. '*Pedi pedi, pedi pedi*!'

'It means half-caste boy, that's what they named me here,' Adam called into the wind.

The motorbike came to a stuttering halt in a dense orchard of palms, beneath which young men and women sat among drifts of coconut hair, drinking *gongo tippas* from a tea bowl. Adam knocked his fingers against everyone else's and handed a purple TSh5 000 bill to the motorcyclist, who roared off, returning after a few minutes with a foil package no bigger than a flower beetle. Adam lit a bit of coconut husk and held a fragment of a tile above it, then unwrapped the tin foil parcel and crushed the *unga* inside with the base of the *gongo* cup. He smoked alone, breaking off only to draw breath and loop spittle around the end of the joint. His phone rang in the grass beside him, and then rang again.

'Me mum says she's finished at the house. I told her she must wait by the road, I'm chilling with my friends.'

The conversations quickly homed in on the bad luck of mutual acquaintances. A boy they had called Gaga, who had played with Adam on the village football team, had been beaten to death after being caught thieving in a nearby village. Another acquaintance, having just bought a new motorbike, had been murdered by a *bodaboda* hijacking racket on one of the area's many bush paths. The gang was known to comprise youths who had grown up in the area, but who had since relocated to Dar es Salaam. Their strategy was to return to the villages in the company of at least one person whom nobody would recognise. The outsider would engage the services of a local *bodaboda* driver, while the others waited in ambush beside the path they knew the *bodaboda* driver would travel. When the motorbike neared they would step out to hail the driver, who would be sure to recognise them and stop. The moment he put the machine in neutral the passenger would knife him in the neck and between the ribs. The friend in question had been found with his eyes stabbed out.

Adam shook his head, and flicked the ash off his cocktail. 'Back in the day you had to leave Dar es Salaam before sunrise if you wanted to get to this village before nighttime. The road was terrible, but at least none of this shit was happening.' It was not clear whether he was referring to the violence or the heroin he was smoking. Probably both.

'Give me one *tippa*,' he demanded of the drinkers, and when it was poured he threw it in the sand.

'God bless the dead,' he croaked.

Suna called again and Adam lost it, became truly furious. 'My mother left me here when I was five years old. She dropped me in the bushes and went away. It made me crazy. It made me hate her. Today I love me mum but she left me, and she knows that. To be honest she can wait for me now.'

When the joint was done he started walking in the direction of the main road, but, with the news out that *pedi pedi* was back, men and women of all ages came streaming towards us, and in the next hour we moved no more than a hundred metres. At sunset we found Suna standing beside a *daladala* on the side of the highway, her eyes flickering between the red-eyed throng surrounding her son and the policemen manning a nearby roadblock. She practically begged Adam to climb in, and even then he kept us and the other passengers waiting for several minutes as he continued to shake hands and swap stories. When the bus eventually departed he was sweating. His mouth, which had not stopped moving for hours, kept up a jawing inertia.

'I'll come here one more time, to visit my grandmother's grave,' he said. 'After that, it is finished. I hate this fucking place.'

◆

Lying awake on the grubby mattress in Sudi's room, the barking of dogs curiously absent from Sinza's nocturnal chorus, I was reminded of the last time I had slept this close to the floor in a room without electricity, running water or furniture. It was in the course of my return to the place of my own upbringing: my grandfather's farm outside the agricultural town of Norton, in Zimbabwe.

In 2001, when the news had come that my grandfather had been frightened off his farm by a powerful politician, I had been working 12-hour night shifts in a Devonshire trifle factory. I had been away from southern Africa for a year, and had found myself unable to engage with these distant events in any significant way. I had experienced a measure of relief, in fact. For much of the nineties, emphysema had been squeezing my tobacco-farming grandfather for breath; parts of the farmhouse and yard had begun to reflect inattention. By the time I had left the continent, orb-weaver spiders had embalmed the pigsties. In the mill, it had been the same: only, the billowing flour would turn the webs into giant silken stalactites.

It had become clear that my grandfather and his wife, who was also in poor health, were determined to farm until their hearts stopped working. What then? Who would the farm pass to? Which of us – now naturalised South Africans, living city lives – was capable of keeping such a place? The expropriation of the farm had simplified, in a sense, what would have been the administration of a complicated estate: 1 500 hectares of mixed-use sandveld, on which roughly fifty workers of mainly Mozambican origin had lived and worked with their families under the Damoclean sword of the Zimbabwean government's xenophobic land-reform policies.

I had returned to South Africa to find my grandfather living on a smallholding in the Western Cape with my Zimbabwean uncle and aunt. My step-grandmother, too ill to leave Zimbabwe by road, had flown to KwaZulu-Natal, where several of her children had lived. A year had passed since their extraction, and I had offered to drive the old man across the country so that he might be reunited with his wife. But on the day of our planned departure he had been diagnosed with cancer of the stomach, and told that, if he wished to live out the year, treatment should commence immediately. So, instead of driving 1 800 kilometres to the east, we had driven 30 kilometres to the west, to the nearest radiology facility. He had lived another four years, as had she; but, both being too frail for travel, they had died without ever seeing each other again.

The experience of watching him wither away in exile had left me at odds with the country of my birth. Seven years had passed before I next crossed the Limpopo River, riding shotgun in Willie Phiri's fifty-ton rig bound for Zambia. On that journey I had resolved to return to the farm. No sooner had I returned to Johannesburg than I had set off again, by bus, for Harare. The country being starved of fuel, I had borrowed a bicycle and a tent from a friend, and had set out on the Bulawayo road in the early morning. Winter had passed through like an overloaded hay cart, leaving a trail of chaff on the shimmering tarmac. I passed the landmarks of my youth: Zanu–PF House, with its imposing cockerel emblem. The gold-painted Sheraton Hotel. The 40-metre-tall, black obelisk in Heroes Acre, topped with a red light signifying the Eternal Flame of the revolution.

I had passed a sign for Warren Hills cemetery and recalled that my grandmother's remains were interred there. She had been weighing pigs when her heart had seized. My brother and I had been in a pen shooing piglets towards the beam scale. The first person to hear our screams had been Bindura, the farmhouse cook, who had just come out to the yard bearing a tray of mid-morning tea. We had remained in Bindura's care when my grandfather had set off for the distant hospital, and it had been in Bindura's care that my parents had left my grieving grandfather after the funeral. Both Bindura and August, the senior cook, had worked in the farmhouse for a decade before I had been born, and it was they who had helped to pack up its possessions at the end.

It had taken me two days to reach the red soils that mark the farm's boundary. A fire had recently swept through the district, marooning a little knoll of rudimentary headstones marking the graves of men, women and children who had lived out their lives on the farm. August had emerged from his house in the workers' village smoking a joint of uncured tobacco rolled in over-inked paper. Although cataracts had blurred his vision, he had recognised my voice from a distance. This had set off his laugh, which infected everyone who heard it. We had hugged and, holding hands, had worked through the roll call of people whose fates had remained a mystery for a decade.

The news of my grandfather's death had hit him physically. He had sat down on his veranda and wept.

'What of Bindura?' I had asked.

August, to my immense relief, had slipped on white gumboots – 'Let's find him'.

I had difficulty keeping up with August, who had led the way on overgrown tracks to Bindura's new homestead on what had once been the neighbouring farm. We had passed the empty silage pits and the deserted pigsties, which had once debouched bright afterbirth into a rancid marsh. We had come to a clearing at a small dam, where three or four huts had been founded alongside an enclosure for goats. A figure in a large green hat had been hoeing an area on the enclosure's margins. He had frozen in his stoop when we had approached, before coming forward with his arms open.

Bindura had become emaciated, his temples scooped-out bowls and his chest quite fleshless. My friend in Harare had given me some salted pork; that night, August had cooked a memorable stew, using curry powder salvaged from the old farmhouse. At one point Bindura had stood up. With his hands flapping deep in the pockets of his oversized coat, he had asked, 'Who am I?' For the tenth time that day we had all been reduced to tears and laughter. My grandfather had never liked the cold. In winter, the short walk from the farmhouse to his farmyard office became a gauntlet across which he had shuffled rapidly in outsized coats. Invariably, he would be intercepted by one, or several, of his employees. As he would listen to their news, he would stamp and flap his coat like an unhappy bull elephant. Bindura's exact and loving caricature had seemed to bring him back to life.

The only dissonance in the evening had resulted from my asking the two to pose for a photograph.

They had glanced nervously at each other. 'We're afraid,' Bindura had said. 'Somebody might see the light from your camera. If the wrong people find you here, there will be trouble. New people are arriving all the time. We don't know each other any more in this place, so everybody lies in his hut at night fearing his neighbour.'

On a grass mat in Bindura's pantry that night, I had remembered the fear I had often felt at night in the farmhouse, especially on Saturday nights when the sounds of drumming and singing had drifted across from the workers' village. My sense of our vulnerability, in that big house, had been underscored by the two shotguns in the gun cabinet, and the fact that the entire house had been rigged with dynamite during the war years. The wooden boxes that had housed the explosives had remained beneath the windows for two decades after independence, as if on standby. I wondered whether this paranoia had transferred to the new residents, who had more to fear, perhaps, because their mismanagement of the property had destroyed the livelihoods of the dozens of men and women now starving in the nearby village. I fantasised about sneaking over to the old house, throwing rocks at the windows in the darkness. Knowing the garden like no other, I could have moved from structure to structure unseen, hooting like a witch.

But my vengeful side had soon disappeared, along with my anger. Unlike Adam's, my rural childhood had been a happy one, and I had found, against expectations, two of the constituents of that happiness alive and well.

◆

Adam took off on his own when we returned from Kiparang'anda, saying he needed to procure emergency travel documents for our coming journey. He did not return the next day, but called to say that Sudi and I should join him in the district of Temeke.

A fine misting rain was falling when we left, just heavy enough to bring down dead leaves all along Morogoro Connect, turning the pavements into mosaics of bright-yellow spearheads. In the low light I could appreciate the colourful *khangas* and headscarves worn by the female pedestrians, who seemed like creatures misplaced in this world of oily puddles and smoking braziers. The billboards called out to them in pinks, purples and reds: Konyago Whisky, Yebo Yebo Braids, Tusker Lite. Hot Deal. Feel Beautiful. Taste the Difference.

On Kigogo Road the second-hand clothes traders (*mitumbas*) were rolling desiccated pairs of Nikes and All Stars up in the plastic sheets on which they had carefully laid them out earlier that morning. The rain came down harder, and the lines of *dukas* on either side of the road became choked with street merchandise hastily stacked under the tiled awnings. There was little of interest in these scenes for Sudi, who stared at the fingernails of the female hand clasping the seatback in front of him.

'You know, Sean, people from Kenya can't understand the Swahili we speak in Dar es Salaam. Even people from Tanga cannot understand us. We have too many names for things – names that you can only know if you live in Dar es Salaam. And even if you are a man from Dar es Salaam, you still cannot understand a woman, if she doesn't want you to. They have their own words for things that men do not know. They have women's words, not really Swahili at all.'

We crossed the railway lines – moisture-bright strips sliding beneath the sea mist to the harbour – and skirted the long wall of the railway reserve, which offered a feast of chalked slogans: *Problems are the fart of life. Disability is not unability. Mr Mphoto, the king of local rhymes.* I wondered about the use of English on these East African walls, and

I wondered why Sudi had not, since my arrival in the city nearly two weeks before, stayed a single night with Sauda, the woman he referred to as his wife.

'Is everything all right with Mama Esau?'

'Everything's all right, but she is angry that I am going to South Africa again. She says Esau is growing up without his father but I tell her there is no better life for us without a ship. If I stay I must feed myself, I must buy myself clothes. Where will that money come from? The money from the rent is already not enough for them. Mama Esau understands this, I think, but she says I must not stay with them in Magomeni East, otherwise Esau will think his daddy is home to stay, and it will be difficult when we go.'

As our *daladala* approached Dar es Salaam University, we veered right onto Nelson Mandela Road and then right again onto Mbagala Road. Midway down, we hopped off and crossed the street to the tavern in which Adam had said he would meet us. Like most taverns in the city it was shed-like, with kitchen fires at the back alongside a concrete block of pit latrines. The tables, a hundred or so, were covered in pink plastic sheets and had blue plastic chairs clustered around them. It being nearly noon, the air was acrid with the smell of *nyama choma* and *pilipili maluzi*.

We found Adam at a table littered with empty Safari lager bottles, sitting across from a man in his early twenties whose fake diamond earring complemented the TSh10 000 notes spread out before him. Adam was wearing the partner earring and an oversized black T-shirt printed with the phrase 'Don't fuck with family'. He had tucked his red bandana under his Chicago Bulls cap, so that it flowed down to his shoulders. Sudi had warned me that Adam had a reputation to keep up in Temeke. This was the community in which Suna had left her son after it became obvious that the village could no longer hold him. With nothing better to do, he had spent his teenage years roaming the streets, befriending the area's toughest strays. The character he had honed in order to do this was bombastic and dangerous. He could still inhabit it.

'This is Gerrard,' he said, introducing his friend. 'I just convinced him to come back to South Africa with us. If he stays here he's going to get in trouble.'

Sudi's eyes had fixed on the notes, which amounted to about half a million Tanzanian shillings.

'Gerrard stole this money from a woman last night. I feel sorry for her, knowing what happened.'

The biggest challenge facing street muggers like Gerrard, he explained, was the local propensity for concealing cash down brassieres, inside knickers and under shoe soles – anywhere but in the obvious bag, purse or wallet. Since very few criminals in Dar es Salaam carry firearms, most victims are happy to empty their bags and invert their pockets in theatrical displays of poverty, the hope being that their attacker will soon run away, knowing that no street is deserted for very long.

Gerrard, however, had hit on a strategy for getting beyond this impasse. It was simple, and quite brutal. He would wait in the shadows and, when his victim passed, he would swing his panga with all his might. The pedestrians would see the broad blade flash – the stuff of nightmares – and feel a clap of shocking pain from their back, neck or skull area. In that moment they knew only one thing: that they had been split open to the bone, and would probably die. Faced with the raised blade once more, they would make their money miraculously appear in outstretched hands – the day's takings, the children's school fees, the contribution to a relative's funeral. Only later, after Gerrard was long gone, would the victim realise that the panga had been turned flat before impact, causing nothing worse than a bad welt.

Our waitress brought a round of perspiring beers and a plastic basket of *mishkaki*, which was followed through from the cooking fires by several blue-bottomed flies. Gerrard grinned broadly, clearly enjoying the attention his temporary wealth had drawn from surrounding tables. Sudi clucked his tongue in disapproval. As a former gangster he could appreciate the brutal logic of Gerrard's methods, but flaunting ill-gotten gains was pure stupidity, and it put us all at risk. I sensed it was only a matter of time before he would challenge Adam over his decision to invite Gerrard to return with us to South Africa. Adam must have sensed the same thing: he pre-emptively laid out his case.

'I warned him this is how you get caught but the boy doesn't want to listen. I can see he has stopped caring what happens to 'imself. That is why I want him to come to South Africa. Gerrard could be me, or you, Sudi. He deserves a chance but nobody ever give him one.'

Gerrard sipped his beer and uncomprehendingly pulled chunks of beef off kebab sticks. I was with Sudi – the guy was trouble. It was hard to say what it was about Gerrard that I found repellent (the details of his methods only emerged later). He had a nice face, a nice smile. If I had been able to speak with him I might have felt differently, but in the absence of shared language anything I chose to say had to go through Adam, and he was in no mood to play interlocutor. In fact, it seemed that, having led me this far into his life, he now wanted to hurry through to the conclusion of his story, to be rid of the burden of constant explication and translation. He spoke fast, drank fast, ate nothing.

Once Gerrard had paid the table's bill, Adam went dancing down the street, throwing his hands up, rapping, cursing, greeting people on the go, walking backwards, stumbling forwards. He led a long trail down a series of dirt roads, cutting through taverns and crossing open sewers until we came to a dirt panhandle dominated by a large white *daladala* up on stocks. It was a Japanese Hino, a thirty-seater with lime, apple and olive stripes going around the middle. Two shirtless men were sitting on blue water drums outside the passenger door, sipping black coffee from teacups. There were several more young men inside the bus, leaning against the dashboard or lounging on the front benches. Adam stepped in to cries of 'KiPaka … KiPaka Memory!'

'This is the clubhouse, where me and my friends used to chill back in the day.'

The bus had belonged to a Chinese woman, he said, but it had broken down and stayed put because she did not have the money to fix it. Adam and his teenage friends had offered to protect it in exchange for a small fee, and they had done this by using it as a base for smoking weed and plotting their juvenile heists. The bus had become a way of life; for many of the original gang members, it remained exactly this. Their clothes and cooking utensils filled the baggage shelf above the seats. A mattress rested atop the white pleather seats, its green sheet embroidered with the image of a peacock rising upwards from a rose.

Adam was instantly offered the driver's seat, where he sat pouring ganja smoke out of his mouth and nose: KiPaka Memory, back at the wheel.

The name had a history, having initially belonged to a famous house robber in Temeke.

'That guy had the skills of a cat, a *paka*,' said Adam. 'This guy would never forget it if you crossed 'im, which is why they added Memory to his name. KiPaka Memory. But in the end someone put witches on that guy and he died, and people started calling me KiPaka Memory because I was now the best house robber in Temeke. In Cape Town the boys took that name and changed it to Memory Card.'

Leaving Adam to his friends I retreated to the back of the bus.

Here, unexpectedly comfortable and suddenly exhausted, I closed my eyes and played an old game, in which I imagine myself turned back into my adolescent self and, from this place of innocence and inexperience, try to make sense of the surrounding sounds and conversations. I was relishing my younger self's abject confusion when the words Chawa Suga stood out from the torrent of Swahili issuing from the front of the bus. I opened my eyes to see Sudi slamming his palms on the dashboard.

'You know what?' Adam shouted down to me. 'These guys say that Chawa Suga was here just a couple of weeks ago. Here in this bus. Can you imagine? We just missed him. He was staying with some guys down the way. If we knew this he would be finished, but these boys say he already left Dar es Salaam. They don't know where he is now.'

For ten days it had been possible to forget about Cape Town and the tensions that had washed through the Foreshore following Aubadeeleh's murder, but Sudi was now back to punching his palm with his fist. The hazing marijuana smoke aside, the bus suddenly felt small and cloying.

Adam's phone rang, and he put his hand up for silence. His voice instantly modulated, losing its fierce edge. He put his shirt back on.

'That was my adoption mama. She says we must meet at her friend's party. We have to go now.'

To save time, we hailed a *Bajaji* and went speeding down Taifa Road. Adam took the opportunity to fill me in on the missing months between his departure from Kiparang'anda and his arrival in Temeke.

'When I was 14 Suna took me to live in a small village on Mafia Island. I was going to take you there, and Suna even bought two mosquito nets for us to sleep under, but we ran out of time.'

Mafia, or Chole Shamba, is the southernmost island of the Zanzibar Archipelago and, of the inhabited islands, easily the least touristic. Suna's only other brother had settled there in the seventies, in a traditional fishing community on the shoreline of Chole Bay. He owned two buildings, and made one available to his sister.

'Suna used to make me carry water every day in these big fucking containers,' Adam continued. 'I used to feel my neck crushing. I used to think I was never going to grow, because the water was always pushing me down.'

Feeling little but hate for his mother, Adam plotted his escape. The plan had come to him some weeks before, when he had watched the village coconut traders pushing their *mashuas* and *ngalawas* out into the bay in the early evening before climbing aboard and unfurling the sea-stained sails. It always amazed him that such wreck-like things could suddenly come to life and move out over the ocean, eventually disappearing into darkness. He knew from listening to the talk around the village that the boats set course for Dar es Salaam, travelling through the night to deliver their cargo to market in the early morning. They would sail into the mouth of the harbour and tie up in the small inlet at the fish market, where the traders would be waiting with their baskets. Adam had studied these boats, and had found only one place where he might be able to hide himself: the wet, dark aperture beneath the bow deck.

'It's where the *pwesa* go,' he said. 'The octopuses. If someone catches one of those things, and it disappears, he knows he will always find it right at the front of the boat, in the furthest, darkest place. They put a piece of wood in there to stop this happening but an octopus as big as a football can fit through a space like this,' he said, isolating the thumbnail of one hand with the fingers of his other. 'I don't know how they do that.'

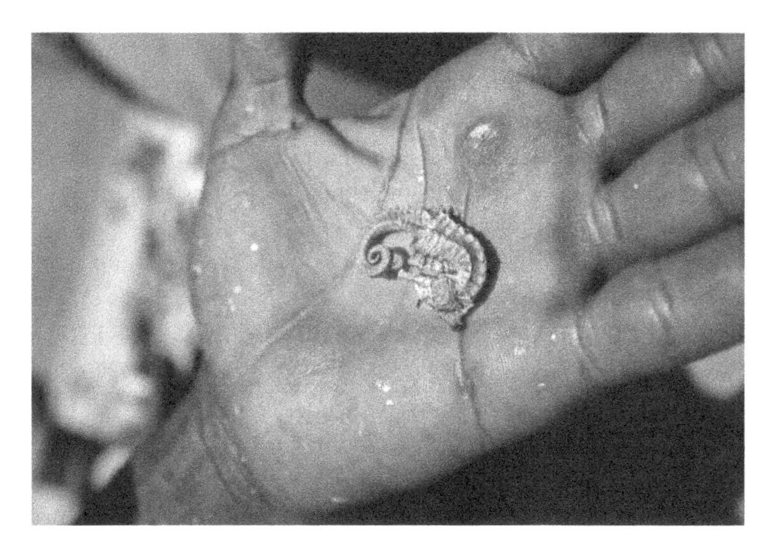

On the appointed afternoon Adam had waded out to his chosen boat and, after clambering aboard, had worked his way into the prow cavity, pulling the octopus barrier into place behind him. When his presence had been discovered it was well after dark, and the vessel was hours from the shore.

'They told me they were going to throw me in the sea when we reached a place where the sharks are, but they were just joking. Actually, they were amazed. They said they never heard of nobody stowing a fishing boat before.'

The traders had made Adam sit out the night on the gunwale. By the time the boat had slipped into the neck of Dar es Salaam harbour, he was as tired as he had ever been. He had taken in the east-facing cityscape for the first time, the morning light caught in the palms on Sokoine Drive, and behind these a series of large white buildings with red roofs: St Joseph's Cathedral, Azania Front Lutheran Church, the rectangular face of the Kilimanjaro Hotel. More impressive, though, were the ships lined up against the long port wall. A container ship with three cranes on its vast deck was just then being tugged out into the channel: an entire city block detaching from the shoreline and sliding out to sea, the wake lifting the *ngalawas* up as if they were sticks, before crashing onto the stone walls of the fish market.

Adam had known the traders would not let him off the boat, even to take a piss, so he had waited until nobody was looking his way before slipping into the water. He had walked down the beach towards the docks, half-expecting to feel a hand on his shoulder at any second. When he had made it into the food market, he'd known he was free. And, just like the boy who had lost his parents over the Eid weekend, Adam had fallen in with the Posta Beachboys. During the day, he'd helped market shoppers to carry their bags to the bus station. At night, he'd smoked joints and slept on the beach.

'It felt better, you know. My family didn't care about me so I stopped caring about them.'

One of the market regulars he used to help was called Rehema. She was younger than Suna, but twice her size. She always looked for Adam and tipped him more than she needed to.

'One day Rehema said she needed me to help her to take the bags to Temeke. I said, "Fine, let's go," and we caught the bus. When we came to her house she showed me an empty room and said, "This one is yours if you want it. You can stay here for as long as you want."'

Adam had lived with Rehema for three years. During the day he would be on the streets but there would always be a hot meal and a bed waiting for him at night, if he wanted it. It was from Rehema's house that he had departed for South Africa for the first time. Eight years had passed before they had spoken again, but when Adam had returned to Dar es Salaam after being deported from England he had made a bee-line for Rehema's house.

'She greeted me like I had just gone out to the tavern for a beer. She said, "Your room is there. Will you be in for dinner tonight?" I started crying, man. That woman was pure kindness.'

Adam had not yet seen Rehema since his arrival in Dar es Salaam, though he had spoken with her on the phone several times. Now, as we approached the meeting place, he looked a little nervous. Mama Rehema was sitting in a *Bajaji* of her own, her body filling the carriage from end to end. She was wearing a pink skirt with a lime-green top that mustered her ample chest into tight bulges. Her eyes had been made up with parabolic mauve strikes and her lips shone purple.

'I love this woman,' said Adam, offering Rehema his hand. 'She understood me at a time when nobody understood me, not even my own mother. Tha's why I call her my adoption mother.'

A woman as narrow as Rehema was wide rushed down from the line of *dukas* and shepherded our party into a small street restaurant, in which we were all served bowls of rice and coconut chicken curry. Sudi and Gerrard were both *tinga*: the condition of being too stoned to talk or keep one's eyes open. Rehema roughly poked their ribs with her spoon whenever their heads slumped, and cackled when their eyes opened in red surprise.

On the other side of the road a DJ was playing to a small crowd of children. Adam wanted to join in but Rehema put a hand on his arm and produced four A4 pages from her handbag, each of which had a passport-sized photograph stuck in a corner. I recognised Sudi, Adam, Gerrard.

'Emergency travel papers,' Adam announced. 'Rehema works for the government, so Gerrard paid her TSh120 000 this morning and she already done it, amazing.'

He started reading from his own document: 'Temporary Travel Permit … Adam Chazili … Central and East Africa. That means we can use these to go through the border into Malawi. It should say Mozambique as well but we will just write it in later. That means we only have to jump one border, from Mozambique into South Africa.'

Adam stowed the documents in my bag and led Rehema across the street to the dance floor, which was now dominated by women of similar dimensions wearing identical pink skirts and lime-green tops.

Sudi, who had sobered up some, explained that the women in Dar es Salaam tend to throw weekly parties, usually on a Sunday. 'They have many different kinds of parties, they can party for any excuse. They even have something called a Kitchen Party, where they dance naked inside a house, no men allowed.'

He followed Adam across the road and joined in, caricaturing the ladies' limited range of movements, pushing his backside out and lifting his elbows to shoulder height. The women encircled him and he threw his hands up in surrender, still dancing from the hips. Gerrard was nowhere to be seen.

'Maybe he felt guilty,' Adam wondered aloud, back at the table for a second course of doughnut-like *mandazi*. 'Maybe all these women remind him of the thing he do last night. Or maybe he's scared to come to South Africa. In Temeke he is somebody, at least, people know 'im. In South Africa nobody knows Gerrard.'

With our benefactor gone we walked the few kilometres to Rehema's place, eventually stopping at a long wall of connected homes. The metal door opened on a large, tiled living room of orange walls and green couches. A large television stared out from an uncluttered console.

'When I first came here I was amazed,' said Adam. 'The toilet outside had a door and it flushed. Up until then I had never seen a toilet like that. I just shit in it and leave, until somebody explained what you must do.'

We sank into the couch and watched music videos while Rehema prepared the evening meal. At a point Gerrard called to say he was at the local *unga* house. He had smoked his remaining money and more, and wanted us to join him, bringing cash to settle his debts. Adam said this was not possible and Gerrard cut the call.

'Fuck him. He know I never go out after dark, not since I was arrested for stabbing that guy. The police know me too well here. If anything happens they come looking for KiPaka Memory, to this day.'

Adam had left Rehema's house for South Africa on his 17th birthday. Now, 14 years on, he was back where he had started, watching Rihanna's 'Diamonds' music video with tired eyes. The situational irony did not seem to bother him. Marlon Brando's generation of Beachboys had stowed away and lived and worked abroad with relative ease, but that was before the Maastricht Treaty integrated the European Union's common migration policy. It was before the worm on population growth charts reared up, especially in poor countries, before 9/11 and the fast-tracked ratification of the ISPS.

I am now more convinced than ever that, for Adam, stowing

away has become an end in itself, a form of extreme sport, like base-jumping, or kayaking over waterfalls. He doesn't need to do it – it is far from rational – but it marshals his energies and gives him a purpose that would otherwise be lacking. It is the thing that separates him from the man his uncle Mageni expected him to become: a toiler in a field. The thing that separates him from the man he would have become: a man like Gerrard, who, incidentally, we never saw again.

◆

Back at Sudi's place, I was woken just after sunrise by the sound of Adam's voice in the yard. He was speaking in Swahili at an explosive rate, only switching to English at the end of the conversation.

'I'm showing my friend around Dar es Salaam first, then I'll take care of fucking business.'

When he returned to the room he went straight for one of the clothes piles and retrieved the Lenovo laptop hidden within.

'Come, we need to make some paper today. Bring your bags, you never know what is gonna 'appen. Maybe we gonna leave tonight already.'

His mood relaxed on the bus to Magomeni East and, stepping out on Morogoro Road, he handed some money to a shopkeeper, who fed three sticks of sugar cane through a grinder and produced three glasses of *juice ya miwa*, with lemon.

Adam winced as the sweet and sour liquid hit his gills.

'Drink it, we need energy today.'

Magomeni was Sudi's territory, and he led the way to a *duka* that sold pirated DVDs and assorted electronics. Adam produced the laptop and a negotiation ensued. He asked for TSh300 000. The burly store owner offered TSh70 000. Adam dropped his price to TSh200 000 but the store owner flicked his fingers to indicate we might as well leave. A triangular yelling match ensued, with Sudi berating Adam passionately for behaving in an offensive manner on his turf. This caused Adam to stalk out of the shop, leaving Sudi to do the deal for TSh70 000.

'Memory is under too much pressure,' said Sudi, allowing Adam to get ahead some distance before explaining the source of his frustration. It had to do with *unga*, as I suspected. Sudi confirmed that the electronic goods I had brought to Dar es Salaam had been given to me by a drug dealer. The plan had been for Adam to sell the items and put the cash towards the purchase of a quantity of heroin, which he and Sudi would take back to Cape Town. Adam had promised the dealer half a kilogram, but this was unrealistic in the current environment. The last time Adam had moved through Dar es Salaam, the price for ten grams of heroin – one *ndonga* – had been TSh150 000, roughly US$100. This time, the lowest quote the Beachboys had sourced for a *ndonga* was TSh300 000. The price hike was a consequence of constrained supply, which the local newspapers, quoting government officials, had ascribed to the good work being done by a task force set up by President Jakaya Kikwete some years before.

On the streets, though, the traffickers were saying the shortage was attributable to the president's son, Ridhiwani Kikwete, widely believed to be one of the nation's biggest importers of heroin. He had been caught – again, street rumours – trying to move a large shipment of the stuff out of China. Ordinarily this would have meant a short stay on death row in a Chinese prison, but Kikwete Jnr, or so ran the allegations, had returned home safe and sound, at about the time that a large gas prospecting concession was mysteriously plucked from the cradle of advanced tender processes and handed to a Chinese company.

Whatever the true causes, the increase in prices had landed Adam in a difficult position. In the days before I had arrived, said Sudi, he and Adam had visited several suppliers known to the Cape Town dealer. They had promised certain of these suppliers that they would be in touch when they had the money together, but it had been nearly a month. This morning one of the suppliers had called Adam's buyer in Cape Town to say he believed Adam was a phony, lacking both the money and the backbone to complete a serious deal. It was this information, relayed by the Cape Town dealer over the phone, which had sent Adam into this morning's defiant rage.

Still, the problem of money remained. Between them, Sudi and Adam had saved R5 000 of the bribe monies paid to them by the agent of the ship on which they had stowed away. The electrical hardware had collectively fetched TSh450 000, a portion of which had already been spent. By leaning on his tenants for their next rent instalments (a request so irregular it had nearly ended in violence), Sudi had manufactured a further TSh1 000 000, bringing the pot to almost TSh2 000 000. In *unga* terms, this equated to 60 grams, or six *ndongas*.

Even before Sudi had concluded his explanation I could feel myself being drawn inwards towards the problem. I braced for the inevitable.

'If you can maybe lend Memory TSh3 000 000,' said Sudi, 'we can buy nine more *ndongas*. I think everyone will be happy then, and we can leave Dar es Salaam.' Back in Cape Town, he said, we would cut the heroin with Panado and the leavened gear would fetch approximately four times the purchasing price, even at the current prices. I would, he assured me, double my investment.

I shook my head regretfully and told him that, as things stood, the amount required was ten times what I had in my bank account, and there was the journey back to South Africa to consider. He cut me off.

'It's okay, Sean, no problem.'

He never asked again.

With the question of my complicity resolved, the air cleared and Adam made his peace with the fact that they would only be able to afford six *ndongas*. After a short discussion with Sudi to determine a preferred seller, we set out in an easterly direction through Magomeni, stopping outside a small house with a red metal door. Sudi entered the house alone, leaving us in the shade of the buildings on the far side of the road. After half an hour he emerged in the company of a man with very dark skin.

'Tha's Senegal,' said Adam. 'He's a proper gangster, proper. The police know 'im. They want 'im.'

The heroin supplier was wearing an unbuttoned jeans vest, and jeans printed with a paint-spatter pattern. Multiple chains swung forwards off his chest when he leaned in to punch our fists.

'We got a deal?' Adam asked.

Sudi and Senegal nodded.

'Unbelievable, boys, unbelievable.' Adam knocked his fist around again, and danced off to fetch three Safari quarts from a nearby *duka*. We clinked the bottles and poured the cold beer into our mouths.

'I think we're ready to go to South Africa now.'

Senegal downed his beer and returned to his house. Adam waited until the red door had shut before saying, 'That nigger has the most expensive *unga* in Dar es Salaam I think, but we chose 'im because his brother lives in Cape Town. He knows that if he sells us shit, we got his brother. It's not really nice but we will be far away when we find out the quality of the drugs, so we must have insurance.'

Sudi stared off at three young girls climbing out of a *Bajaji*. They looked at us and giggled. He stood up, grabbed a sandalled foot, and stretched his thigh. This was a bittersweet moment for him. He would be leaving his wife and child again for an indeterminate period, and wanted to go directly to them now.

Adam downed his beer. 'Let's go.'

We followed Sudi into a quarter of Magomeni called Mwembechai, crossed a sandy football pitch and descended a long flight of cracked steps, stopping at a house that verged on the milky blue stream, overlooking a dumpsite.

'Nice, innit,' said Adam, jumping up to grab some green bananas from one of the plants flourishing by the water's edge. We found Sauda playing a game of bau indoors with Esau and her sister. They remained indoors, shy, but in due course spread their reed mats on the ground outside. The afternoon passed in quiet conversation and games of bau, and later Mama Esau served a meal of *ugali* and beans. Esau sat on his haunches, watching his father sitting shirtless against the wall of their home, balling pap and beans. When the meal was over he went to him with water and a dish. Sudi washed and dried his hands, and asked me for a piece of paper and a pen. Using my journal as a backboard he wrote a four-line note, which he handed back to Esau. The boy folded it and went scampering up the stairs, which had grown gloomy in the fading light.

'Time for us to take a walk too,' said Adam.

Two teams were going at it on the football pitch, kicking up dust. The mouths of the surrounding *dukas* were bright with hurricane lamps, and the chairs put out by the owners were all occupied by spectators. Adam bought two beers, handing over more than the required amount.

'I bet on the team with no shirts on. There's a game here every evening, and betting on it is the big entertainment in Magomeni. The team that wins gets some of the money, so if you're in a good team you don't need a job, you can just play. Sudi used to be in a good team back in the day. He's a big guy here in Magomeni East, people respect 'im, and if they don't respect 'im, they fear him at least.'

Esau approached, skirting the crowd at the edge of the pitch. Adam took three strips of paper off him, each covered in Arabic sentences, written in red koki.

'The imam made a du'a for each of us and blessed it, so that we can have good luck on our journey.' Adam pocketed the precious slips. He made Esau stand beside us.

'Sudi need some more time alone with Sauda.'

The players played until the only light left was burning in the *dukas*. We remained, nursing our Serengetis until the shop owner came for his chairs. At Sauda's place we found Sudi packing his bag by the light of a paraffin lamp while his wife wound tape around the *ndongas*, increasing the girth of each until they resembled small grenades.

'Yow,' Adam gulped.

In Cape Town I had given Sudi an old pair of trainers, roughly five sizes too big for his feet, and it was these clown shoes that he laced up now before shouldering his pack and leaving the house. He and his wife walked hand in hand. At the top of the stairs they kissed and hugged, and then she turned and went back down into darkness. Esau continued walking, and would have followed us to the ends of the earth if Sudi hadn't stopped and told him to go home. He shook the boy's hand formally and cuffed his head. The boy ran off without a word.

With the aim of acquiring a small store of *unga* for travel purposes, Sudi led a route down narrow alleyways flooded with sewage into which bricks had been dropped at regular intervals. He picked these out with his cellphone's torch beam, and we proceeded carefully from one brick to the next, hands on the walls on either side, until we reached the Magomeni *maskani*. Heroin had been the great constant of our days in Dar es Salaam, and wherever we happened to travel – Sinza, Kigamboni, Posta, Magomeni, Temeke – part of the day or night had been spent in the local *unga* house. In Temeke, this had been a yard between three houses, accessible at the front from the road and at the back through the house in which the dealer and his family lived (although as a rule this was only used as an escape route in case of police raids). In Posta, it had been tents on the beach.

The *maskani* we turned into now comprised a series of lean-tos at the back of a double-storey building. Panels of plywood propped on tyres served as tables; around each of these, thirty to forty men sat smoking. It was all they were doing. There was no *gongo*, no beer, only smouldering cocktails and the detritus of cocktail production: marijuana stalks and pips, broken tiles, bits of metal, burned-up matches and twisted boxes of Sportsman cigarettes, which the smokers call Sports. Strips of *kattes* were being passed around, long as the tails of kites. Sealed into every inch was a grain of heroin no bigger than the Imodium tablets I'd been taking for my chronically unsettled stomach. Each table seemed to have its own psychic weather. At some, the men said nothing at all, and seemed not to notice what was happening beyond their own hands. At others, conversation burned like boiler fire, rising in anabatic walls.

I mentioned this observation to Adam, who said it was quite normal. 'People sit here for hours, days even. When they are high, everyone is high together. When one person is *tinga*, all the others at his table will soon be *tinga*, too.'

Just occasionally, he said, the tables fell into step.

'When this happens you get what we call a beach fire, a party you have to see with your own eyes to believe it is possible.'

We joined the table of euphorics, Adam scuttling around with TSh10 000 notes, posing for photographs with his face alongside long, humpy lines of heroin. I was given a prime seat and offered a line to sniff. For perhaps half an hour the air became hot and the volume of conversations increased dramatically. Then quite suddenly everyone fell silent, closed their eyes and turned their palms upwards in front of their chests. Sudi began chanting a well-known supplication for travel.

Allahu Akbar, Allahu Akbar, Allahu Akbar, Subhanalazi Sakharalanaa haza wa ma kunna lahu muqrineena wa innaa ilaa rabbinaa lamunqalibun, Allahuma nina nas'aluka fi safarina hazal Biraa wal Taqwa, wa minal Amali ma tardha, Allahumma hawwin alayna safarana haza watwiannaa bu'dah Allahumma anta as-Sahibu fi safar, wal khalifatu fil ahl, Allahumma inni auzubika min wa'thaa'i as-safar, wa kaabati al mandhar wa soow'i al munqalab fil maali wal Ahl.

'Amin,' the smokers all said at once, 'Amin', and they came in search of our hands, shaking them meaningfully and saying good luck, good luck, Allah be with you. Then we were off, once again picking out bricks in sewage.

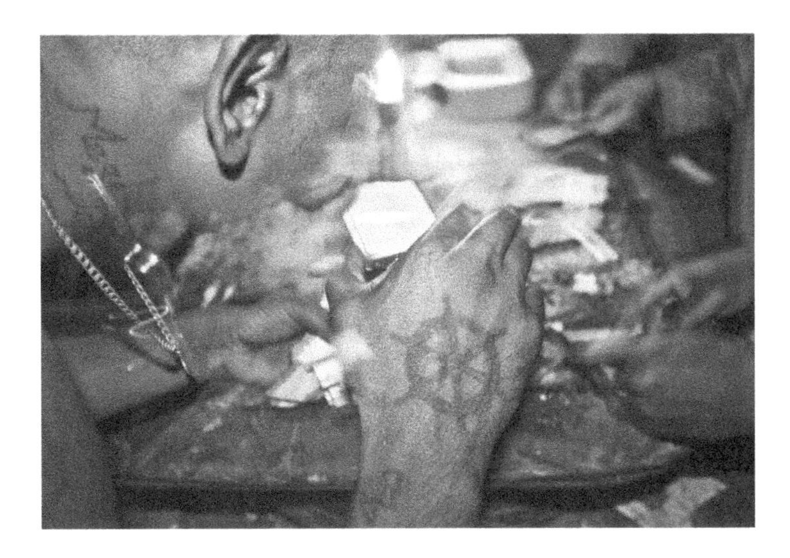

I wanted to throw up when we reached the hitchhiking point on the side of Morogoro Road, a place called Kimala. I started stumbling off towards the banks of a small river but Adam called after me.

'Yow Sean, we going.'

I looked back to see a newspaper delivery truck idling in the road. One at a time we clambered over the tailgate into a dark Tetris-scape of newspaper parcels.

'*Chukua safari ki*,' said Sudi, and giggled.

Our small, dark capsule travelled southwards at high speeds, and each bump in the road caused our bodies to sink deeper into the freight. Blind and covered in parcels we passed through or skirted some of the places tourists come to Tanzania to see – Kitulanghalo Forest Reserve, Mikumi National Park, Udzungwa Mountains National Park. We saw nothing, only the shut-up *dukas* in the deserted towns we stopped in to make newspaper drops: Kibaha, Mlandizi, Morogoro, Mikumi, Iringa. Every stop was a blow to our comfort, as more and more of the relatively soft parcels disappeared until we were left sitting on the bones of the truck bed.

By the time we reached Makambako, it was light. We had covered 655 kilometres in six hours with six stops. Allah, said Sudi, was watching over us. We all sat up on the last stretch to Mbeya, light shafting through the partially open door, catching the swirling smoke from the morning joints. Adam opened one of the brown-paper packages and studied the front page of *The Citizen* newspaper.

'It say here that the government has been kicking thousands of foreigners out of the country. Malawians are being beaten and raped in Iringa Province.'

'Not good,' said Sudi. 'The Malawian police are going to be angry.'

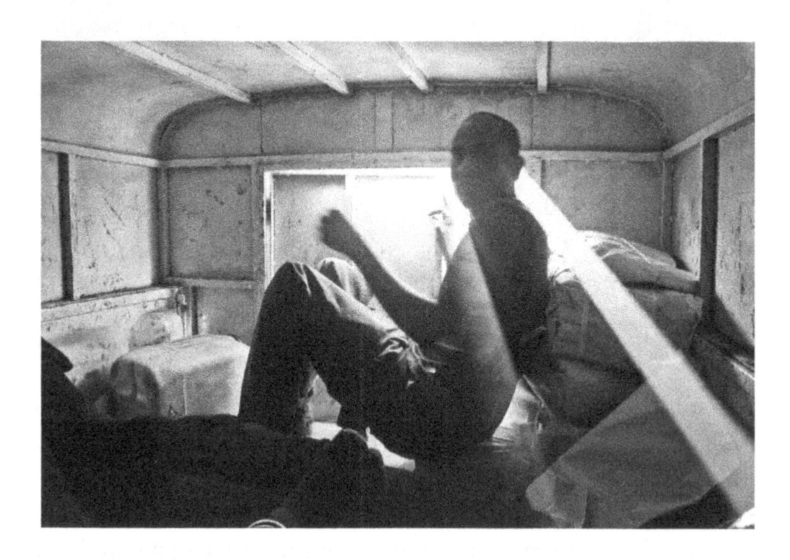

At the Mbeya bus terminus, the driver shooed us out of the cab lest anyone from his company cotton on to his racket. Minutes later we were rolling again, standing in the aisle of a packed *daladala*. The vehicle climbed slowly through the tea-covered hills around Ipinda, and descended much more quickly to the Tanzania–Malawi border post on the Songwe River. We clambered out at the main intersection of Kasumulu town and headed for the market, where Adam and Sudi bought a few cobs of weed and three yellow fever certificates. They took turns entering the dealer's long drop to stow their *ndongas*. Then they called for bottles of water. When these arrived they removed the Qur'anic prayer papers from their pockets and fed them down the necks of the bottles. We watched the paper relax and slowly sink, the red ink drifting free in hazy trails. I followed their example and we all took several sips while Sudi led us in another du'a.

Tension filled our bodies on the short walk to the border. I went into the immigration office first. When I exited, a large-bodied man in slacks and a polo shirt was pointing at Sudi's *kofia*.

'Are you a holy man?' he asked. 'Are you going to say a du'a for us?'

Sudi said, 'No, why do you need a du'a? You don't need a du'a?'

The man flashed an identity card.

'Tanzanian intelligence, come with me.'

Adam was exiting the office as they passed. 'You too, beach-y boy,' the officer said.

I positioned myself on the loading wall of the truck bay, feigning calm under the gaze of interested officials. Half an hour passed before the friends reappeared. Adam signalled that I should follow. We walked in silence to the bridge over the Songwe.

When we were closer to the Malawian post than the Tanzanian, Adam said, 'I was honest with 'im. I said we are going to South Africa to look for ships, hoping for a better life. I told him you were with us, to tell our story. He took TSh20 000 and told us to go.'

On the other side we were swarmed by money traders, and I realised I was sick. I had put my chronically sore throat down to smoking too many Sports in Dar es Salaam's *unga* houses, but now my head hurt and my skin felt clammy. I thought, *Please, just not malaria*.

We had our documents stamped by Malawian officials, who could not have seemed less interested in our travel plans.

'I know a place where you can rest,' said Adam. 'The bus to Lilongwe is only leaving tonight, in any case.'

The traders fell away as we turned off the road and started to climb into the hills above the river. Our path bisected a small village of adobe huts and continued towards a line of trees growing alongside a dry riverbed. On the far bank, under a canopy of knitted branches, a dozen young men were sitting around on tyres and paint drums, playing bau or filling shopping bags from an enormous pile of dried marijuana plants.

They greeted Adam warmly.

'Back so soon!'

Taking a bucket, Adam walked down to the riverbed and began to dig. Sudi joined him and soon the hole they had scooped out was full of water. Adam ladled it into the bucket with a sawn-off Coca-Cola bottle.

'Have a wash,' he said. 'Nobody will mind.'

The water was cold – earth water. I brushed my teeth with it, rinsed my mouth and felt better. Sudi stripped off his pants a few metres down the course and had a shit.

'There are good places on this road,' said Adam. 'Some good people, too, like these guys. They never go nowhere, just sit here every day and smoke weed, but they're good guys. You can come back to this *maskani* anytime now and you will be welcomed.'

Taking a different path back to the road, Adam ran ahead to see about buying tickets for the evening bus to Lilongwe. Sudi and I passed a group of teenagers sitting in the grass, who pointed at us and said some things I did not catch. Sudi evidently did, because he walked over and punched the first of them to stand and face him. The youth fell to the ground and put his knees up in surrender. Sudi was not done. He stood over them and gave a short lecture, emphasising his points with shakes of a crooked finger. When he was done the boys stood and shook my hand, saying, 'Sorry, sorry.'

'They said a bad thing about us,' said Sudi. 'They saw us walking out of the bushes and thought we must be doing something there. This one,' he pointed to the boy with the swollen cheek, 'said it must be that we are gay, because I am wearing an earring in my right ear. I told them I am a seaman, and seamen are allowed to wear an earring in this ear. Now they understand.'

Adam came running up the path.

'Hurry, the bus is leaving.'

We sprinted after him and clambered aboard, taking seats in different rows. The prospect of progressing all night without incident was delicious, but the bus had hardly hit its cruising speed when we struck a roadblock, outside Kaporo. Three policemen in white uniforms boarded the bus and did the you, you and you thing, unerringly picking out all the Tanzanian passengers without having to ask for their travel documents. A collective grumble went up from the Malawians.

'Why do they stop these people?' asked the man sitting next to me, an apple and orange salesman from Mzuzu. 'Do they think they will find something wrong with their documentation that the immigration officials did not?'

In time the Tanzanians were permitted to return to the bus, all except Adam and Sudi. Then they appeared too, and the bus started moving.

'They locked us up,' said Adam. 'They read about the Tanzanians killing Malawians in Iringa. They said we were going to have to take a punishment for this violence. They just wanted money, really, but when they could see that we were going to give them *fokol* they let us go.'

A roadblock outside Mwenitete was a copy of the earlier experience and in Karonga, where the bus stopped in the transport terminal for an hour, an off-duty policeman sidled up to Sudi and began questioning him. I tried to intervene by asking why he and his associates were so hard on travellers with legitimate, stamped documents. The ploy worked, and the policeman became philosophical.

'When you have something it is easier to accept that everyone has a struggle, and you don't need to make life more difficult than it has to be. But sometimes you have nothing, and then you must look for opportunity.'

The bus pulled into Lilongwe's Old Town precinct at about noon the next day and by mid afternoon we were on a taxi bound for the border with Mozambique, just beyond the town of Dedza. The officials on the Mozambican side knew all about opportunity. They wanted a bribe each from the Beachboys for stamping their emergency papers, and MT3 000 on top of this because their names and addresses weren't inscribed on the inside of their yellow fever certificates (they were written on the outside). Their ploy with me was to claim that I would not be able to enter the country on a transit visa, as their transit visa stamp was malfunctioning. Instead, I would have to pay three times the amount for a holiday visa. Adam and Sudi were nowhere to be seen when I emerged from the post, virtually broke. A young woman approached me to say that they would be back soon and, if I would follow her, she would take me to the lift she had negotiated on our behalf.

'Yolanda,' she said, shaking my hand firmly.

The ride was a yellow, long-nose truck joined to an empty trailer.

'We must wait for your friends before getting in,' Yolanda said, as taxi touts began to gather around, shouting at us in Nyanja. The problem, she whispered, was that the taxi criers did not appreciate truckers taking their business.

She became restless. 'Where are your friends? We need to move.' When Adam and Sudi finally appeared at a run, the threat of violence was in the air. The truck driver took off at speed, rocks clattering on his trailer.

The Beachboys clambered onto the back bunk alongside Yolanda and the trucker's turn boy. Her face was waxy with travel, but her eyes were alert. She looked to be in her mid thirties.

'Sister, you really helped us,' said Adam. 'You are our first angel of the road.'

The three of them hit it off instantly. The Beachboys had travelled these roads a dozen times each, but Yolanda lived on them. She explained that she had been married to a good man, the man of a lifetime, but he had been murdered in 2008 in South Africa, a victim of the xenophobic violence that had exploded in the country's townships in the month of May. To keep ahead of her grief she had focused on business, using the region's trucks as transport to fetch goods that were scarce in her home city of Beira.

Her stories lifted the mood in the cab, though Sudi had fallen sick with withdrawal. When darkness fell, the smell of burning *unga* wafted through from the back bunks. '*Nime pona* [I feel better],' he cried, in a shrill falsetto. We had a problem with money, though. Between us we were MT200 short of the fare that Yolanda had negotiated with the driver. When we made this known on the outskirts of Tete, the driver promptly pulled over and dumped us on the side of the road – Yolanda, too. This was no minor inconvenience, because the discovery of the nearby Moatize coalfields had pushed the city limits out by ten kilometres in under a decade. And since this was a boomtown, with all the criminal issues that come with rapid expansion, nobody in their right mind would stop to pick up a group of men after dark. To get around this, Yolanda took off her jacket, rolled her shirt up beneath her breasts and put out her thumb, telling us to hang back in the shadows.

It wasn't long before a pickup stopped. The driver, appreciating the ruse, invited us to clamber aboard. With the wind in our clothes we felt cooler than we had in days. Samora Machel Bridge was lit up, the Zambezi River a dark abyss below.

Our ride dropped us beside the night market at the riverside. This, Yolanda said, was the place for catching southbound trucks. She doubted any would be leaving in the night but promised to ask around. We sat in the dust beside the road. Adam bought a beer and a friendly Mozambican businessman bought one for me. Prostitutes paraded among us but left when it became clear that we had no money. I was still not feeling particularly well; since the Beachboys seemed in no hurry to resolve our transport problem, I joined Yolanda, who was drinking with two truckers – one an elderly mestizo, moustachioed and wearing a red vest, and the other a Somali who looked to be in his early forties.

'You have a lift to Inchope tomorrow, I think. This Somali man will take two, and his friend will take one. They will sleep here tonight and leave at about 3 a.m. You can relax on the back of the trucks tonight, because they are carrying no loads. In the morning you can sleep in the cabs on the road. I'll be going with.'

We had spent all our meticais, however, and although Sudi had R800 stowed up his backside the truckers doubted they would be able to convert this to local currency along their route, and refused to take payment in rands. I produced my BlackBerry. 'That will work,' said Yolanda. She thought for a minute, made a phone call, and then proposed buying the phone off me herself for the price of three fares to Inchope, with dinner thrown in. Satisfied with the arrangement, the truckers drained their Laurentina Blacks and walked over to their rigs.

Yolanda opened her luggage and produced two colourful *khangas*, which she said we could spread on the cold metal of the trailer, humping our shoes under the edges to make pillows. The Saturday night revelry in the riverside bars continued until after midnight; when the music dimmed and then ended, the sound of mosquitoes came up. Light broke over the Zambezi at about 4.30 a.m. and, at six, the drivers cracked open their doors, pissed at the roadside and washed their faces with bottled water. At about seven, the Somali invited us up into his cab, and then walked a little way down the road, trying to call Yolanda, who was nowhere to be seen.

'Did you already give the girl the phone?' Adam asked.

'Yes.'

'Then she's gone, man. We're fucked.'

Preoccupied with this new predicament, I hardly noticed Adam's hand whistling past my head. He burrowed into the storage space in the upper console porthole and came away with the trucker's fat wallet.

'Nah man, put it back,' I hissed.

'Chill,' said Adam. 'This man has too much money. Is he coming?'

'Uh –' I glanced at the trucker, still with his phone to his ear, '– no.'

'And now?'

'No.'

When the Somali turned to face the cab, the wallet was back in its place.

'It's all right, Sean,' said Adam, stowing his takings under the inner sole of his right shoe. 'We don't take everything, just a little. This trucker was drunk last night, and I know he hasn't counted his money this morning. Trust me, this is how we do it.'

Adam had taken MT1 200, about R300. If Yolanda had run off with my phone, it was possibly just enough to get us to Inchope, as planned. Yolanda did appear, though, at a run. She arrived out of breath and smelling of spirits.

'I overslept, I'm so sorry. I was drinking till 5 a.m., then I went to this other place to sleep.'

With Sudi installed in the second cab, the truckers pressurised their brakes and started off. Yolanda and Adam were soon snoring away on the bottom and top bunks, leaving me to undergo the mortification of the Somali's first stop alone. He grabbed his wallet, went through his money slowly and pulled some notes out. When he clambered back in with a haul of potatoes and charcoal, his expression was untroubled. Steering the truck down the 102, he asked what our business was. I explained that the other two were full-time stowaways, and I was planning to tell their stories.

'Lot of stories on this road,' he said.

His own story eclipsed most for interest. He said he had lived the life of a trucker since the late eighties, first as a turn boy in Somalia, fagging for older truckers on the increasingly fraught Mogadishu–Addis and Mogadishu–Nairobi routes, and then as a licensed driver of super rigs in Kenya. He had worked out of Mombasa first and then Dar es Salaam, moving goods inland to Kigali, Lusaka, Lilongwe, even as far west as Kinshasa, along the delta of roads known collectively as the Trans-African Highway.

In 2003, he started to hear of opportunities to the south.

'Everyone knew that you can sell anything in Zimbabwe at this time – clothes, food, even soap, you could sell it, because in the shops there was nothing.'

There was also, of course, the diamond game – the opportunity to mule rough stones from Zimbabwe's Chiadzwa diamond fields over the Machipanda border, taking them on to Chimoio, which has an airport.

'That was a good time,' said Yolanda, now awake and sitting on the bunk. 'If you are interested in diamonds, I can still get them for you.' Or, if I knew the right people, she offered to show me where she had buried a sizeable rhino horn in a field on the outskirts of Beira. The Somali smiled. The two, clearly, were old confederates.

We made several more stops for provisions, which included a chicken, two pigeons in a reed cage, several more sacks of charcoal, a goat and a large bunch of sugar-cane stalks. The pigeons were layered one on top of the other in the tiny reed cage, and whenever the cab jounced they pecked at each other's heads for a few seconds before falling still again. The chicken hid itself behind my seat and merely panted, if chickens can be said to pant. Yolanda clambered out in Chimoio and met her brother, who gave her money for the BlackBerry, enough for our passage and an additional MT200 for good measure. We thanked her profusely.

'God bless you, sister,' said Adam.

Inchope was the end of the line for the two truckers, but, before they continued eastwards to Beira, Adam insisted they both sit down for a chicken lunch, which he paid for with the stolen notes. I wanted a wash, and struck it lucky at the Estalagem Bambamba, a trucker's lodge, restaurant and bar. The proprietor handed me a full bucket of well water and a begrimed plastic cup, and pointed in the direction of the toilet. Like so many bathrooms on Africa's east coast, the sheet-metal room comprised a large keyhole of porcelain above a pit latrine. Elevated slightly above this was the bathing slab, designed to drain directly into the pit. The stench was bad but the water was cool and the road dirt came off with my shampoo and disappeared into the dark latrine.

I returned to find Sudi in an agitated state. He knew that Adam had been arrested in Inchope in 2010, so he considered the place cursed. Nothing Adam said could convince him to walk with us along the EN1 highway to the hitchhiking spot. Instead, he went snaking between the roadside huts and houses, and across a ploughed field.

'Sudi spent six months in a prison in Senegal,' Adam explained. 'It was the worst experience of his life. He went in with three other Beachboys, and the other prisoners told them straight that they would all die there, in that prison. The other three guys did die. Sudi was the only one who made it out. He said it was kill or be killed in there. He doesn't really talk about it, but now he takes no chances.'

We arrived at the hitchhiking place, which was also the local *maskani*. Several Inchope youths lounged around on reed mats, spread next to a stall at which you could charge your cellphone, if need be.

'*Oya*,' said Adam.

'*Oya vipi*,' replied one of the sitters, who was wearing a yellow T-shirt emblazoned with the face of Jacob Zuma.

Adam and the youth carried on a conversation in halting Swahili. Sudi translated.

'This brother learnt to speak Swahili from a Beachboy called Kacho Lee. Kacho came here in 2001, and he stayed in Inchope for 11 years. He still got a child here, with a Mozambique woman. They say this brother went to South Africa last year but Memory told him we haven't seen him yet. They want us to tell Kacho that his girlfriend already gave her pussy to another man.'

The man in the Zuma shirt remembered Adam from a previous trip, and invited us to sit on the mat while he ran off to rustle up some marijuana. Set back from the road a hundred metres or so was a small army camp, outside which off-duty soldiers went to and fro carrying large containers of water. Sudi couldn't take his eyes off it.

'It's okay, Sudi,' said Adam. 'These boys told me the army don't care about smoking. They're here because terrorists have been attacking some trucks on the road.'

I'd read about this. A month before I had flown to Dar es Salaam, a militant wing of Mozambique's opposition party, Renamo, had attacked a passenger bus and a truck on the EN1 in Sofala Province, not far south of where we were. The ambush had sparked fears of a bloody afterword to the civil war of the seventies, but the Frelimo-controlled army had been quick to react, overrunning the provincial base of the Renamo leader, Afonso Dhlakama. But the threat of hit-and-run ambushes by the retreating militants remained very real – at least, that had been the situation before I had left Cape Town.

Adam confirmed that little had changed. 'These boys say we gonna struggle to pick a truck on this road because it's already late in the day, and the drivers are too scared to drive at night. They say there's a bus coming, though, from Nacala. It was supposed to pass this way already but it had a breakdown, so the company sent another bus from Nampula to pick up the passengers.'

The lads asked how much money we had.

Sudi produced his R800, and put it together with Adam's remaining meticais.

'Hmm, *dogo* [little].'

Nevertheless, when the bus arrived the wide boys crowded around the door and thrust our money at the conductor, imploring him to take it. 'Come,' the conductor grunted, waving us in with a beefy arm. It was just after 5 p.m., and before long the thorn scrub of the north had ceded to forests of palms. An hour later the bus stopped in a small roadside village, and the passengers began disembarking.

'The bus is stoppin' for the night,' said Adam. 'The driver is too scared to carry on.'

We took up residence on the porch of a small shop, and the Beachboys wasted no time placing some *unga* on a piece of broken glass, which they heated with burning corn husks. They smoked a cocktail in plain sight and began jabbering away. I was having difficulty keeping up, and when my head started nodding Sudi went off and found me a sack to lie on, Culemborg-style. I found the gesture deeply moving. Both Sudi and Adam had, for weeks now, put my comfort and safety ahead of their own – I who had left a comfortable life just for a time, and would soon be comfortable again. Their behaviour towards me had been a requirement of my ignorance and helplessness initially, but now something else was going on. I had been steadily growing into the role of the group moderator, cautioning against behaviour that might disrupt our progress and anticipating crises that we may steer clear of disaster. In Dar es Salaam I had merely functioned, at times, as a patron. Here, under the palms of this anonymous village in Mozambique, all of us virtually penniless, I felt I was being recognised, by Sudi's gesture, for other values. We were, finally, a team of friends on a journey, quite equal.

Not long after I bedded down, Sudi made his own bed on the porch of the neighbouring shop, wrapping the strap of my bag around one of his arms. The village became very quiet, save for the occasional growling of dogs and, deep in the night, a horrific wail from Sudi. By the light of a slender moon I saw him leave his sleeping place and kneel on the ground, where he mumbled to himself for several minutes, beating his chest with a fist. When the bus driver turned the ignition on at 3 a.m., we woke up and clambered aboard. Sudi explained that he'd had a nightmare. Someone without a face had put hands around his throat, and he had been unable to break the grip.

The journey onwards was a long one, with many stops. Passing through the village of Muxungue the bus went over a dog, and from my seat at the back I saw the poor creature rolling down the road behind us. Remarkably, it ended upright, and limped off the road, mouth open in a howl I could not hear over the roar of the engine. At Xai-Xai, where the Limpopo River meets the Indian Ocean, a young policeman boarded the bus and looked hard at Adam and Sudi's papers, but became distracted by the kid sitting next to Sudi, who had no identification documents of any kind.

'Off the bus,' the officer ordered.

The boy did not understand, so the officer pulled him out of his seat. Several surrounding passengers implored him to stop, saying that the boy belonged to a group of northern Mozambicans scattered around the bus who could vouch for his nationality. The officer put this to the boy's travel companions and they nodded, which won them a rebuke for being too cowardly to speak up for their brother.

The distances between police stops shortened as we neared the capital city, and the mood in the bus became correspondingly tense. At a stop near Maputo International Airport, Adam said, 'Let's go,' and unexpectedly left the bus. Sudi grabbed my bag and followed.

I had to jog to catch up with them. Our sudden disembarkation made no sense. The skyscrapers of the city centre were matchboxes in the distance.

'Why are we getting out here?'

Adam retrieved a red Nokia phone from his pants.

'Oh.'

'Sudi took this from the boy sitting next to him, the one with no papers.'

I winced. The phone was almost certainly the most valuable thing the boy had owned, his connection, perhaps, to the rural home he was clearly leaving for the first time. Adam caught my expression.

'Sean, remember when I said there's always a way? Well, this is the way. Come, we need to move if we gonna make it to the city centre by night.'

There was no talk as we crossed the bridge over Avenida Joaquim Chissano, going down the on-ramp to the lanes coming out from the city. We slipped under Rua Carlos Morgada and Adam said, 'We're back in bridge country, brothers.'

Sudi kept on at a punishing pace, reiterating Adam's point about the importance of finding lodgings before sunset. I required no further encouragement, and broke into a jog. 'Yes, yes,' said Sudi, leading us right at a run down Avenida Angola. We entered Mafalala, the city's oldest township, on the unpaved Rua Da Guine, coming to a halt under a large flame tree, the roots of which had broken through the pavement.

'Sudi reminded me now that we need to explain something. You must not talk about *chakula* here,' Adam whispered, using the Cape code for heroin. 'There are many Tanzanians living in Maputo, many Beach-boys, but they are not all good. The ones who have killed in South Africa, the big criminals, they run to Maputo, and they stay around this area, which we call Strela Market. If the wrong people hear we have stuff, they will rob us, maybe even kill us. Or they will call the police to arrest us, and then share the *chakula* with them. That is how it works here.'

A queue had formed outside a nearby bakery, and one of the men standing there raised his hand as we passed.

'*Vipi* Memory!'

'Ah, Moshe, respect man.'

Adam and Sudi took turns hugging the man, who had shed all vestiges of youth. His front teeth were missing from his broad smile and, like most of the men going about the street, he was dressed in shorts, a vest and sandals.

'Moshe's a Beachboy from Richards Bay community,' Adam explained. 'He was nineties generation, with Dullah Macho Mzungu and the boys, but he had to run away a few years ago.'

The reason for this was simple. Positioned midway between the Mozambican border and the city of Durban, the Richards Bay Beachboys had been able to establish a degree of control over the heroin flow into South Africa from Africa's east coast. They would either buy or steal the stuff from the independent mules who stopped in, or they would travel to Maputo to fetch it from the Tanzanian suppliers there. To protect their patch, the controlling clique of Richards Bay Beachboys had been in the habit of giving new arrivals the taxi fare to Durban, and suggesting that they leave while they were still able to walk. But even these measures failed to prevent chronic infighting – 'Bad *unga* politics' – and Richards Bay had developed a reputation for 'bongo-to-bongo' killings. The last murder had occurred in 2012: a denizen of the Richards Bay community had been accused of stealing another dealer's stash, and a group of Beachboys had beaten the suspect to death and buried his body in the forest. Not only had it come to light that the victim had been innocent, but the police had found the body, and practically the whole community had fled over the border to Maputo – Moshe included.

'He's been in Maputo a year and a half now,' said Adam. 'I feel sorry for him. He can't go back to Dar es Salaam because he has spent more time out of Tanzania than in. He can't go back to South Africa, because the police want him. He has no choice but to stay here, where he is nobody, really. So he just smokes *unga* and drinks. That's why he looks so old.'

Adam tried to break the end off the small baguette Moshe had just bought but the older man knocked his hand away with a smile.

'See what I mean about Maputo? Every Beachboy just thinks about hisself here.'

With light draining from the street, Sudi pushed the issue of accommodation.

'Come,' said the veteran Beachboy, leading us down a series of narrow alleyways. The houses had the grey, drowned look of all mature slums, the stained, windowless walls suggesting that another Mafalala – the real Mafalala – lay on the other side. At the end of a cul-de-sac Moshe rapped lightly on a door, which opened an inch. An eye appeared through the slat and at ground level I could see a foot in a sandal, running up into a brown shin covered in light hair. The door opened wider and a wiry mestizo in red-and-green plus fours slipped out. Moshe introduced him as Tony Moto. He did not look pleased to see us. He shouted at Moshe in Portuguese. Adam had already turned to leave when Moshe said, 'Tony says you can stay, MT20 each, but you must leave early tomorrow, as soon as the sun comes up.'

The room we entered was lit by a single halogen strip light, the casement hanging free of the ceiling on one side. Three men on plastic chairs craned their heads towards a small battery-powered radio, listening to an animated Portuguese newscast. We crossed into the next room, where a hi-fi system wired up to a car battery blasted scratchy Marrabenta tunes. On the opposite side of the room, a dented pot bubbled away on a blackened coal stove.

Tony Moto took up the head of a grass broom and lightly swept the area next to the stove.

'Can't expect no more for MT20,' said Adam.

Outside in the back yard, two old drunkards were nursing a half-jack of *kachasu*, their backs against the breeze-block perimeter wall. There was a door in the wall, and every few minutes someone knocked on it. If nobody came to lift the latch, a piece of metal would appear between the wall and the door and the latch would be knocked upwards from the outside. The world beyond that door, said Moshe, was dangerous, a slum within the slum, dense with rickety *mchondolos*. It was feared by women especially. A woman or a girl could be walking one of its many narrow paths, he said, and an arm might shoot out from a hovel. They could scream, but nobody would come looking for them. The only ones who could walk the labyrinth unmolested at night were sinewy old mestizo drunkards, like the two men before us.

Tony came out, shirtless, a white towel around his waist. Before disappearing around the corner for his evening wash he hung a blanket up on the wash line, and said it was ours for sleeping on. The moon rose and showed up the holes in the blanket.

Adam produced the red Nokia from his pants. 'Sudi, go make paper please,' he said, handing it over. Sudi left with Moshe, returning after half an hour with MT350.

Adam made no effort to hide his disappointment. 'Sudi, this is fuck-all man, you bin robbed.'

He stood and motioned Moshe to follow him, and the pair returned an hour later with a plastic bag full of fried rice and two bottles of Laurentina Black. To pay for our dinner Adam had pawned a silver medallion he had bought in England, the only physical thing he had left from this time. We moved inside and sat on the floor around the bag, balling rice, eating in silence. Adam said something out of the side of a full mouth, and Sudi grew visibly tense.

'You know who I just saw, outside in the street? You'll never believe it.'

I didn't have to be told. For the first time in weeks I felt my cheeks go cold with worry. Sudi, grim-faced, set about sweeping the fallen rice grains together with a piece of cardboard, pinching up the strays with his fingers.

'Did he see you?' Sudi asked.

'Nah, he never saw me.'

When he was done cleaning up Sudi poured Swahili into our small circle at an incredible rate. I could not understand a word, but it was quite clear what he was proposing.

'Chill, Sudi,' said Adam. 'Let's discuss.'

Out on the bench in the yard, the Beachboys conferred with Moshe, who pointed at the steel door in the yard wall. Adam jumped up and put his hands to his head.

'No way. What you telling me, Mosh?'

He turned to me.

'Moshe say our boy stays in there, less than fifty metres away. He even comes in here sometime, to buy his drink. I don't know what we gonna do now. Sudi say it's like Allah has led us to 'im, or maybe Aubadeeleh is leading us – Aubadeeleh's ghost.'

The conference resumed in low tones. Sudi was out for vengeance, that much was clear. Tonight, he said. It had to be tonight.

'If we do something we gonna have to run,' said Adam. 'In this place we not gonna have the support of the other Beachboys. Too many of them have killed before. If we do something against 'im, it's like we attack them all.'

Tony Moto came out into the yard and looked at the moon.

'You got a Rizla, bra?' Adam asked.

'No,' said Tony, and walked back inside.

Sudi asked Moshe where he could get his hands on a small container of petrol. The old Beachboy became angry, flipping over to English to limit the potential for eavesdropping.

'If you put a fire in this place it will go to other houses. Everything is touching in this place.'

Adam and I both agreed: burning Chawa Suga alive in his *mchondolo* was a very bad idea.

The mood became less awful the longer the Beachboys talked. Sudi seemed to take some comfort in Moshe's description of the murderer's arrival in Maputo. From day one he had smoked *unga*, said Moshe, starting early in the morning and going until he could hardly stand. One night he had passed out in an *unga* house in the neighbouring slum of Malhangalene. A group of middle-aged Tanzanians had taken turns raping him. Since that time, he had been like a dead man in a living body. He was hard, though, Moshe admitted. He never cried. He still smoked in the same *unga* house. The men who had raped him no longer did.

'Allah judge him already,' Sudi mumbled, and that seemed to be the end of it. The conversation turned to the next leg of our journey.

'Where are you going to jump the border?' Moshe wanted to know.

Adam explained the plan. We would head east to Namaacha on the border with Swaziland. After jumping the border we would catch a truck or taxi north-east to the Jeppes Reef border post with South Africa, near Driekoppies Dam, where we would jump again, and take a taxi directly to Malelane, alongside the N4. From Malelane we would proceed directly to Johannesburg.

'We will be there tomorrow tonight,' Adam reckoned.

Moshe did not think so. Things were not what they once were on the eastern borders, he said. The South African government had deployed soldiers, and the Swazis were cracking down, too. The better strategy, he felt, would be to cross the mouth of Maputo harbour and head for the southernmost border with South Africa, just beyond Ponta do Ouro. Moshe said he smuggled cigarettes through that portion of the border all the time. Sudi nodded vigorously. He said it was true: he had crossed that way five times himself without experiencing any hassles.

'Okay, we trust you Moshe. Sea Power.' Adam took MT50 from his shoe and handed it over. The middle-aged Beachboy's face brightened, and he hurried out of the yard through the metal door. We moved into the kitchen.

'Do you trust Moshe?'

'Don't worry about it, we're safe tonight,' Adam assured me, spreading the holey blanket on the floor.

Sudi said a du'a for good measure and wrapped the straps of my rucksack around his feet. We lay back and closed our eyes against the light and the music. I sat up in the dark much later, woken by the sound of the latch in the yard being knocked up. Footsteps approached the kitchen door and stopped. Sudi, up on one elbow, had his *kisu* gripped tightly in his left hand. In the moonlight we could both see the silver door handle moving up and down, a thing swimming in the gloom.

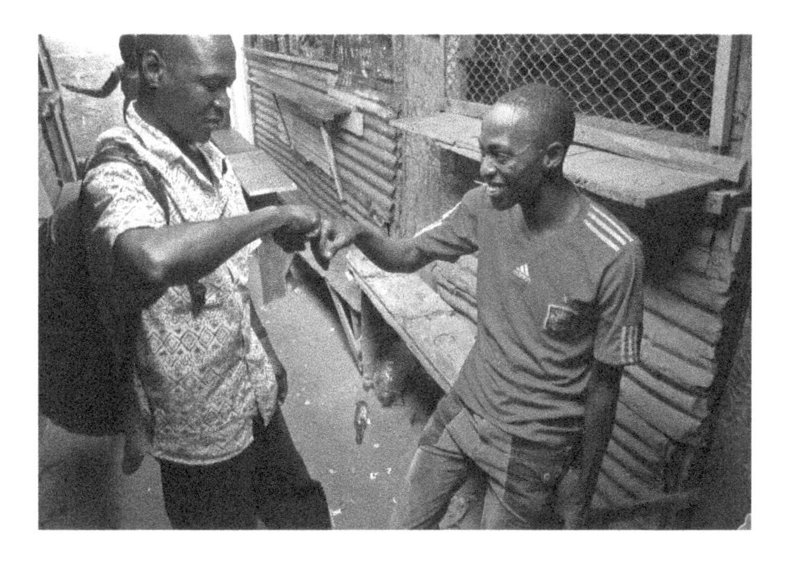

'*Oya*, who there?' he growled.

'Me, Moshe.'

The door banged open and the old Beachboy stumbled in carrying an old car seat, which he set down alongside our blanket. The backrest had been snapped to make a mattress of sorts. After some grunting he lay back on it and pulled some plastic sheets over his body, to keep off the mosquitoes. He passed out within seconds, the alcohol on his breath infecting the room.

◆

The house was up and in the back yard at about 6 a.m., enjoying the cool while it lasted.

Three moustachioed mestizos came through the metal door and took up their regular seats. They were neatly dressed in chinos and collared shirts, but their faces were parched and the one's feet and ankles were messes of peeling skin, dense with flies in no time at all. Tony Moto produced a half-jack of Big Boss whisky and a fluted pewter cup, which was filled, downed and passed on. More people joined the group of boozers and by 7 a.m. they were through a second bottle of Boss. Tony, who seemed to have decided we were not such bad guys after all, came over with some marijuana and a section of toilet-roll wrapper, which he tore up into make-do rolling papers. Adam thanked him at length and the two smoked together and talked about their children. Tony said he had two under school age. The mother was not around so he was raising them. He wouldn't have turned his place into a doss house and shebeen otherwise, he said. He worried about their safety, quite frankly, what with all the people coming and going. Adam said he thanked Allah every day that his daughter was in England, and that her mother was a strong woman.

Moshe came back from his morning wash and pulled his socks and shoes on in the yard.

'Time to go,' he said. 'The border is near but the road is bad.'

By 9 a.m. we were in the labyrinthine central market off Avenida 25 de Setembro, eating bloody chicken legs off a bed of doughy noodles and salad. As we entered downtown Maputo, Adam and Sudi fell behind. This irritated Moshe.

'What do they think? That they are on holiday?'

We walked onto the jetty of the Vodacom Ferry Dock as the main ferry was pulling off. Moshe cursed.

'Fuck, man. Fuck. The police stopped your friends. I knew this was going to happen. They're so slow today. What do they think this is? Where are their heads, really?'

He backtracked and deliberated with the police. When I approached he waved me away. After a few minutes the two Beachboys came walking down the jetty, passing me without acknowledgement. Moshe came behind, wiping his sweating brow with a blue bandana.

'Mozambique police are no good. These boys have their documents, but the police still want MT150 to let them pass. I don't have papers. I haven't had papers for twenty years. Nobody stops me.'

Small cuddy boats picked up travellers between ferries, and one of these was about to leave. We clambered on and squeezed into the hot cabin, where we were ordered to sit down. Adam was sullen. 'Same thing gon' happen to us on the other side. This is not my style. There's no way to run.'

I was concerned that events had been several seconds ahead of us today, and that the Beachboys had not had the time to stow their *ndongas*. If this was the case, the heroin would be in their underpants, perhaps even in my bag. And just as Adam had feared, several officers were waiting for us on the other side.

In the south bank police station, Moshe ranted at the officers until two of them forcibly ejected him from the room. A female officer studied the Beachboys' emergency travel documents.

'We are going to search you, one by one.'

Sudi stood and emptied his pockets of lint and wrappers. He took off his *kofia*, and poured the meagre contents of his drawstring bag onto the table: a single T-shirt and a toothbrush. The only male officer left in the room made him loosen his pants, and was busy folding over the top of his belt, feeling the stitching of his trousers for lumps, when Sudi unexpectedly dropped his pants to his ankles, eliciting a grunt of surprise from the female officer.

'What are you doing?'

'I'm helping this man. I can see he is struggling here.'

The insolence was reassuring. Adam went next and was one step ahead of the officer all the way, turning out every pocket and cranny they might have wanted to search before being asked to do so. He took off his shirt.

'Put it back on,' said the female officer.

'It's hot,' said Adam. 'I'll keep it off.'

By the time I was searched, the game of cat and mouse was over. Now it was just a case of paying a bribe. I saw Moshe hand some notes to the officers outside. 'Come, come,' he said, ushering us out. An argument broke out between the officers inside and those who had been outside.

'How much did you pay them?' the female officer demanded.

'One hundred.'

'What about us?'

Adam handed her another hundred, an overpayment that upset Moshe to such a degree that Sudi had to escort him outdoors by an elbow before he gave the officers cause to re-arrest us.

'It's okay, Mosh. We spent more on breakfast. Let's go.'

In the taxi rank Moshe talked with his hand on Adam's head, as if he were about to deliver a benediction. Adam let him keep it there. He bought us a strip of Big Boss whisky sachets and some peanuts, and only reluctantly said goodbye when it became clear that our taxi would not be leaving anytime soon.

'Second angel of the road,' said Adam. 'Salut-eh!'

The taxi was a VW Syncro, a 4×4 version of the minibus taxis that rule South Africa's roads. It had just gone midday and the taxi was half-full. We were no more than one hundred and sixty kilometres from the border, but already the passengers were lobbying the driver to cut his losses and leave immediately, arguing that we were already in danger of arriving at the border after its closure at 6 p.m. The driver pretended not to hear them. The seats filled up in half-hour increments. An old man with nodule-covered hands. A woman with a baby strapped to her back, a wet spot on her shoulder where its sleeping mouth had been. When all the seats had been taken, we still did not move.

'He's waiting for the roof to be full,' a passenger explained. A woman arrived with a sealed cardboard box, paid the driver, and left. He lifted it to the roof.

Eventually, at about 1.30 p.m., the driver slung his body into the vehicle and fired up the engine. The dirt road traced the coastline, passing huts beneath palms overlooking deserted beaches. The views of Maputo across the bay were spectacular. I could appreciate the scenes particularly well from my seat next to the driver, who seemed to know what he was doing even though the vehicle was too heavily loaded on my side, causing the tyres to whirr against the chassis whenever we plunged into a pothole. The smell of burning rubber came up from the footwell.

After eighty kilometres the road became much sandier. Red-tinged at first, it gradually turned powder white. Twenty kilometres from the border, it was as if someone had cut a narrow corridor through the coastal bush and set about creating the world's longest sandpit. To keep going, the driver kept his foot flat on the accelerator, cooking the drive-shaft. We crested several deep drifts this way, but he was no longer in control. As we careened crazily from one hummock to the next, the driver's foot inevitably slipped off the accelerator, causing the vehicle to stall. The doors opened and, without needing to be told, the male passengers took up positions at the rear. *Um*, *dois*, *três*, the driver shouted, and we all heaved. The minibus started moving, gradually at first and then so rapidly that Adam fell to the ground and stayed there. I ran over to find his face wet with tears.

'Hooo,' he cried. 'Sudi just told me he pushed so hard a *ndonga* shot out his backside.'

The final section of road was littered with marooned minibuses. In fact, it was no longer a road – more a delta of tyre tracks weaving on the flat coastal plain. Our driver navigated these with supreme ability, too absorbed in his work even to acknowledge the stricken drivers we were passing. With ten kilometres to go the engine overheated, but we were moving again within fifteen minutes. Adam and Sudi were seated on the back bench, sealed in by bodies and bags, and they only noticed how near we were to the border when we were one kilometre out.

'Sean, get him to stop,' Adam shouted. The driver slowed, but with minutes to go before the post was due to shut the other passengers overruled the request and we surged forward again. In another minute we had arrived beside a line of rammed-earth buildings. A handful of minibuses faced the way we had just come; one by one they took off, loaded with the last of the day's border crossers. Our fellow passengers stripped their bags from the roof and sprinted for the immigration office, outside which a soldier stood lowering the Mozambican flag from a flagpole. The driver made a three-point turn, quickly filled his seats, and took off.

'Let's go,' said Adam, breaking right from the road into ankle-high coastal scrub. It was five hundred metres to the border fence, and there was no cover whatsoever. We were fifty metres in when a soldier wandering down the road from the Maputo side ordered us to stop.

'In here,' said Adam, crossing to a solitary reed outhouse a few feet away. One after the other we pretended to use it, before walking back to the road.

'Passports,' the soldier demanded. The Beachboys reluctantly produced their much-folded, now entirely irrelevant Central and East Africa emergency travel papers. He looked them over and ordered us to accompany him to a nearby bar, where soldiers in civilian clothes were playing pool. Several more men studied the travel delineations, but they must not have been able to read in English or Swahili, because they refolded the documents and handed them back.

'The border is closed. It opens again at eight,' said one.

'Is there somewhere we can go to sleep?'

My question provoked a discussion. Fingers were pointed at the line of shops at the roadside.

'You're not going to try and jump the border or anything? No? Then you can sleep there.'

We chose one that was painted washing-powder blue, and slumped down on the porch with our backs to the wall. Sudi put his hands to his head and prayed fervently. Adam gazed across at the border fence.

'Nah man, I can't handle this. We need to go.'

The soldiers clearly had eyes on us, though, and we agreed that it was essential to wait for total darkness, at the very least. Privately, I was preparing to say goodbye. I was in possession of a perfectly valid passport, with a dozen empty pages left to fill. I could sit out the night and cross the next morning, perhaps even link up with Adam and Sudi in the nearby town of Manguzi, if they made it across. I felt a very strong urge to call my wife, to let her know where I was and that all was well. But, since pawning my BlackBerry, I had been using a steel-body Nokia that Adam had lifted from a pocket on the Grand Parade months before. The battery was weak and had not held any charge for days. I walked over to the soldiers' bar and asked the barman if he would mind plugging it in.

'Five rands.'

'Fine.' I handed over the R5 coin that had been swimming around in my documents wallet since Cape Town. I was now completely without cash of any kind.

Back on the porch, the Beachboys watched the sun set in lavender tones. Adam cursed Moshe's intervention. 'I knew we should have gone through Swaziland. I know that way, there are no problems. I should have said something. We were supposed to be in Johannesburg some time tonight already.'

There was nothing to do but smoke and wait. Nobody felt like talking. I heard my ringtone go in the bar and went to fetch my phone. It was the first of six weeks' worth of South African SMSs coming through, a response to an advertisement I had placed on OLX months before.

Do you still have the dog kennel? Thanks. Chrystal.

Being too nerve-wracked to think straight, I started to respond, but the phone battery died before I could send the message. I handed the phone back to the barman. No point denying it now: I wanted to be home. Returning to the porch, I felt a sharp pain in my stomach. I stopped, breathed in. The moment I started off again my stomach twisted. I doubled over, then staggered back over to the soldiers' bar.

'Where will I find a toilet?'

'Big or small?'

'Big.'

I realised I hadn't gone 'big' since leaving Dar es Salaam.

'You'll have to go out there,' the barman advised, pointing at the area of scrubland between the shops and the borderline, now lost in darkness.

He fished around behind the bar and came up with a half-depleted toilet roll.

'Nobody going to shoot me?'

'It's fine. Go.'

I clumped through the scrub until I came to a bush a little taller than I am. I squatted, facing the buildings. Each shop had a lamp above its entrance, angled upwards on a short length of pipe, like the lure of a deep-sea anglerfish waiting for its quarry to emerge from the darkness. Behind the haze of insects around our lamp I could make out Sudi's *kofia*, but couldn't see Adam. I refocused my eyes on the dark plain and immediately noticed movement nearby: a human shape, low to the ground and moving towards me so slowly I wondered if it wasn't simply a trick of exhaustion. The shape rose, however, and closed the distance between us in one surge.

'Yow Sean, you had a good idea. I brought your things.' In his hands Adam had my rucksack and camera bag.

'I'm taking a shit, man.'

'Finish quickly, it's time to go.'

'The phone is still charging.'

'Leave it.'

'I can't.'

'Come back quickly, then, and bring Sudi, he didn't see us go.'

I returned to the bar with the toilet roll and collected the Nokia without meeting the barman's eyes. Sudi was looking out at the dark when I reached him. He seemed to read everything from my face.

'Come, this way,' he said, and we walked off in the opposite direction from the border, circling around the soldiers' living quarters to get beyond the portion of the road that was illuminated by the shop lights.

Once we were across, we crawled towards the silhouette of the bush where I had left Adam. Sudi made some kissing sounds and received a series back in response. Adam scrambled over. We all lay flat for a bit watching a soldier progress down the border fence, his presence betrayed by the cherry of his cigarette. Off in the direction of Maputo the trees wore a penumbral headdress of moonshine. 'Fucking moon,' said Sudi. In a matter of minutes, the thing would be up and the scrub would turn silver.

Adam led off at a crouching run, with periodic drops into the bushes. We halted one last time at the fence, which was about eight feet tall and laddered with taut, barbed strands, each no more than ten centimetres below the next. Adam again led the way, taking hold of a shaky post. He made it up and over. Sudi went next, and was over in no time. I made it over, too, but for the first time since leaving the buildings I patted my money belt and realised my ID and passport were missing. The others groaned in sympathy but there was nothing to be done about it. We were in South Africa, and making a lot of noise on the fallen leaves and branches in the eucalyptus forest that verged on the border. It was time to run.

We headed upslope, fanning out. When torches appeared in the distance our speed increased. The torch beams wriggled crazily in pursuit. I could no longer see the others but followed the sound of snapping branches downslope and, after a few minutes, broke out of the forest to find the Beachboys walking comfortably at the side of the Kosi Bay road. They removed their travel documents from their trousers, ripped them to shreds and threw the pieces up in the air.

'We don't need these any more. We're South Africans now.'

A lone jogger went by, a soldier most likely. The Beachboys called out to him in their best Zulu, gleaned from the prisons of Durban and Johannesburg.

'*Sawubona.*'

'*Unjani?*'

'*Ngikhona, ngiyabonga. Wena unjani?*'

'*Ngikhona.*'

'*Wosh.*'

'How far is Manguzi?'

'Twenty-six.'

'No way!'

Since the road ended at the closed border post, no vehicles came or went. Adrenalin turned into fatigue. We stopped talking.

Finally, with Manguzi's skyglow visible above some low hills, a set of headlights approached. As Yolanda had done outside Tete, I ordered the Beachboys down into the culvert, and tried to look as white as possible. The pickup came to a stop ten metres beyond us, and the driver shuddered visibly when the two Beachboys appeared at my side. He quickly regained his composure, though, and quoted R20 each for the lift. He said the Engen Service Station on the town's main road doubled as an after-hours taxi rank, and dropped us there. It looked promising – all the parking bays were occupied by minibus taxis – but a short, muscular Zulu soon informed us that the last ride to Johannesburg had left an hour before. 'I can take you in my car,' he offered. 'If you pay me R4 000 we can leave right now.'

I could practically see the cat's eyes on those eastern roads disappearing under the bonnet of his Jetta as we sailed through the night at high speed, stopping for KFC in Ermelo before continuing on to Johannesburg with dawn breaking in the rear window. But, of course, we were broke. Sudi set about securing accommodation. He had recognised a Bongoman from previous journeys, a man called Musa, who had a *mchondolo* on the nearby Gesiza River. It was this man's business to approach late-night border crossers like us with offers of shelter and supper; although the fee he quoted was reasonable, Adam took against him, calling him a *poes* to his face. This left us with two options: we could loiter on the main road in the hope of flagging down an insomniac trucker, or we could seek out the Manguzi *maskani*, where we would at least be beyond the attention of police cruisers.

Sudi led the way down the main road, turning right up a gentle slope and following the dirt road to a large property with no gate. In a corner of the overgrown stand there was a ruin, outside which a dozen Beachboys had arranged their bodies in depressions in the rubble. The walls of the ruin were densely marked with seaman names and slogans.

Adebayor. Mafegi Tenaa. Dogo Visheta. Ommy Jey. Crazy Sailor.

Adam approached like a prize fighter, shouting '*Oyaa, oyaa, oyaaa,*' and letting everyone know that we were no common delegation. He explained who I was and what we had just done. My camera was passed around to illustrate where we had been. 'Sean-y *shavu moja*,' they shouted. 'Sean-y mah cheeky'. Adrenalin was still kicking in my system, and it felt good to be sitting there as the group mood took off, the moon rising above the missing roof. Everyone wanted his picture taken, with me, with us. They took their own pictures. We smoked the little bits of weed the group had left; when it was done some of the boys went indoors, shifting a panel of corrugated roofing away from the doorway and climbing into a midden of plastic on the floor. Those of us still outside talked in lower tones, and a young man called Jimmy London led us in a long du'a, which was the most beautiful I have yet heard.

Then the temperature dropped, and I decided I would return to the service station and try for transport after all.

Adam and Sudi walked with me, but Sudi stopped at the main road. The town was too quiet now, he said – the cops would notice us for sure. Adam remonstrated with him but Sudi was adamant. The two of us would be okay, he said, with our paler skins and command of English, but South African cops would pick him out as a foreigner in seconds. He turned back, saying he would return after sunrise. If we were not there, he would know we had found a lift. He would follow, meet us in Johannesburg perhaps, or back in Cape Town.

'Good luck for you,' he said, and vanished into the shadows thrown by the tall roadside trees.

The garage was very quiet by the time we arrived. The drivers of the minibus taxis were all asleep on their front seats. Three young women working the night shift in the 24-hour store had locked the doors for the sake of security and were serving through a reinforced glass window. There was a single petrol attendant on duty, called Dumisani, and a single security guard, called Sipho Mthembu, both Tsongas. They were pleasant characters who came over one at a time to chat and smoke with us at the edge of the paved forecourt. These gatherings drew the attention of an elderly drunk with a well-fed white dog at his heel, called Kanga. Kanga loved her master, never straying more than a few feet from his legs.

When the old man heard Adam was Tanzanian he became animated.

'Nyerere,' he grunted. 'Great man.'

'Nah, he was a *poes*,' said Adam.

'Angry young man,' said the drunk, cackling. 'Angry. Young. Man.'

'What do you know?'

'I was there,' said the old man. 'I served with Umkhonto we Sizwe [the former military arm of the ANC]. Mbeya. Bagamoyo. Morogoro. Kongwa. I knew all the camps.'

'You know Tanzania, father, you know,' said Adam, now genuinely interested.

'I know Africa,' the drunk rejoined. 'Angola, Uganda. I was there, in the camps.'

Our gathering attracted another drunk, a much younger man clothed in an extraordinary, colourful robe.

Sipho, the security guard, circled his forefinger around his temple. 'He's not right.'

The man sang a song, then fought the older drunk for half a beer Adam had offered around. Adam seized it back and downed it.

'What the fuck, you think I'd give you people half a beer?'

The former soldier produced some marijuana and rolled it up in a strip of light cardboard. Adam took the joint from him and smoked most of it, then pulled his arms inside the sleeves of his football shirt and fell asleep with his head on my bag. Sipho talked to me about the annual Tsonga marula festival, which occurs annually in mid summer, when the marula fruit ripens.

'People come from all over the country to visit the place of the Tsonga king. There's a tap that you turn to fill your cup with marula beer, for free. You must come back for that one, you will enjoy it so much.'

The robed madman curled up next to Adam and was soon snoring away. The old freedom fighter wandered off, leaving his bags, and returned with a full beer.

'Why is it that the people who have nothing end up getting drunker than the people who have something?' Sipho wondered aloud. The old man listened to the snoring at his feet and said that he never sleeps. Then he was off again. 'Kanga, tsk, come Kanga,' he snapped, and the faithful bitch jumped to her feet and trotted after him, into the night.

At 3 a.m. Sipho excused himself, and went into the staff utility area to sleep. The town was still, and would be for another two hours. At about 5 a.m. the first pedestrians would begin to appear, traders with bags of merchandise on their heads. The first cars would turn in for Dumisani to fill their tanks; he would be looking forward to his 6 a.m. handover. The taxi drivers would wake, stretch, and walk over to the toilet block to wash up. By 8 a.m. the town would be fully alive, and we would be there to see it all.

But, until then, there was nothing for it but to follow Adam's example and lie down on the cold bricks, pulling my arms inside my sleeves.

◆

At about 8 a.m. we parted ways.

It had been my intention to stick with the Beachboys all the way to Cape Town, but when I awoke it was light – well after dawn, in fact. Sipho was standing above me – possibly he had shaken me awake – saying I should get up before the owner arrived. For a second I failed to recognise him, or recall where I was. My throat felt terribly hot, and my right arm was painfully asleep. In another ten minutes I had my hand back and I was using it to pour purple Energade into my mouth. I still felt far from composed. SMSs had continued to crowd into my cellphone inbox: bank statements, cock pill solicitations from Men's Health International.

I was back on grid, geolocated.

If you're looking for perspective on your life, switch off your phone for six weeks. Then switch it back on. You're in debt. Your copy is late. Your wife loves you, misses you. You could do with a harder erection. The phone pinged again, an advisory from Marcia, the bride-to-be:

BRING GUMBOOTS!!! HEAVY RAINS FORECAST THIS WEEKEND!!

'What day is it?' I asked Sipho.

'Thursday.'

'Goddamn it.'

'What's wrong?' Adam asked.

'I promised my wife I would be back by Friday. I thought today was Wednesday. If it was Wednesday there would be just enough time.'

Seven hundred kilometres from Manguzi to Johannesburg. Fourteen hundred from Johannesburg to Cape Town.

'It is Thursday today, Sean. There's no way you can make it, unless you fly.'

I had air miles, thousands of them. I could be in Durban by midday, home by evening.

Sudi came strolling up the main road, shoulder-bumped us both.

'Sean need to fly home today,' Adam announced, taking the decision out of my hands.

Sudi nodded.

'It's good.'

Minutes later, I had booked a place in a Durban-bound minibus. I handed the Beachboys what I felt I could afford from my remaining funds, drawn from my credit card account, which I was now able to access. We hugged.

'Sea Power,' said Adam.

'See you in Cape Town,' said Sudi.

The taxi crier slammed the sliding door shut and the driver pulled out of the garage. Sipho, waiting for a taxi of his own, waved.

A friend from school days picked me up in the parking lot of the La Lucia Mall, to the north of Durban. 'You stink,' he said, but insisted I use his car for the day, after dropping him off at his ocean-view offices in Umhlanga.

It seemed a reckless dose of power and freedom. Five minutes to the beach. Ten to the airport. A few hours to the middle of nowhere, if I really put my foot down. I drove to a mall I once swore I would never again set foot in and bought gumboots, then carried on down to the beach, aiming to take the sort of swim that resets the nerves. Adam called while I was stripping down, to say they were R400 short for their taxi fares to Johannesburg. He explained I could send the money through Shoprite. I put my clothes back on and returned to the mall, only to learn that I could not send money without my ID, which was lying somewhere out on the border, a mist of moisture between the book and its plastic sleeve, no doubt.

'Don't worry, bra, we'll find the way,' said Adam.

The way, as it turned out, constituted two minor robberies en route to Johannesburg and a slightly more serious one in Hillbrow. The minibus taxi they boarded for Cape Town was stopped short in Laingsburg, a small town in the arid Karoo, where the driver was incarcerated over unpaid fines. The friends called from a trucker's cellphone at 10 p.m. on Friday night. They had made it to Kraaifontein, thirty minutes outside Cape Town, and owed the driver the price of their passage – R50 each.

'Go,' said my wife. 'Finish the trip.'

The Beachboys were in high spirits when they clambered into the Conquest, though Sudi was again sick with withdrawal. They thanked the trucker, called him father.

We made a stop at the Maskani railway bridge so that Adam could buy weed, and continued up to University Estate and parked outside the block of flats in which the dealer lived.

'You coming in?'

'No, go ahead. I'll find you tomorrow.'

At 4 a.m. my phone rattled on the bedside table.

My wife sat up. 'What's wrong?'

'Nothing, everything's fine.'

I smiled in the darkness, shook my head and switched off my phone.

AFTERWORD

Adam's departure on the very same night of their return to Cape Town was a real blow for Sudi. After handing over their *ndongas* to the Woodstock dealer, they had returned to Maskani with a portion of their payment, much of which they had spent on vodka and *unga*. Sudi, who has no head for hard tack, had passed out the moment they returned to The Kitchen, at about 1 a.m. He had woken to find Adam missing, but had not for one second suspected the reason.

No Beachboy had ever stowed away on the very same night of their return to Cape Town. No Beachboy had even thought to try.

When I shared Adam's news, Sudi took my hand. 'Let's make a du'a for him. We must pray that we never see him again. Memory Card is my brother, but if I never see him again I will be happy, because it will mean he made it somewhere.'

Sudi took a ship of his own six months later. He had hated every intervening moment. The dealer to whom he had handed his *ndongas* had been Adam's contact, and in Adam's absence the deal had gone cold, which put Sudi back to threatening drugmen with mortal violence. Worse, he found he was unable to forgive Cape Town for the murder of his friend Aubadeeleh. Several of the *mwiba mwitu* who had backed Chawa Suga remained living under the Foreshore bridges, and Sudi refused to pass that way. Temba, the Beachboy who had handed Chawa Suga the murder weapon, had moved to Delft, and Sudi knew exactly where. Naturally, he wanted to burn the house down. He tried on several occasions to get me to sign on as his driver, and was visibly disappointed when I refused.

By night he threw himself at the port, and eventually made it onto the *Warnow Moon*, which took him *nyuma mlima*, to Durban. After being flown back to Dar es Salaam he called to say that he had broken off relations with Sauda: his old friend Ayoub had exposed her relationship with another man from the neighbourhood. When Sudi confronted her, he learnt that there had been several men in his long absence. He resolved to take Esau to his place in Sinza, but before the details could be worked out he had set fire to the car belonging to Sauda's lover and then robbed every single other man she had allegedly slept with in his absence. These actions put a price on his head – he was forced to relocate to Ukonga, a township out near the airport. In January 2016, after paying for Esau's coming school year, he headed south again, with a kilogram of *unga* in his stomach. Adam suspects that Sudi will head for Durban, a city in which his enemies have limited influence.

Barak's appendix burst in September 2015, and his life was saved by the surgeons in Groote Schuur Hospital's F ward. He moved to the Blikkiesdorp sick house to recuperate but developed an infection, which brought him even closer to death's door. It took another month in Groote Schuur and several courses of antibiotics to save him. I would often find Morieda at his bedside when I visited. She, too, was very sick, with cancer of the brain. She said her two grown children seemed relieved by her diagnosis, because in their eyes the tumour explained her relationship with Barak, a homeless Tanzanian man half her age.

Barak's outlook on life was fundamentally altered by these experiences. The moment he was back on his feet he asked me to help him find a job and, to demonstrate intent, he relocated from his highway *mchondolo* to a unit in Blikkiesdorp, where he would be able to keep his body washed and his clothes clean. I hooked him up with a Zimbabwean friend called Felix, who runs a cupboard-spraying business from his garage in Athlone. The first week went well. Felix reported that Barak worked hard, and seemed a fast learner. In the second week, however, Barak failed to pitch up two mornings in a row. He initially complained that it was dangerous to cross from Blikkiesdorp to the Delft taxi rank while it was still dark, but later he admitted to punching an influential Blikkiesdorp dealer during an argument, a rush of blood that had forced him to leave Blikkiesdorp for two nights. He wouldn't say where he had slept, but based on the state of his clothes I suspected the Port Jackson forest between Blikkiesdorp and the airport.

This on-off approach to his work persisted for a month or so. Stretches of attendance would be followed by inexplicable disappearances. After a particularly long period of absence, Felix called to say that his patience was wearing thin. I begged him to give Barak another chance. Things blew up on Barak's first day back. Felix's other employees

– two young Zimbabweans – had asked Barak why the *mzungu* continued to intervene on his behalf, beyond reason. What was he doing for the white man in return? they probed, while showing off some lewd hip movements.

They will probably never know how close they came to bleeding out on the floor of that Athlone garage. Barak had been in a state of intense agitation for weeks. After his run-in with the Blikkiesdorp dealer, he had started carrying a fold-out Okapi lockback. In my experience, the period between a Beachboy's decision to carry a blade and his violent use of it is never very long. Fortunately, instead of knifing the young men, Barak had complained to Felix, who had wisely ordered his employees to take the afternoon off and to return the next day with cooler heads, or not at all.

At the Athlone taxi rank Barak, still fuming, had bumped into some Tanga Boys who told him about a new *maskani* they had started in the Athlone railway reserve. Barak had not touched a single cocktail since his first operation but felt he needed something now, and followed them there. Instead of smoking *unga* he accepted a puff on a tik bulb, and another. The smoking continued late into the night and culminated in a fight with an abrasive Tanga youth, during which Barak used his Okapi. He fled, and spent the next week sleeping rough in secret locations. Another Beachboy had been stabbed and killed in that same *maskani* on the same night. When Barak heard this he threw up, believing he was the murderer. Barak's victim survived, though, and after another month tensions had cooled, enabling him to return to his *mchondolo* in The Kitchen.

He smoked tik day and night for a month, and became gaunt. To kick the habit he started smoking cocktails again, and slowly gained weight and calmed down. He is back to spending his days as he spent them before his operation. I see him often, but our conversations have become wooden and awkward. There is no mention of the terrible pain, fear and depression he experienced in hospital, or of the rare opportunities he squandered afterwards because he could not control his temper. His eyes convey his desperation, but his pride will not permit him to ask for more help; I have not offered any, nor will I.

That said, I did try to help him find Morieda, with whom he had lost contact during his time in Blikkiesdorp. Staying with Morieda had never been an option for Barak, as she had lived with her children and they had forbidden it. Their relationship had always been conducted in his territory, and on her terms. When apart, they had remained connected by their phones, but one day her number had gone dead. Months had passed before he heard from some Grand Parade shopkeepers that she had been admitted to Somerset Hospital for aggressive treatment of her cancer. We visited the hospital only to be told that Morieda's treatment had been suspended, and that she had been transferred to St Luke's Hospice in the southern suburbs for terminal care. I called, but the receptionist could not locate any record of a Morieda Swart ever having been admitted.

'Try Morieda Hussen,' said Barak. 'Maybe she used her married name.'

I could hear the receptionist typing in the new details, and then a pause.

'Yes, we had a Morieda Hussen here, but I'm sorry to say, sir, that she passed some weeks back.'

Barak received the news without flinching, but did not say another word until I dropped him at the Beachboy Office. Later that night, he called to thank me for my help. 'I'm happy,' he said, 'because I know Morieda kept her own mind until the end. If she used our married name it means her family was not controlling her. I will never forget her. I never had a mother, and if I'm honest I must tell you that Morieda was more like a mother to me than a wife. I know she's in a better place now, a beautiful place. I can see it in my mind. I even feel jealous, you know, when I think of that nice place she gone to.'

Daniel Peter returned to Cape Town in late 2013, and has been in and out of Pollsmoor Prison since. He is no longer the clear-featured boy I met in 2011. His fighting abilities, repeatedly tested in the prison environment, have made him bold to the point of recklessness. In 2015 he ripped a gold chain from the neck of a male tourist on Darling Street, and later pawned it for R12 000. He sent much of this back to his sister in Dar es Salaam, and used the remainder to buy a considerable stash of marijuana from Swaziland, in this way setting himself up as a major dealer under the Foreshore bridges. In January 2016, he was openly smoking a joint on his corner near the Grand Parade toilet blocks when two cops he did not recognise came for him. They demanded he hand over the joint. He refused, and swallowed it. The officers arrested him anyway, claiming on the charge sheet that he had swallowed hard drugs. The judge accepted this version of events and, taking into account the young Tanzanian's 11 previous convictions, sentenced him to three years' imprisonment. I have neither seen nor heard from him since.

Mege JoJo was cured of TB in 2014, although he remains living in the Blikkiesdorp sick house, where he has appointed himself chief medical adviser and housemaster, overseeing the convalescence of the seriously ill and injured. His efforts have earned him the deepest respect in Beachboy circles.

I've heard from several people that P Diddy is alive and well and living in Pretoria, where he bought an old scooter with the money I gave him for the journey back to Dar es Salaam. He still harbours hopes of returning to Dar es Salaam a rich man, apparently, so that he can reclaim the affections of his childhood sweetheart.

Feisal's run of bad luck continued. He called from Pollsmoor in late 2013 after being arrested for possession and, in 2014, a nurse called from Somerset Hospital to say that he had been found walking down Long Street naked in the middle of the night. When the CCID guards picked him up, he was jabbering and in a highly distressed state.

'He says you are going to send him home,' the nurse said.

While resting in hospital he sent me a series of reflective SMSs, all in characteristic upper-case script.

BEING IN SOUTH AFRICA I LEARNED A LOT OF THINGS. EVERYONE HAS GOT HIS OWN WAY OF HOW TO SURVIVE AND ON MY SIDE I AM AN UNTALKETIVE PERSON. AINT BOASTING MYSELF BUT AM TRULY THE NON TALKATIVE ONE. I DON'T LIKE A LUXURY LIFE ALTHOUGH I HAD WHEN I WAS BORN BUT I AINT REALLY PASSED THROUGH THAT WAY FOR A LONG TIME NOW.

WHAT I CAN SAY TO U IS THAT MY LIFE IS NOT COMFORTABLE.

WHAT I HATE IS GOSSPING AND HATERS. THOSE ARE MOST WHAT I HATE ALTHOUGH THERE'S A LOT THAT I DO HATE.

BEACHES LIFE NEEDS HEART AND NOT JUST HEART BUT A REALLY STRONG HEART, OTHERWISE YOU WONT SURVIVE. THAT IS WHAT I GRASP ON MY SIDE, ALTHOUGH THERE ARE MANY STAGES – STEPS LIKE BECOMING A DRUG DEALER AND ROBING PEOPLE, WHICH CAN MAKE YOU AFFORD A BETER LIFE ON THE BEACH.

WHAT I MISS SINCE BEING HERE IS TO GO HOME FIRST FOR A WHILE THEN TO COME BACK FOR ANOTHER PURPOSE, NOTHING ELSE. I BELIEVE WHEN I REACH HOME AND BEFORE I COME BACK EVERYTHING IS GONNA BE ALRIGHT AND MY LIFE GONNA BE CHANGED HERE IN SOUTH AFRICA.

BUT WHAT IS NECESSARY FOR ME IS TO GO HOME FIRST.

On being discharged from hospital, Feisal walked directly to Cape Town Central Police Station, just up from the Grand Parade. He stood in the queue for an hour. When he reached the front, he confessed to the duty officer that he was an undocumented foreigner and should be deported. The officer laughed at him.

'You're not the first one to try to get a free ticket home,' she said, before ordering him out onto Buitenkant Street.

To try to establish which avenues an undocumented and penniless African like Feisal could pursue to leave the country legally, I wrote to Corey Johnson on the advocacy desk at the Scalabrini Centre.

'The media narrative in this country is all about foreigners fighting to get in', he replied, 'but I can think of more than a few people who are desperate to find a way back out, who have sickened of or become disillusioned by the economic opportunities, or who have endured community hatred, violence, harassment, detention and so forth. The list goes on and on.'

He suggested I check out the International Organization for Migration's Assisted Voluntary Return and Reintegration programme, but warned that it was a long shot: 'I'm aware of only a handful of cases that have ever been approved in South Africa. The logistics are breath-taking. Contact needs to be established with the applicant's family in their home country, and they must express willingness to take this person back. Once this has been established an escort with medical qualifications needs to be booked to accompany the migrant in question on the flight, and then onwards to their living environment, where the escort needs to provide reintegration assistance. This might extend to vocational training, education, further medical assistance, and so forth, depending on the donor funding the IOM is able to access.'

At the time of our exchange, the global news stations were running daily footage of boats wallowing in the Mediterranean's waters, hopelessly overloaded with Syrian families fleeing war. They were washing up, dead and alive, on European shores – not just Syrians but Kosovans, Afghans, Eritreans, Nigerians, Somalians, Ukrainians, Gambians … 'the greatest trans-national human migration seen since the start of the Second World War', the newspapers decreed. In the face of such a crisis, the IOM's AVRR programme seemed akin to walking a single grain of sand from the bottom to the top of a mighty sand dune in the middle of the Sahara.

In the end, I walked with Feisal to Cape Town station, and booked him a seat on a bus leaving for Johannesburg that night, and another from Johannesburg to Lilongwe, Malawi, leaving three days later. I gave him R2 000 towards managing the remainder of the journey and said goodbye. More than a year later, on 25 September 2015, he sent the following SMS:

HELO SEAN. LONGTIME. HW Z EVRYTIN? THIS MONTH AM GETTING MARRIED TO ANOTHER WOMAN COUSE I DEVORCE MY FIRST WIFE. PLIZ WOULD U CONTIBUTE 5,000 RAND 4MY CELEBRATION. ITS ME FEISAL, TANZANIA.

I am happy to hear you made it home, I replied, and left it at that.

In 2014, Dave Southwood exhibited his extraordinary photographs of Cape Town's stowaways at the University of the South, Tennessee. In the same year, he published them in broadsheet newspaper format, under the title MEMORY CARD SEA POWER. Often, since, I have passed under bridges in Cape Town and spotted pages of the newspaper pasted to the walls, the images stained by rainwater and stripped by the wind, just as he intended. I will forever be indebted to him for introducing me to Adam and the others all the way back in 2011.

On 13 August 2014, my wife gave birth to a healthy boy. We decided to call him Ruwa, which means 'water' in Hausa and 'the land' in archaic Shona. This met with Adam's approval: 'Your boy can travel either way, cross-country and in the sea.'

Ruwa's arrival in the world changed everything, not least the way I interacted with the Beachboys. Tanzanian etiquette is based on the acknowledgement of family, so the time taken over greetings has increased markedly. How is Ruwa? I am asked. Then, How is Mama Ruwa? And finally, How are you, Baba Ruwa? As my relationships with certain Beachboys have deepened I have increasingly been able to hold up my end, asking about individual sisters, mothers and grandmothers at home in Tanzania. I never ask after the fathers, though. Of all the Beachboys I have come to know, not a single one knows where his father is. In fact, most have never met their fathers. As a consequence, my Beachboy friends are constantly exhorting me: look after Ruwa. Teach him. Do anything you can. Never forget about him.

I nod. Thank you, I will try.

Adam returned to Cape Town in early 2014. The ship he had stowed away on ended up in Santos, Brazil, where he was put up for a month in a portside hotel while the details of his deportation were worked out. He caught another ship in mid 2015, and ended up back in Dar es Salaam during the lead-up to the general elections. It was a tense time, he said – soldiers everywhere, dispersing public gatherings of any description. The government had even warned politicians to refrain from engaging in witchcraft, admitting for the first time that killings of people with albinism tended to rise discernibly during election periods.

The mood infected the whole city. Adam stopped visiting the *maskanis* in Posta, Temeke and Magomeni, because he encountered too much fighting. He wanted to leave for South Africa immediately, but was told the Iringa highway had become a gauntlet of roadblocks run by violent and grasping policemen. In the end, he sat out the election at Mama Suna's place on the Kigamboni Peninsula. This allowed him to reconnect with his half-brother Mohamed, who had just completed his matric exams and was selling peanuts down at the ferry terminal while waiting for his results. Once a day the brothers would both walk to the shoreline, and watch the workmen hammering away on the long-overdue Kigamboni Bridge. Dar es Salaam, Adam felt, was changing – had already changed. Some of the changes were clearly for the best, but it was no longer his city. He understood for the first time why older Beachboys in places like Maputo and Richards Bay feared being forced to return to Tanzania, a country they he had spent more time out of than in.

The moment the election results were in, giving the Chama Cha Mapinduzi party yet another term (the CCM has been in power since 1977, making it Africa's longest-reigning ruling party), Adam returned to Kiparang'anda, the village in which he had spent his childhood. His grandmother, Halima, who had been born in Mbwera before the First World War, had died in her sleep in 2014, almost a year to the day after our visit. She had been buried under the stand of cashew trees growing at the bottom of his uncle's small farm. Adam said that village parents now warned their children to avoid the place, and especially to avoid picking Uncle Mageni's cashew fruit.

'Even in death she got power,' he said.

To her grave he brought a picture of himself, taken when he was a teen. Suna had showed it to me: a grainy print of a shy, good-looking boy in a blue tracksuit top. He placed it on the grave, and put a sizeable rock on top, to prevent it from blowing away. When he walked away, hand in hand with Mama Suna, he said he felt a strange peace. He had known love as a child, thanks to Halima. His mother had been absent, but she was with him now, and he knew she would love him until her own death, or his.

Back in Dar es Salaam, Adam had one more stop to make before continuing on to South Africa. Rehema had died, too, just a few months before his deportation. 'It was her heart I think, she was a big woman,' he said. When he returned to Rehema's place on Yombo Street in Temeke, an old local called Sekhota informed him that the family had already sold up. Adam stared hard at the familiar blue door in its long concrete wall, and tried to recall every detail that lay behind it: What the tiles had looked like, which ones had cracked and why. What the kitchen curtains had looked like the night they caught fire.

It was all there. The closest thing he had ever known to a happy home may now be closed to him, but he knew he would carry it in his mind forever. Rehema's body had been buried in Kisutu Cemetery, said Sekhota, but he did not know in which quadrant, and Adam was not about to wander aimlessly around a place of death. Instead, he knocked on the blue door and asked the new owners, 'Do you have beer, whisky? Anything. I need to pour one drink for my adoption mama, who lived here before you.' A glass of warm Tusker was duly produced, and Adam tipped some on the house steps before draining the rest. From here he proceeded directly to Morogoro Road and, ten days later, stepped out of a minibus taxi on the deck above Cape Town Station.

As he has done so many times before, Adam landed on his feet. When a young *mwiba mwitu* called Suleiman Issa was shot and killed by a Woodstock policeman right up against the port fence, Adam took control of the funeral collection, winning the respect of Issa's many friends. But Cape Town, like Dar es Salaam, is no longer a city he wants to live in. The physical environment of the Foreshore has changed significantly since his arrival in 2011. The traffic islands around Hertzog Boulevard have been fenced off, and a large part of the Nelson Mandela Boulevard underpass has been turned into a boomed parking lot. The dock-facing perimeter of the Culemborg industrial park has also been re-fenced, and hundreds of millions of rands has been spent on new Fore-shore skyscrapers and building upgrades. The gentrification of lower Woodstock and Salt River has continued apace; as the local business community has grown in strength, the Passenger Rail Agency of South Africa, which owns the rail yards, has come under significant pressure to clear out the tents and keep them from being re-established.

Already, many of the encampments described in this book are no more. The Beachboys are slowly being pushed northwards, out of the old city suburbs and away from the port. When the physical connection to the port is lost, Adam believes the Sea Power code will die out. 'When the boys move away from the sea they are not Beachboys any more. They become more like South Africans. Away from the sea all you have is the streets. When you're in the streets you play by street rules. You can't bring your own rules there.'

Port and ship security measures have tightened. Captains have become increasingly wise to stowaway techniques. 'For example,' says Adam, 'they used to tie up with just one big rope, which we knew how to climb, but now they tie with two smaller ropes next to each other. Not even Sudi can climb something like this.'

Squeezed between the city and the sea, the Beachboys increasingly take their frustrations out in internecine fashion, stabbing each other and gouging out eyes with broken bottles. 'Violence is all the young ones know,' says Adam, no longer hopeful that the situation can be solved from within. 'Soon we will start seeing bodies, same as what happened in 2009, except this time it will go on and on.'

His escape plan is simple. He seeks one more ship. If it takes him somewhere new, so be it – he will consider this divine direction, and live the experience through. If it results in his being flown back to Dar es Salaam, he intends applying for a Tanzanian passport so that he can enrol in the Merchant Marine Institute on Zanzibar Island. Once he has his 'seaman book' (Able Seaman certification), he plans to head north, to seek work not on ships but on fishing trawlers. Ultimately, he hopes to reach and explore the ports of the Gulf of Aden and the Red Sea.

I have repeatedly offered to look into his prospects of being allowed to return to England, but he has always put me off.

'I need to do something in the sea first, before I go back. My father was a seaman, and I have his blood. I don't belong in Africa and I don't belong in England. I belong in the sea, so this is where I must go.'

ACKNOWLEDGEMENTS

I owe thanks to David Southwood for introducing me to the Beachboys, and for encouraging me to go ahead when our collaborative work came to an end. I am also grateful to Dave for permitting me to use his powerful images in this book at no cost.

I have Ingeborg Pelser to thank for convincing me there was a book to be written, and for making this a contractual reality. When Ingeborg departed Jonathan Ball Publishers Ester Levinrad drove this project with care and enthusiasm, and her valuable insights helped transform a dossier into a work of crafted non-fiction. Hedley Twidle and Anna Hartford also provided excellent feedback on the manuscript, twice. Thanks also to Kerri von Geusau and Tammy Joubert, who read and reported back on early drafts. I would also like to mention Angela Voges, who edited the manuscript with great skill and feeling.

Able Seaman-turned-academic Amaha Senu, who heard many of these Beachboys tales from the Beachboys themselves, answered many questions about the seafarers' experiences of stowaways, in addition to providing me with valuable source materials. I am also thankful to Benyam Bouyalew for allowing me to summarise his published life story, *Benyam*, and to use his 'stowaway tips'.

The idea to divide the book into the seasons of a year came from Tom Devriendt, who organised an early article of mine this way. I also owe thanks to Tanya Pampalone, Billy Kahora, Carlos Amato, the team at African Cities Reader and Anton Harber for publishing and supporting my early articles about the Beachboys.

In Tanzania, thanks to Ian Boyd, and also Tania and Hamish Hamilton, for beds and meals and other forms of support.

Final thanks must go to my parents, Brian and Shirley Christie, who helped in so many ways, and most of all to my wife, Andret, whose support for this project kept me going.

Printed in December 2022
by Rotomail Italia S.p.A., Vignate (MI) - Italy